SCUBA DIVING

MALTA · GOZO · COMINO

FOURTH EDITION

PETER G. LEMON

Sharon and Ian enjoying the marine life and a photo shoot with the Tugboat Rozi in the background.
PHOTO: PETER G. LEMON

All rights reserved. No part of this publication may be reproduced, stored in any retrieval system or transmitted in any form or by any means, mechanical, electronic, recording or otherwise, without the prior written permission of the Publisher, Peter G. Lemon.

All requests for permission should be addressed in writing to Peter G. Lemon.

Although every care has been taken in compiling this book, using the latest information available at the time of going to press, some details are liable to change and cannot therefore be guaranteed. The Publisher/Author does not accept any liability whatsoever arising from errors or omissions, however caused.

Would readers please note that the illustrations of the underwater plans and road maps to be found in the following pages have been made as accurate as possible. They are to compass bearings but not to scale, information for distance and time can be found within the text. The author accepts no responsibility for the loss, injury or inconvenience sustained by any person using these illustrations.

PUBLISHER Peter G. Lemon

PROJECT MANAGER Sue Lemon

PRINT PRODUCTION George Lanham

Printed and bound in the UK by

THANK YOU
Peter and Sue would like to thank all persons who helped in any way to the production of this book

ACKNOWLEDGEMENTS
A list of names appear on page 221

ISBN 978-0-9541789-3-2

Front cover designed by George Lanham and Stephen Clough

Front and back cover photos: Sharon Forder, Joe Formosa and Peter G. Lemon

Planned and produced by
Peter G. Lemon and Sue Lemon
7 Earls Hill Gardens, Royston
Herts SG8 9DA

www.scubadivingmalta.co.uk
www.scubadivinggozo.co.uk
www.scubadivingmaltagozocomino.com

Copyright © Peter G. Lemon

Contents

The little hamlet Wied iz-Zurrieq entry point for the Um el Faroud and where the colourful boats leave for the Blue Grotto.

SPECIAL PAGES

	PAGE
Ian & Sharon Forder	16
Joe Formosa	95
Calypso BS-AC Malta	110
Atlam BS-AC Malta	181
Sue Lemon	198
Professional Diving Schools Association	210

The Author!
PHOTO: SHARON FORDER

	PAGE
Shore Diving Index	5
Boat Diving Index	7
Foreword	8
A Note from the Author	9
Introduction	10
Travelling to the Maltese Islands	11
The Maltese Islands	12
Weather Chart	13
Dive Centre License Authority	15
Islands for Divers	17
Key to Symbols	20
Malta Shore Dives	21
Gozo Shore Dives	120
Malta Boat Dives	168
Gozo Boat Dives	182
Comino Boat Dives	188
Places to visit in Malta	199
Places to visit in Gozo	205
Professional Diving Schools Ass	210
Dive Centre Locations	211
Dive Centre Information	212
Acknowledgements	221
Indexes	222

Shore diving site locations

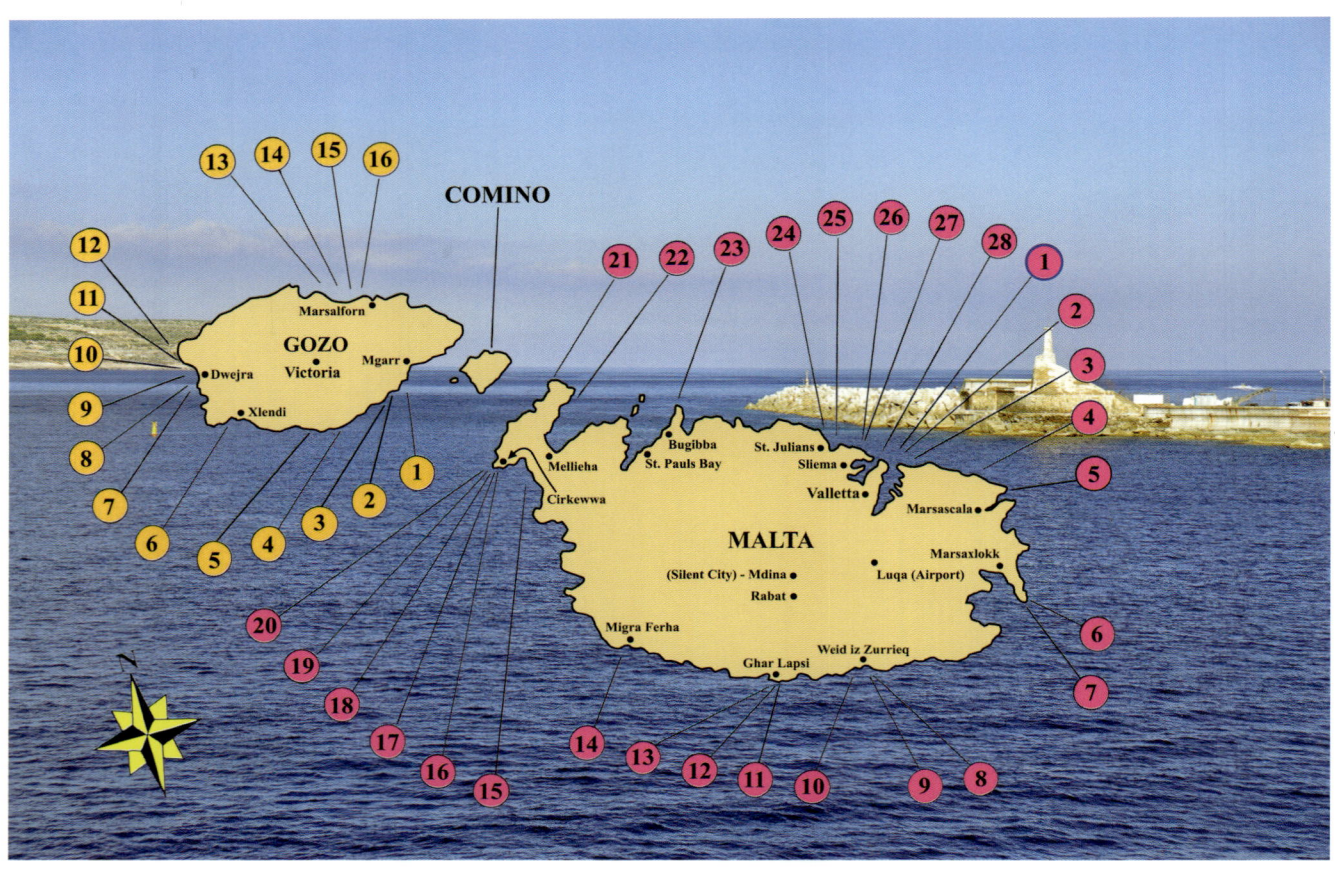

Dwejra, Gozo. INSET: *The Blue Hole.*

Shore diving index

Malta

#	Site	PAGE	Description
1	St Elmo Bay – HMS *Maori*	21	Interesting wreck 10m-14m – lots of marine life
2	Valletta – Fort St Elmo	26	A good rummage and reef dive – 20m drop off down to a maximum depth of 35m
3	Kalkara Creek – SS *Margit*	28	WW2 wreck – good dive in right conditions – 22m
4	Marsascala – Mini Blue Hole	38	Interesting for training or second dive 5m-14m
5	Marsascala – Zonqor Point Tugboats	34	*St Michael* and Tugboat *10* both at 20m
6	Delimara Point – East Reef	40	Long walk – well worth the effort 3m-34m
7	Delimara Point – South reef	44	Long walk – the reefs are excellent 3m-30m
8	Wied iz Zurrieq – East reef	54	Visibility here can be excellent 40m plus
9	Wied iz Zurrieq – West Reef	52	Drop-offs, ledges, gullies and caves 4m-28m
10	Wied iz Zurrieq – *Um el Faroud*	46	A large wreck possibly the best in the Med. Depths on the wreck range from 20m-35m
11	Ghar Lapsi – Middle Reef	64	Good for navigation or second dive 0m-14m
12	Ghar Lapsi – Finger Reef & Crib	60	Reef, crib and cave – a long dive 22m
13	Ghar Lapsi – Black John	56	Difficult walk out of the way dive 3m-38m
14	Migra Ferha	66	Only for the fit – 90 steps – excellent reef 14m-45m+
15	Anchor Bay	70	Reef and cave dive – good training area 2m-21m
	Cirkewwa /Marfa Point	74	Malta's most popular diving area
16	Cirkewwa – Paradise Bay	88	Variable depths around the headland 33m
17	Cirkewwa – Patrol Boat *P29*	85	Scuttled in 2007 on the seabed at 38m
18	Cirkewwa – Sugar Loaf & Madonna	82	The Madonna stands silently in a recess 28m
19	Cirkewwa – Tug boat *Rozi*	79	Possibly the best known tug boat in Europe 5m-35m
20	Cirkewwa – Cirkewwa Arch	76	Great photographic opportunities found here 4m-20m
21	L'Ahrax Point – South Reef & Tunnel	90	Long swim to the reef, tunnel and inland sea 12m
	L'Ahrax Point – North Reef	94	10m reef with drop offs of 12m depths 2m-28m
22	Slugs Bay	96	The name does not do this dive site justice 1m-10m
23	Qawra Point – Reef & Cave	98	Good dive for experienced and novice divers 1m-12m
	Qawra Point – North Reef	100	A deeper dive for experienced divers 35m
24	Paceville – Mercanti Reef	103	Navigate yourself to this excellent reef 2m-12m
25	Sliema – Exiles – Tugboat *2* & Reef	106	A nice wreck at 22m with a reef to enjoy 22m
26	Sliema – Fortizza	111	Good dive with small tunnels and arches 4m-15m
27	Sliema – Coral Gardens	114	Unique limestone rocks – a very pretty dive 4m-14m
28	Manoel Island – Lighter *X127*	116	This WW1 barge makes a good dive 4m-23m

Gozo

#	Site	PAGE	Description
1	Xatt l'Ahmar – Red Bay	128	A quiet dive site with an excellent reef 35m+
2	MV *Karwela* & MV *Cominoland*	124	Scuttled in 2006 upright on seabed at 42m
3	MV *Xlendi*	120	This up-turned wreck still offers a good dive 42m
4	Ras il-Hobz Middle Finger	130	A unique dive only metres from the shore 50m+
5	Mgarr ix Xini	135	Great place for a night or second dive 16m
6	Xlendi – Reef & Tunnel	138	A 70 metre tunnel and a reef to explore 3m-25m
	Dwejra Inland Sea /Blue Hole	142	Gozo's most popular diving area
7	Dwejra – Little Bear /Crocodile Rock	144	Excellent visibility – reef with 25m drop offs 5m-34m+
8	Dwejra – Big Bear /Coral Gardens	146	Good reef and cave dive 1m-45m+
9	Dwejra – Blue Hole /Coral Gardens	148	Underwater headland with drop offs of 40m+
10	Dwejra – Blue Hole /Azure Window	150	Unique rock formation Blue Hole and window 15m-38m
11	Dwejra – Inland Sea to Blue Hole	152	Inland Sea tunnel, reef, arch, Window, Blue Hole makes this long swim a great dive 3m-45m+
12	Dwejra – Inland Sea /Tunnel	154	Tunnel and reef dive 3m-45m+
13	Ghasri Valley – Cathedral Cave	165	100 steps – well worth the effort 0m-33m
14	Marsalforn – Reqqa Point	162	Possibly the best – but its only my opinion 2m-45m+
15	Marsalforn – Anchor Reef	160	Excellent reef an abundance of marine life 9m-50m+
16	Marsalforn – Double Arch	156	Spectacular dive great for photography 45m

Boat diving site locations

There are many dive sites around Malta, Gozo and Comino which are not accessable from the shore. The following boat dives that I have selected are just a few and possibly the most popular.

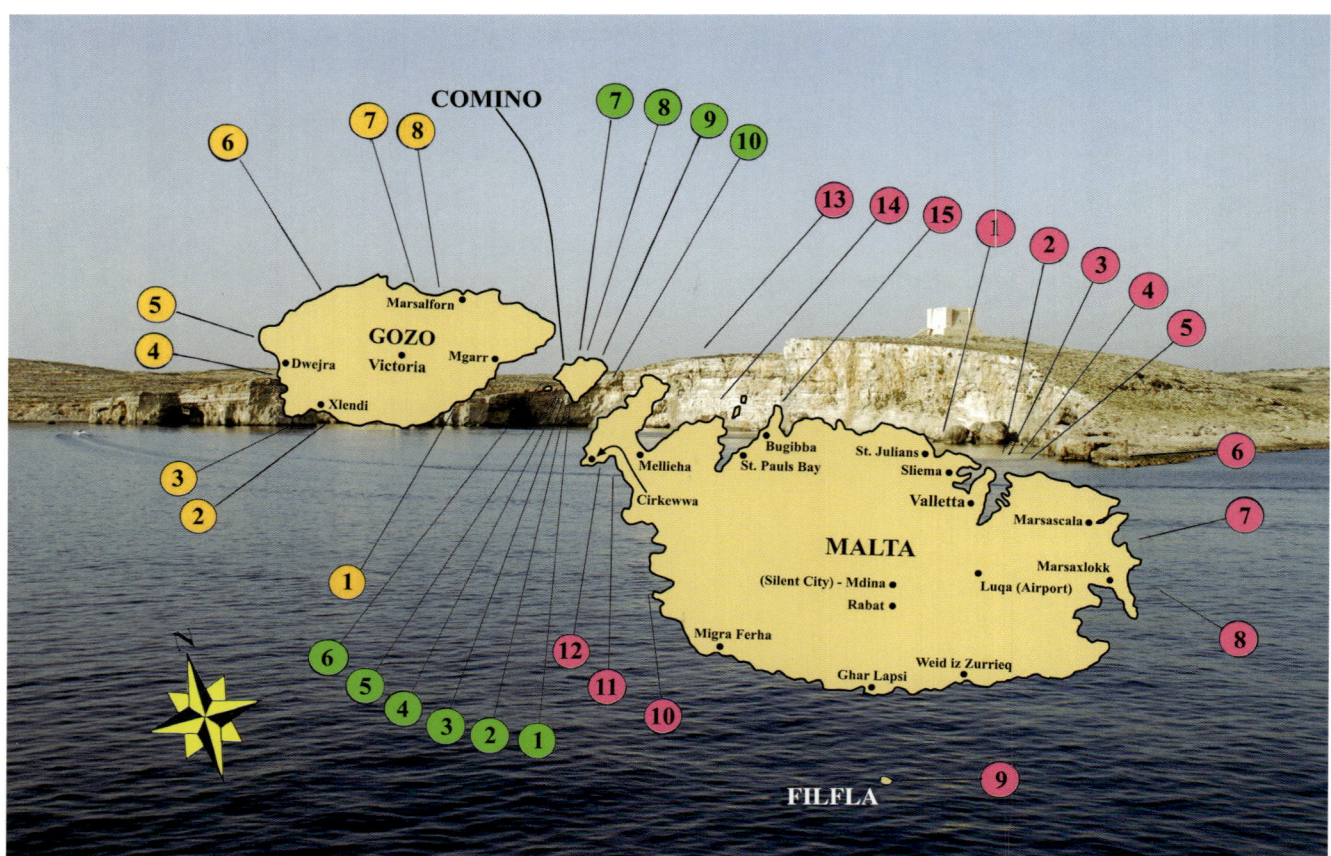

Lantern Point, background Blue Lagoon, Comino. INSET: *Maltese Luzzu*.

Boat diving index

Malta

		PAGE	
1	The Bristol Beaufighter	168	The upturned wreckage of this WW2 plane is almost intact on a sandy seabed at a depth of 38m
2	HMS *Hellespont*	169	Stunning wreck which is remakably intact 45m
3	HM Drifter *Eddy*	169	Carried out duties in WW1 and WW2 56m
4	HMS *St Angelo*	170	Sunk in 1942 now upright on the seabed at 55m
5	Schnellboot *S-31* (E boat)	170	Good Trimix dive at a depth of 73m
6	HMS *Southwold*	171	In two sections on a sandy seabed 300m apart 65m-75m
7	*Le Polynesien*	173	She lies on a sandy seabed almost intact 53m-70m
8	Bristol Blenheim	174	A highly rated dive of this WW2 aircraft 42m
9	Filfla Island	175	Off-shore island seldom dived 6m-40m
10	Ras ir-Raheb	175	The wreck of a yacht here as well as nice reef 18m-32m
11	*Scotscraig*	176	Started life as passenger ferry in UK 21m
12	Qammieh Point	177	The reef drops away almost vertically 4m-45m+
13	HMS *Stubborn*	177	Remarkably well preserved wreck a good dive at 57m
14	MV *Pippo*	178	This small wreck makes a nice dive 35m
15	MV *Imperial Eagle*	179	Scuttled in 1999 as a diver attraction sitting upright at 38m

Gozo

1	Fesse Rock	182	An abundance of marine life can be found here 45m+
2	Dawra Tas-Sanap	183	This is a great dive with much to explore 45m
3	Ulysses Cave	183	The rock formation here is quite spectacular 45m
4	Fungus Rock	184	Originally named 'The Generals Rock' – good dive 45m
5	San Dimitri Point	185	Spot the barracuda, dentex and tuna in the blue 40m+
6	Hekka Point	186	View from the cave is quite breathtaking 20m+
7	Billinghurst Cave	187	Look out for anemones,sponges and corals 27m
8	Calypso Tunnel/Cave	187	A very impressive and interesting dive 35m

Comino

1	Lantern Point	188	Good reef and chimney tunnel – an excellent dive 3m-45m+
2	Lantern Point West	189	Sometimes referred to as inner Lantern Point 30m
3	Crystal Lagoon	190	The lagoon is a nursey for young fish 3m-14m
4	Patrol boat *P31*	191	Scuttled in 2009 as a diver attraction 22m
5	Alex's Cave	194	Popular second dive – suitable for all levels of diver 12m
6	Cominotto Reef (Anchor reef)	195	Normal depth for this dive 25m – WW2 anchor at 35m
7	Santa Marija Reef	195	Gullies, caverns, swim-throughs and caves 10m-22m
8	Santa Marija Caves	193	Almost the perfect dive? 9m-16m
9	Elephant Rock	197	Often referred to as the Santa Marija Tunnel 6m
10	Sultan Rock	197	Around the rock the seabed is littered with boulders 18m

Shore diving plays an important part of the attraction of diving Malta and Gozo. The entry points do vary considerably, some are reasonably easy, the more difficult ones some divers prefer to boat dive: it is really down to personal choice. Gozo dive centres sometimes boat dive some of the dives I have listed on Malta as shore dives, likewise Malta dive centres will boat dive some of the Gozo dive sites.

MALTA

FOREWORD – FIRST EDITION 2001

Earlier this year Peter and Sue Lemon called to give me a preview of a book which Peter has just finished. As I scanned the manuscript and listened to their account of anecdotes and mini-adventures which go with the writing of every book, the more convinced I became that the mission which he had set himself was indeed a labour of love.

Peter Lemon's first visit to Malta dates back to 1983. He has since returned many times. Following his retirement in 1997 from a thirty seven year career with the Hertfordshire Fire and Rescue Service his visits became even more frequent and much longer. With the sole aim of sharing with others the delights and excitement that the underwater world of the Maltese Islands has to offer, the author, himself a qualified Advanced Instructor and a member of the British Sub Aqua Club, has dedicated many hours to researching and compiling this book.

Peter Lemon has completed more than two thousand dives, a quarter of which around Malta, Gozo and Comino. His book is replete with accounts of personal experiences and all underwater plans, maps and routes have been personally surveyed and illustrated by him.

The book covers all aspects of Shore Diving around the Maltese Islands. Peter Lemon has discovered thirty six dive sites and in his book he shares all his experiences with the reader. Professional divers as well as diving enthusiasts will find the book of great interest as the author has prepared descriptive and easily understood maps which act as a guide to the dive site. They show the most favourable entry and exit points, depths, the underwater landscape and provide other information to allow the diver to plan and complete the dive safely.

Every graphic is accompanied by a short text which gives routes details, local information and a description of the dive. An aerial photograph showing the coastline of the site's immediate area and matching the underwater landscape further enhances the book's technical and artistic value. The author provides a vast compendium of additional information which includes laws governing diving, emergency telephone numbers, the best parking locality, the nearest public telephone and other facilities of interest to the diver.

While other authors give us the benefit of their equally important experiences at deep sea diving Peter Lemon's literary contribution to what has become one of Malta's most popular niche markets is definitely a first. He has written a book for everyone. It is a book which I commend to the experienced diver who will find this volume extremely useful when planning his dives, to the beginner who will discover an excellent and painstaking guide, as well as to the enthusiast who wishes to take home a souvenir following an enjoyable diving holiday around our shores.

Well done and thank you Peter Lemon.

DR MICHAEL REFALO, KOM, BA(Hons), LLD, FRSA
1936-2015

Minister of Tourism – 1987-1994, 1998-2003   Minister of Youth and Arts – 1994-1996
Minister of Justice – 1995-1996   High Commissioner for Malta in London – 2005-2009

Dr Michael Refalo (right) with the author.

The above is reproduced in memory of Dr Michael Refalo. We first met on the 23rd May, 2000, at the Palazzo Spinola, St Julians, Malta, where he looked at our manuscript and listened to our accounts of writing our first book and kindly agreed to write the above Foreword.

On the 29th June, 2007, we met once again and he agreed to write a Foreword for our second edition. On the 9th May, 2012, we visited him in his office, when he was the High Commissioner for Malta in London, when he kindly wrote the Foreword for the third edition of *Scuba Diving Malta Gozo Comino*.

We always found him to be a gentleman with a great interest in what we were doing. He will be greatly missed and our thoughts are with his family. Thank you.

Notes from the Author

It was in 1983 when I first visited the Maltese Islands and enjoyed my first dive in the warm clear waters around these islands at the pretty little inlet known as the Blue Grotto (Wied iz Zurrieq). Just before Christmas in 2001 we, my wife Sue and I, released our first diving guide for Malta Gozo Comino, now in 2016 after almost 100 visits we have completed and released, this, our fourth edition. All this would not have been possible without the help of many friends, far too many to name individually, but one or two have to have a special mention, of course my wife Sue, George Lanham, Joe Abdilla, Paul Gauci and Sharon Forder.

In February 2015 Dr Michael Refalo sadly passed away after a long illness. We had the pleasure of meeting him on four occasions, in relation to our book both in Malta and London. He had kindly written the Forewords for our first three editions and always viewed our manuscripts with enthusiasm and interest. In this, our fourth edition, we have used the original Foreword along with a few words of our own.

2014 was not a good year for us as we lost our lovely daughter, Katie to a sudden illness and she is very sadly missed. She was of course introduced to the Maltese Islands by her Mum and I and although she did not take up diving she did enjoy her visits, she was always supportive of my diving guide. On behalf of myself, Sue, John, Hannah and Ben, I would like to take this opportunity to thank everyone for their kind messages of sympathy and support which we received.

I would like to dedicate this, my fourth book, to my daughter Katie.

PETER G. LEMON

Katie, with Mum and Dad, in better times.

In the early hours of Wednesday 2nd September 1998, the Um el Faroud *leaves Grand Harbour on her last journey before slipping slowly beneath the surface at Wied iz Zurrieq, to form Malta's largest artificial reef.*
PHOTO: ANTHONY CHETCUTI

Introduction

This guide to diving the Maltese Islands has been written by a diver for divers who wish to make the most of their time underwater. For your first visit to these islands I would recommend that dive guiding would be the best option. If you are a returning diver then you could use this book as a guide, for information or souvenir.

Although the Islands are small, navigating your way to some of the dive sites can prove to be difficult, therefore I would suggest that you arm yourself with a good road map and confirm your directions with the dive shop before you leave.

Each dive location begins with a short introduction giving information on how to arrive at your chosen destination; to assist you with this there is a map of the local area. These road maps have been surveyed and drawn by myself, they are not to scale, but you will find details of times and distances within the text. They show details of parking, entry/exit points and amenities. Please note some telephone boxes are no longer in use.

Divers entry point Susie's pool, Cirkewwa.

It should be noted that in some areas mobile phones do not work. There is also a brief description given on the area of the dive site, followed by my suggested dive plan with a recommended minimum dive time. It is important before selecting your dive site and making a dive plan that the accompanying text is read and understood.

There is an aerial photograph for each dive site and on the opposite page an underwater dive plan, both will show your entry/exit points which will enable you to relate one to the other. I feel sure that all experienced divers would check the immediate coastline for entry/exit points to be used other than those identified. You can of course make your own dive plan.

These underwater dive plans, which are to compass bearings and not to scale, have also been surveyed and drawn by myself; you will find details of times taken to cover distances within the text of each dive location. They are based on my average speed under the water which is, whilst exploring and moving slowly, approximately 10/12 metres per minute.

Although every effort has been made to obtain the correct depths, you may find that they may vary by one or two metres. This is due to the undulating seabed and of course you could be slightly off the position of the depth marked on the plan.

There is a section in this book of boat diving the Maltese Islands. My selection, of possibly the most popular, are just a few of the many sites available, there is also an identification map showing their location.

If you have not chosen or pre-booked your dive centre and wish to find the nearest one to your accommodation, refer to the dive centre map which shows their locations, for all further information and details enquire at your chosen dive centre or school. An index can be found at the back of this book.

Emergency telephone number
Police – Fire – Ambulance   112
Nature Trust Marine Rescue
Malta – Gozo – Comino   99999505

After their brief a group of young divers are about to experience their first dive.

Travelling information

To the Maltese Islands
Luqa is Malta's International Airport; it is very modern with all amenities. Air Malta and major international airlines operate regular scheduled services from most major European cities. Scheduled flights by Air Malta operate from most UK airports; some of these services are not available in the winter months. Flying time is approximately 3 hours, Malta time is 1 hour ahead of GMT. It is normal for Air Malta to recognise the needs of scuba divers with their sports equipment; there is a reasonable charge for this, which is sometimes free in the winter months.

Passport and Visa regulations
All visitors to the Maltese Islands require a full passport; it must have at least 3 months to run before expiry. Visitors from the European Union, Australia, Canada and America do not require a visa, others should check with the immigration authorities.

A traditional way to see the sights is to take a Kartozzin; they are found in the most popular tourist areas.

Car hire and traffic laws
Car hire can be booked with your holiday or alternatively, you will find many companies hiring cars and you just may find a better deal. The requirements for hiring a car are, minimum age of 25, if the hirer is over 70 proof of a medical from a doctor is required. Remember to take your driving license and passport when hiring a car; they drive on the left and the laws are similar to those in the UK. If requested to produce your license by either the Police or a Traffic Warden, you have 48 hours to present it at the nearest Police Station. If you are unfortunate enough to be involved in an accident, vehicles must not be moved until the Police/Traffic Warden arrive. There are couple warnings, do not park within 5 metres of a corner and do not cross a single white line even to park on the opposite side of the road, these actions could result in receiving a fine.

The local bus service is good and reasonable, there is also an open top bus service on both islands.

Ferry Service – Malta Gozo
There is a regular passenger/car ferry service between Malta's northernmost point at Cirkewwa and Gozo's harbour at Mgarr, a journey that takes approximately 30 minutes. During public holidays and the summer season extra trips are organised, often on a shuttle basis. The fares for both passengers and cars are very reasonable.

Public Transport – buses
Malta and Gozo's public transport systems offer a very reasonable and efficient way of getting around the Islands. The main bus terminus is in Valletta in Malta and Victoria in Gozo from where the buses operate to all parts of the islands.

Little and large – the large one being the Gozo Channel Car Ferry MV Melita *which sails between Malta and Gozo.*

The Maltese Islands

You or your group will not be the first to land in these delightful Mediterranean islands. You will be following a tradition that started some 6,000 years ago. Throughout recorded history, Malta has been at the heart of world events. The islands have been a haven, battleground, home and refuge to a host of famous figures through various episodes of European history. It is this essence of history, which has helped forge their unique Maltese character.

St Paul's Islands where in AD60 the Apostle Paul was shipwrecked.

The Maltese archipelago consists of three inhabited islands; they lie in the middle of the Mediterranean Sea approximately 93 km south of Sicily and 230 km from the North African (Tunisian) coast. Malta, being the largest of the three with a total land area of 246 square km. Gozo is somewhat smaller with a land area of 67 square km. The smallest is Comino, which lies between the two and has a land area of 2.7 square km. There are also a number of small un-inhabited islands, such as Filfla; Cominetto and the most well chronicled St. Paul's Islands where the Apostle Paul was shipwrecked in AD 60.

Dockyard Creek, a good place to sit and relax watching the boat traffic, in the background is Malta's Naval Museum.

The People of Malta and Gozo

The rare sense of hospitality and friendliness of these people invariably strike visitors to the Islands.

The Apostle Paul was probably the first long stay winter visitor to the Island and the hospitality shown him by the locals is well recorded in the Acts of the Apostles. Two thousand years later their hospitality remains as warm and as unaffected as it was then. The Maltese people welcome the company of foreigners and being helpful to them comes naturally. Also, they take great interest in what is happening to the rest of the world, and, with their flair for languages, communication with visitors is easy. They have an admirable sense of humour and like most Mediterranean people, tend to be rather jovial. These qualities endear the inhabitants of the Islands to the foreign visitor. It is generally said that foreigners are tourists to the Islands only on their first visit; on their second and subsequent visits they return as their established friends.

Republic Street, Valletta, which is the main shopping area in the capital.

They are proud of their independence, having one of the highest electoral turnouts in the world. Their patriotism was at its most evident during World War II, when they fought so bravely that Great Britain awarded them its highest award for civil bravery, the George Cross, in 1942.

The pace of life is very relaxed by European standards. They enjoy life and their broad smiles tell you they are a happy people. They find great strength and unity in their common language, religion and strong family ties.

One of the favourite sports of the Islanders is football, and their National Stadium is on the island of Malta at Ta'Qali. There is strong support for world and European football especially the English Premier and Italian Serie A leagues, and their supporters clubs are to be found in many towns and villages. The matches can be seen live, here on television and if the team they support wins, they celebrate in style by driving around the streets waving team flags and blowing their hooters.

The Islanders love festivals and the warm climate makes it possible to enjoy these colourful events throughout the year.

Between May and October every town and village in Malta and Gozo celebrates the feast day or 'festa' of its patron saint. The festa is the most important event in each village's annual calendar and the villagers eagerly look forward to this very special day. Considerable preparation goes into these celebrations. The village church is draped with red damask and decorated with beautiful flowers. All its gold and silver treasures are put on display thus creating a fitting setting for the statue of the patron saint, which is placed in a prominent position in the Church. The church façade is illuminated with hundreds of multicoloured bulbs, as also are the streets, across which are suspended massive and colourful drapes. Hundreds of flags are flown from rooftops whilst drapes and light bulbs are hung across the width of the covered balconies, which are typical of the traditional houses.

Traditional Gozo farmhouse covered in bougainvillea.

On the festa day, as the statue of the saint is carried shoulder-high along the streets of the village the church bells ring and massed bands play marches. Children throw confetti from balconies on to the passing procession. The nougat and candy floss stands do excellent business whilst the crowds walk up and down the village streets stopping every now and then for a drink or to greet an old friend. The noise reaches a crescendo, as the statue is about to re-enter the church; at this point there is normally a colourful fireworks display.

The Maltese people specialise in the manufacture of fireworks and, in the inter-village rivalry, fireworks often constitute the benchmark for comparing the success of the various festas. During the summer season there is a festa practically every weekend and no holidaymaker should leave the Islands without visiting one.

Language

Most of the local people speak Maltese, the national language that is closely related to Arabic. However, they also have English as a second official language, and Italian is widely spoken as well.

The church of St Philip in the village of Zebbug is illuminated with hundreds of multi coloured light bulbs for the festa, the most important event in any village's calendar.

Religion

Predominantly Roman Catholic but the Maltese Constitution guarantees freedom of worship. There are also churches belonging to various other religious denomination.

The weather

The climate is warm and pleasant. There are no biting winds, fog, snow or frost. Rain falls for only very short periods, mostly during the late autumn and mid-winter, with the hottest period being from mid-July to mid-September, where the temperature will not normally rise above 37°C.

Month	Daily Sunshine hours	Monthly Rainfall mm	Air Temp. °C	Sea Temp. °C
January	7	95	13	17
February	8	63	13	16
March	9	37	14	16
April	11	26	16	17
May	12	9	20	19
June	13	5	23	22
July	14	0	27	26
August	13	6	27	27
September	10	67	25	26
October	9	77	21	24
November	8	109	17	22
December	7	108	14	19

Maltese annual average weather chart.

The dramatic cliffs at the entrance to Xlendi Bay, Gozo which is only part of this pretty and popular seaside village.

Medical care

The Maltese Islands enjoy a high standard of medical care. There is a large General Hospital; Mater Dei in Malta and Craig Hospital Victoria in Gozo, there are also government health clinics in various towns. British nationals holidaying on the islands are entitled to one month's free medical and hospital care in Malta and Gozo. It is advisable to carry your EU Health Insurance card. Persons who are receiving medical treatment and who may need to carry medicine into the Maltese Islands or purchase fresh supplies locally would be well advised to carry a letter of introduction from their family doctor. Most British drugs are available.

Chadwick Lakes which are at their most picturesque in the spring, also the surrounding countryside with colourful flowers in bloom.

Shopping

Shops are usually open between the hours of 9am and 7.00pm, with a three or four hour lunch break (siesta) Most well-known brands of all items you may require are available in pharmacies, shops and supermarkets. In commercial areas frequented by tourists however, most shops remain open until approximately 10.00pm. but close earlier during the winter months. Half the joy of planning a day out in Malta or Gozo is that it is easy to combine both sightseeing and shopping; there are many bargains to be had.

You may be able to pick up a painting by one of the many local artists or find an unusual piece of jewellery, made from gold or silver and very reasonably priced. Maltese lace can be bought in the form of shawls, soft furnishings or trimmings. Hand knitted woollens and Arran styles can be purchased and are of exceptional value and anyone who is fond of glass or pottery is spoiled for choice. If you want to get all your shopping out of the way in one go, visit the Crafts Village at Ta'Qali in Malta or the Craft Village near San Lawrenz in Gozo. At both these villages you can watch potters, glassblowers, and filigree craftsmen at work.

Many of these green grocery stalls are to be found at the side of the road selling lovely local fresh fruit and vegetables.

Currency

Currency is the Euro which can be obtained in banks, ATM's and some shops. Major credit cards, travellers' cheques and euro cheques are accepted at most hotels, shops and restaurants.

Electricity

Electricity supply is 240 volts, single phase, 50 cycles. The square fitting standard three-pin British plugs and sockets are used.

Water

Although the tap water is safe to drink I would recommend that you use bottled water for drinking, which is reasonably priced and can be purchased almost anywhere, and use tap water for making hot drinks and cooking.

Dive Centre Licence Authority

All diving centres in the Maltese Islands must be authorized by the Malta Tourism Authority, which is the official agency responsible for issuing operating licenses to diving centres, who offer Recreational Diving Services. This is defined in local legislation as training, education, accompanied diving and the provision of equipment for unaccompanied diving. Diving centres are inspected by officials of the Authority at least once a year; the centres must conform to the highest standards. The legislation which had been designed around the European standard for recreational diving service providers EN14467. Full details of the Maltese scuba diving legislation may be found on the website at www.visitmalta.com or www.pdsa.org.mt

An example of a Dive Centre Cylinder Charging Room.

Instructors must be officially registered to act as such through a licensed dive centre, where all training, education will be undertaken. Equipment will be issued by a licensed dive centre where you can be assured that it has undergone regular maintenance, servicing and testing by technical qualified persons, unless of course you have brought your own. Officials from the Enforcement section of the Authority have the executive powers which enable them to stop any activity from taking place if it is considered to be illegal. Legal action would be taken against that individual, not yourself as a consumer, if they are found to be providing illicit recreational diving services, your dive would be ordered to cease. Freelance instructors would not operate from licensed premises and therefore their operations are not open to inspections by the local government agency. This is all planned with the best interest of the consumer in mind and there are some 50 licensed diving centers to choose from around the islands.

In order to enjoy the crystal clear waters of the Maltese Islands make sure you take along your Certification card and your Dive Log. These will be required when you register at any of the licensed diving centers, for equipment rental, training courses, accompanied or unaccompanied dives, to confirm your qualifications and experience. Any diver who is in possession of a diving qualification less than CMAS Two Star, BS-AC Sports Diver, PADI Advanced or its equivalent must dive in the company of a certified diving instructor, who will be solely responsible for the safety of these persons.

PADI Bubble maker can be undertaken at the age of eight within an enclosed environment and must be accompanied by a parent or guardian, at the age of ten Junior Open Water may be commenced. BS-AC allow minors to 'try dive' at the age of twelve and continue training to Ocean Diver. These are the regulations of PADI and BS-AC and are accepted at the majority of dive centres in the Maltese Islands.

At the dive centre you will be asked to fill in a short Registration Form with your personal details and a self-assessed medical form. If the form indicates any illnesses or conditions which may hamper the safety of your planned dive, you will be required to undergo a direct medical assessment conducted by one of the hyperbaric doctors available on the Islands. Medical checks are inexpensive and can be done within hours of registration. You may be required by the director of the dive centre to undergo a medical check to ascertain that you are medically fit to dive. The Maltese Islands have a strong and positive track record for safety in diving and all do their best to ensure that you have the safety you require.

Regulatory Officer Diving Sector,
Malta Tourism Authority

www.visitmalta.com
www.maltatourismauthority.com

An instructor guides his group into the water at an entry point.

Islands for divers

The Maltese Archipelago – the main Island of Malta, the smaller island of Gozo and the tiny island of Comino – is a real paradise for divers and snorkelers. These Islands have fortunately retained their natural state due, to a large extent, to the sea and its fauna.

Apart from other positive aspects, one of the most important is that the Maltese Islands are an all year round destination for the diver. During the summer the sea temperatures can rise to 26°C gradually reducing in February and March to 16°C The climate and duration of sunshine at this time of year is similar to an average North European summer.

In stormy weather, these Islands still offer a sufficient number of sheltered interesting dive sites.

My eldest Granddaughter enjoys her first try dive in the Maltese Islands.

Diving Centres/Schools

The islands offer a well-developed infrastructure for divers, representing a high standard and are capable of coping with the most sophisticated demands. The Professional Diving Schools Association has been formed to promote diving within the regulations. Courses leading to international dive qualifications can be undertaken with a majority of dive centres on the islands. It is not necessary to take along your own equipment, as it is possible to hire all your diving equipment at favourable rates.

The Government have official inspectors who regularly check the centres and their equipment. Beginners and advanced divers will receive all help and assistance from the centres to ensure that their diving holiday in Malta is trouble-free and enjoyable. Diver safety is of primary concern.

The diver, who wishes to dive independently and hire equipment, has to present a qualification certificate to the chosen dive centre, equivalent to at least the CMAS/2-Star (BS-AC Sports Diver) or PADI Advanced Open Water. All divers will be required to complete a self certificated medical form, any queries

Friendly Grouper (Epinephelus guaza).

arising from completing this form could require a Doctors medical, and the cost of this is minimal. The dive centres have the right to request a doctors medical. This also applies to the individual who is undertaking diver training.

A diver enjoys the reef using a Torpedo diver propulsion vehicle (DPV); these may be hired at some dive centres.

ISLANDS FOR DIVERS

Diving for the disabled in Malta

The International Association for Handicapped Divers is an association whose aim is to promote, develop and conduct programmes for the training of the physically disabled in scuba diving. Since its introduction in 1993 the IAHD has conducted numerous professional and non-professional programmes around the world. There are a number of centres in Malta who offer introductory dives and diver training for the disabled.

Dive boats which are normally for hire during the summer periods, go to the Café and ask for Michael.

Government: protection of the sea and divers

Diving has a prominent position in the Maltese Islands, and with the assistance of the Maltese Government three aims are being followed
1. **Safety Standards for Diving.**
2. **Protection of the sea, its flora and fauna.**
3. **Protection of finds of cultural value.**

The bow of the P31 Patrol Boat, Comino.

A number of conservations areas have been established around wrecks located in Maltese waters it also includes the shore line. It is unlawful to fish from boats or spear fish in these areas. Spear fishing is allowed if you have a license without aqua lung and away from conservation areas.

Removal and non-reporting of any cultural finds is unlawful. It is a criminal act, which will lead to prosecution. Do not let temptation spoil your holiday, report any such findings to the officials directly or to your dive centre.

Speedboat traffic becomes increasingly busy in the height of the summer season. It is mandatory for dive boats to fly the 'A' flag when people are diving. Permission must be obtained for diving in a main harbour where the use of a Surface Marker Buoy is mandatory and I would also suggest it is used for your own safety when away from the protection of a reef.

These guidelines are in the diver's main interest and are practically self evident to any serious sports diver and coincide with regulations of practically all international diving clubs and centres. All of which are pledged to maintain the fascination, freedom and contribution to the protection of the sea and its fauna and flora, also for the safety of this wonderful sport for future generations.

Useful information can be found in the diving section of www.visitmalta.com.

One of the many caves to explore.
PHOTO: MAX VALLI – ORANGE SHARK H2O

The sea around the Maltese Islands

The seas around Malta are virtually tideless; however sometimes there are under-water currents even when the sea is calm. At times these underwater currents will travel in the opposite direction to the wind and the surface sea conditions. The waters are still extremely clear and clean around the islands and for that reason certain rare species of fish can be found.

The individual diving site and the weather conditions influence the underwater visibility, but thanks to the overwhelmingly rocky coasts and the unpolluted water the visibility can be 30 metres.

The rather strong topographic structures of the Maltese Islands continue beneath the surface. In this most bizarre underwater landscape of the Mediterranean, you will find many caves, some large enough for a double decker bus, arches, grotto's, crevices and undulating reefs with their magnificent and dramatic drop-offs, all these areas are home to many species of fish and an abundance of rich marine life.

During recent years the government has arranged for eleven boats and ships, which have been made environmentally safe to be scuttled. These have become artificial reefs/divers attractions and now conger, moray eels, groupers and a multitude of other marine life live and hide within these wrecks. Add these to the number of existing wrecks and the variety of reefs and caves; it is no wonder these islands are a mecca for divers.

Marine life

It would be difficult to list and comment on the many various species of fauna and flora to be found in the waters around the islands. It is important to say that the chance of meeting 'Big Game' fish or certain species

The release of rehabilitated turtles into the sea.

of shark which maybe dangerous to man, is almost non-existent. Very seldom does anyone see tuna, dolphins or turtles as they rarely come close to shore.

Species which the diver will find around the Maltese Islands are barracuda, groupers, amberjack, various bream, various wrasse, damsel fish, octopus, squid, flying gurnard, stingrays, meagre, bogue, red mullet, painted combers, cardinal fish, parrot fish and sea hares to name but a few, the structure of the coast and the rocks seem to offer ideal living conditions for them. Also John Dory can be found, mostly during wintertime since normally it lives at greater depths. Sea horses are here too, possibly the best time to see them is July and August, but they are so small and very well camouflaged, you have to be very careful and patient to find them.

There are a few sea animals, which are beautiful to watch but dangerous to touch; they are not deadly but could be very painful. These include scorpion fish, jellyfish, the bristle worm, the weaver and the stingray.

Underwater photography

Maybe it's the crystal blue waters of the Mediterranean and the visibility below the surface that entices divers to the shores of the Maltese Islands, bringing with them their cameras to capture the delights of this underwater world. But first of all you need a buddy with good buoyancy skills and the patience to match. He needs to be a hunter to find some of the elusive marine life, gently persuading it towards the waiting camera, and in the meantime keeping himself as part of the backdrop if required.

Around the islands' coastline there are a variety of underwater landscapes and artificial reefs, ranging

A cuttlefish is just one of the many subjects for underwater photographers to be found in Maltese waters.

from areas of sand, fields of sea grass tall and green, shallow reefs where the marine growth sparkles in the rays of the sun to the dramatic sheer drop-offs that disappear into the abyss. There is a kaleidoscope of colour to be found amongst the corals and marine life. Here the coral is not of gigantic size – sometimes small can be beautiful – with the vivid red and orange colours of the soft coral and sponges together with the not so colourful hard coral. Together with the many species of tubeworm gently swaying to catch their prey, and many other wonderful sights, all this adds up to the underwater photographer's paradise. Many of the local divers take very seriously the art of underwater photography; they enter many competitions within their dive clubs.

Although there is a good selection of cameras to be hired or purchased and some spares are available for

ISLANDS FOR DIVERS

A Maltese Luzzu leaves harbour with divers on board.

emergency repairs of popular brands. I would suggest that you bring a spare set of O rings and any other small items you may require for running repairs.

Diving in winter offers the advantage that many species of fish move inshore to shallower, slightly warmer waters and as they are not disturbed by swimmers during this season, the diver has even better opportunities for observation and photography than in summer.

Night diving

Night diving opens a whole new dimension for the experienced diver, and Malta is ideally suited for this kind of diving. At night the diver sees an entirely different variety of fish and the colours seen are more vibrant under a diver's torch. Most dive centres feature night diving in their programme and in the right conditions competent divers should enjoy this experience.

A group of happy divers leave Marsalforn harbour.

PHOTO: BRIAN AZZOPARDI – ATLANTIS DIVING CENTRE

Key to Symbols chart.

SPECIAL NOTES

If this is your first visit to the Maltese Islands or you have any doubts in your dive planning or navigational skills I would strongly recommend that you visit a local dive centre for an orientation dive or escorted diving. You will find that they are friendly and only too pleased to assist you in any way they can.

It is a requirement of Maltese law that a Surface Marker Buoy should be used when diving in a harbour and in some cases permission must be granted from the Harbour Master to dive there. I would also strongly recommend when your dive plan takes you away from the reef into open sea that you carry a DSMB.

Would readers please note that the illustrations of the underwater plans and road maps to be found in the following pages have been made as accurate as possible. They are to compass bearings: but not to scale, information for distance and time can be found within the text.

Although every effort to ensure that the information given on the dive sites was as accurate as possible, other information given in this book was correct at the time of going to press, the author accepts no responsibility for any loss, injury or inconvenience sustained by any person using this book.

VALLETTA & ST. ELMO BAY

PHOTO: JOE ABDILLA & PAUL GAUCI

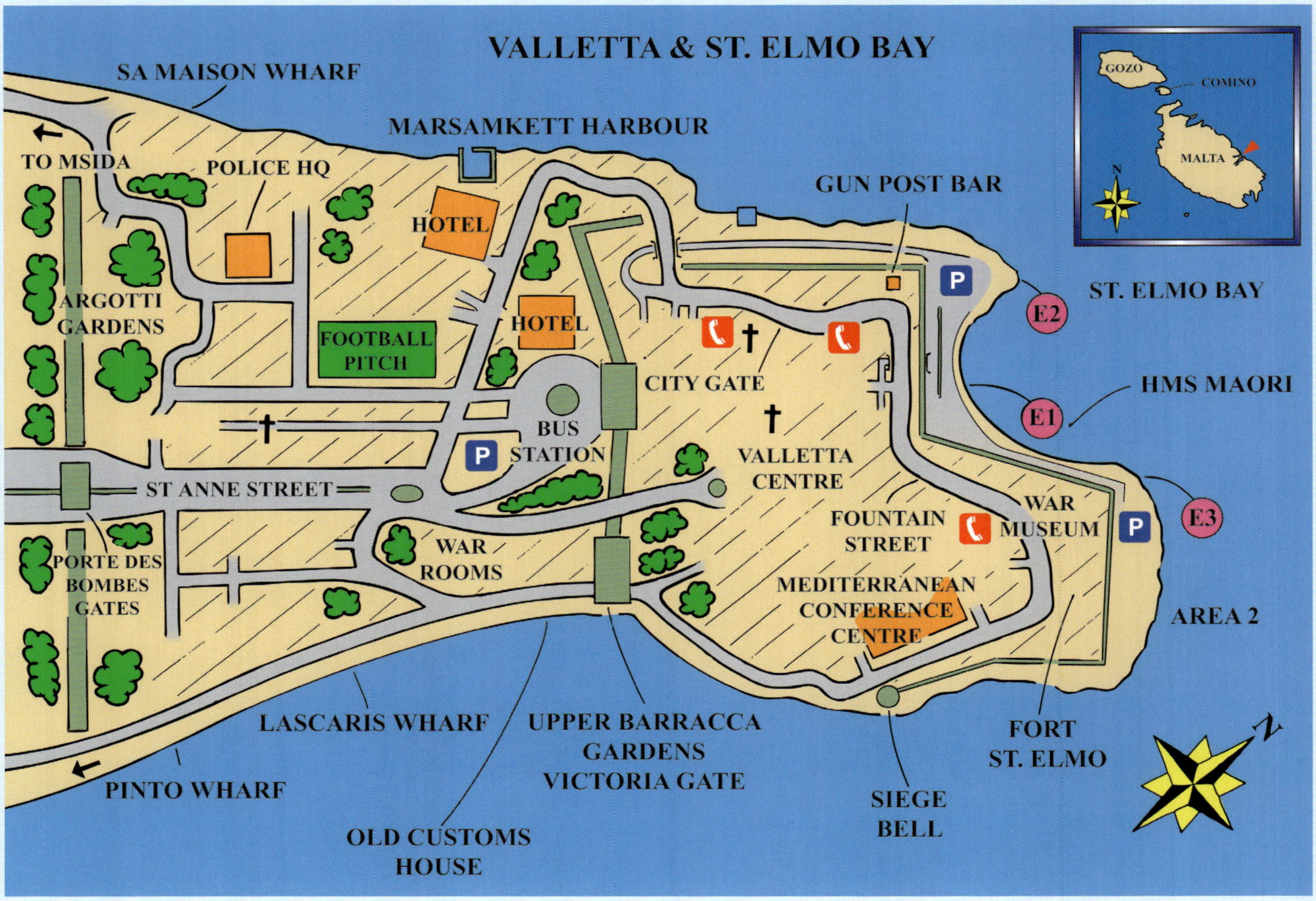

VALLETTA & ST. ELMO BAY

- SA MAISON WHARF
- MARSAMKETT HARBOUR
- TO MSIDA
- POLICE HQ
- HOTEL
- GUN POST BAR
- ST. ELMO BAY
- E2
- ARGOTTI GARDENS
- FOOTBALL PITCH
- HOTEL
- CITY GATE
- HMS MAORI
- E1
- BUS STATION
- VALLETTA CENTRE
- ST ANNE STREET
- FOUNTAIN STREET
- WAR MUSEUM
- E3
- PORTE DES BOMBES GATES
- WAR ROOMS
- MEDITERRANEAN CONFERENCE CENTRE
- AREA 2
- LASCARIS WHARF
- UPPER BARRACCA GARDENS
- VICTORIA GATE
- FORT ST. ELMO
- PINTO WHARF
- SIEGE BELL
- OLD CUSTOMS HOUSE

GOZO · COMINO · MALTA

HMS MAORI

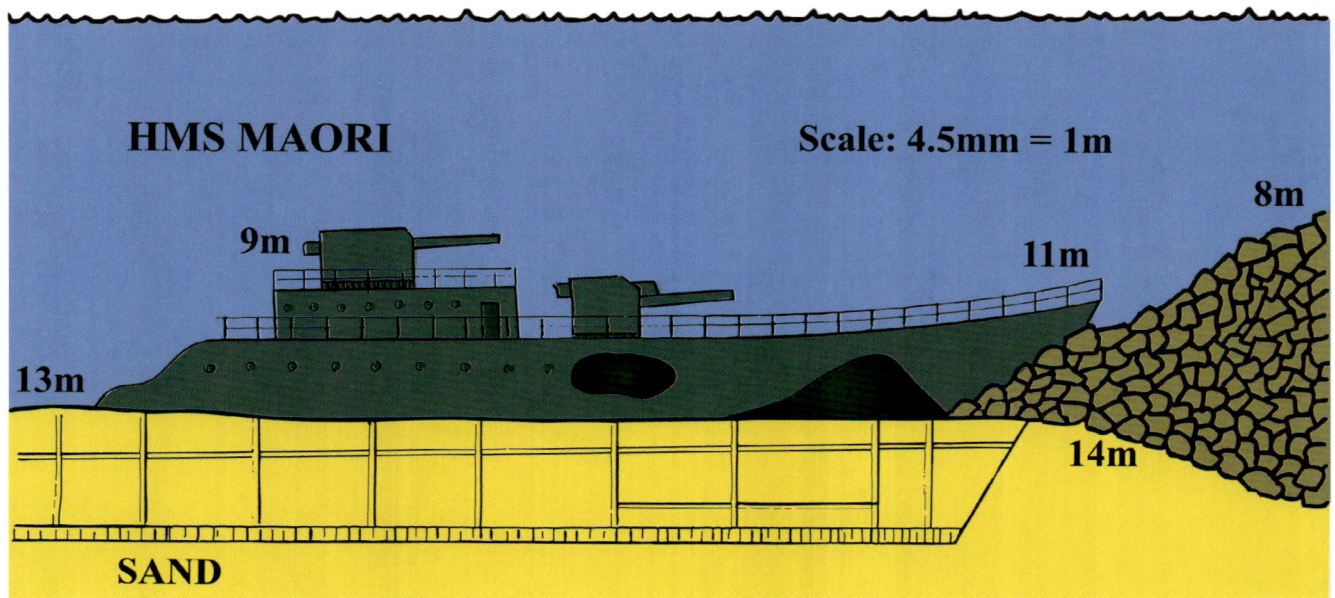

Details of HMS Maori under the water showing the wreckage which is above and below the seabed. The two guns shown in the diagram were removed and used as shore batteries.

HMS Maori outside Grand Harbour and in the foreground two Maltese gondolas. PHOTO: BY KIND PERMISSION OF JOSEPH BONNICI, AUTHOR OF "A CENTURY OF THE ROYAL NAVY IN MALTA".

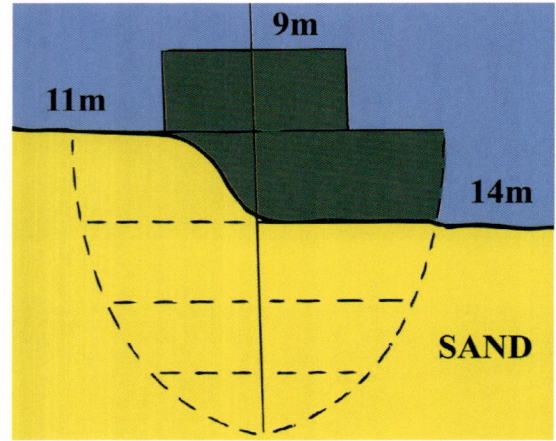

HMS Maori leaving Grand Harbour with Fort St Angelo in the background. Numerous attempts have been made to trace the owner of this photograph, which is displayed in many dive centres in Malta.

St. Elmo Bay – Valletta

St Elmo Bay is situated on the south side of the entrance to Marsamxett harbour, on the lower level road, below the city walls on the northern side of Valletta. Divers normally use this dive site when the weather conditions do not permit diving at the more popular dive sites, but in my opinion the *Maori* should be dived when the sea conditions elsewhere are good, your reward would be to find that you are the only divers here.

During weekdays parking can be a problem at this dive site, but you do have a choice of three entry points, all leading to HMS *Maori*.

Wreckage of the bow section against the wall.

HMS *Maori*

This 1870-ton Tribal-class British destroyer built by Fairfield, Govan, England was launched on 2nd September 1937. Other details, overall length 115m, breadth 11m, main armament 8 x 4.7 guns, 4 x 21 torpedo tubes, twin screws with a speed of 36 knots and a crew of 190 men. During World War Two HMS *Maori* was involved in the following campaigns:, April/May 1940 – Norway; May 1942 – Bismark; Malta Convoys – during 1941 and 1942. She was one of four destroyers which sank two Italian cruisers near Cape Bon on the 13th December 1941.

During the early hours of 12th February 1942 HMS *Maori* was moored in Grand Harbour, Valletta, when a parachute flare dropped by enemy aircraft became trapped in her foremast. Soon after the illuminated destroyer received a direct hit by a bomb and caught fire.

She was abandoned and shortly afterwards the aft magazine exploded. The destroyer sank stern first causing the bows to rise out of the sea, during that afternoon she slowly filled with water and sank. In 1945 she was cut in two and the forepart was re-floated, then towed to St Elmo Bay. The aft section was re-floated and sunk in deep water off the island.

Divers at the most popular entry/exit point for HMS Maori.

Area 1 – Route 1

THE DIVE Minimum time – 30 mins

Route 1 is to use the most popular entry point E1 at the bottom of the steps, which can be very slippery; the depth here is less than 2m so care must be taken when entering the water. From this point take a compass bearing of 20°/30°. The distance is some 120 metres to wreck and it will take you around 6 minutes at a slow fin to reach the top of the rocky slope, here the depth will be 8 or 9m. Continue down and over the rocky slope onto the sand. Your direction now depends on the depth, if you find yourself at 13m or more, turn right or if less than 10m turn left. The *Maori*'s bows are against the rocky slope, see plan.

The rocky slope which will lead the diver to the resting place of HMS Maori. PHOTO: SHARON FORDER

Area 1 – Route 2

THE DIVE Minimum time – 50 mins

If this route is your choice I would suggest you check out your route to E2 before kitting up and maybe consider E1 as your exit point. From the sea wall you will have to walk over the rocks to the most northerly point, where you will find a gentle slope giving easy access to the water, E2. When under the water take a north compass bearing and in less than 2 minutes you will reach the top of the rocky slope at 10m. Continue down and over the rocky slope to your chosen depth or to the sandy bottom at 30m. Now, keeping the rocky slope on your right, head in an easterly direction. It will take you approximately 10 minutes at a slow swim to reach the *Maori* at 14m. At a depth of 18m you will find a smooth step/slope in the sand, turn away from the rocky slope and head out over the sand for about 2 minutes, you will find a single rock called Photo Rock – a great place for macro photography.

Area 1 – Route 3

THE DIVE Minimum time – 30 mins

At E3 in the little pool there will normally be a ladder, but this is removed during the winter, there are steps cut out in the rocks as an alternative. Once under the water and down to a depth of 7m, take a compass bear of 240/250°. Moving over the reef and down onto the sand at 14m, continue over the sand until you reach the wreck or the stony wall, if the latter and your depth is more than 14m turn left or right if its less than 10m. The distance and time are almost identical to route one, 120 metres approx. 6 mins.

Care must be taken – this wreckage has been here for over 70 years!
PHOTO: JESPER KJOLLER

Divers at the entry point E3 used for both dive areas here.

Exploring HMS *Maori* and return route

The deepest part of this dive is on the starboard side; you could enter the wreck, but I suggest you don't bearing in mind that the wreck has been here for well over seventy years, so the weak structure could be dangerous. At the bow of the wreck, two winches and bollards remain, the brass base of the forward gun is still in place, unfortunately both guns have been removed and were reused as shore battery guns. Move away from the main structure and explore the wreckage, which lies on the sand in an area at the rear of the *Maori*. The marine growth, the many small fish and occasionally seahorses are to be found here, with good visibility and sunlight it makes this an ideal spot for photography.

Return route to E1 – leave the wreck by the bows and continue up the rocky slope, from here your exit point has a compass bearing of 200°. This shallow area allows you to spend time, if you have the air, to look around on your way back, if you are lucky you may see large shoals of salema fish. Just to the right of entry point E1, there are two smooth flat steps in the rock below the water level, which I call the 'Throne', making an easy exit, even when there is a small swell.

Return route to E2 – go to the top of the rocky slope and head in a westerly direction until you reach a marker which you hopefully placed at the start of your dive. Now head in a southerly direction to E2.

Return route to E3 – leave the wreck on the port side once away from the wreckage take a compass bearing of 80/90°. Continue over the sand until you reach the reef, then follow it along where it meets the sand until reaching a depth of 14m or if you have left one, your marker stone. Move up and over the reef on a compass bearing of 60/70° towards your exit point.

You can of course plan your own dive to the *Maori* using alternative routes.

HMS *MAORI* – ST. ELMO BAY – VALLETTA

PHOTO: JOE ABDILLA & PAUL GAUCI

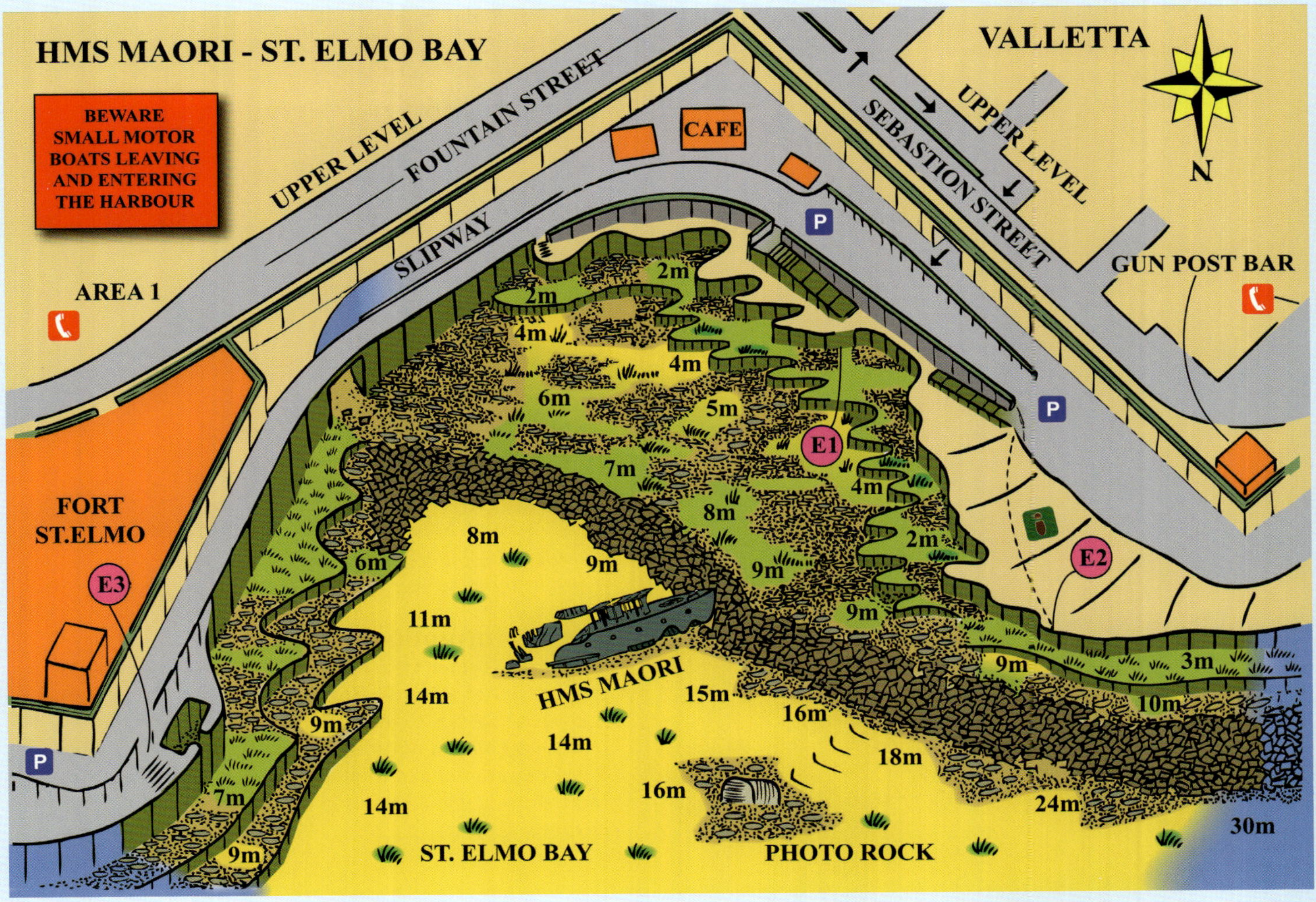

HMS MAORI - ST. ELMO BAY

BEWARE SMALL MOTOR BOATS LEAVING AND ENTERING THE HARBOUR

VALLETTA

N

UPPER LEVEL
FOUNTAIN STREET
SLIPWAY
CAFE
SEBASTION STREET
UPPER LEVEL

AREA 1

GUN POST BAR

FORT ST.ELMO

E3
E1
E2

2m, 2m, 4m, 4m, 6m, 5m, 7m, 8m, 4m, 2m, 6m, 8m, 9m, 9m, 9m, 3m, 8m, 9m, 11m, 14m, 9m, 10m, 9m, 15m, 16m, 18m, 24m, 7m, 14m, 14m, 16m, 30m

HMS MAORI

ST. ELMO BAY

PHOTO ROCK

Fort St. Elmo – Valletta

This dive site is situated between the entrance to Grand Harbour and Marsamxett Harbour, to find this site, continue along the lower level road past the café to the furthest point. This dive should not be attempted in rough sea conditions, as exit would be difficult.

Area 2

THE DIVE   Minimum time – 40 mins

The entry point I would normally use would be E3, it is almost on the corner right by the car parking area, where you will find a number of steps cut into the rocks, however it is extremely difficult to exit the water here even with a de-kit exit routine. Your exit points, of which there are three, are marked with an E on the plan. Normally I would exit the water from one of the two little pools, one each side of entry point E3, they both have steps cut in the rock to enable you to exit the water. The exit point to the south of your entry point, E3, requires the use of a stepladder to enable you to reach road level. Be sure to check that the ladders are there, as they are usually removed during the winter months.

Using entry point E3 surface swim round in an easterly direction until in front of the black post, descend to the seabed, from here take a north to northeast compass bearing and within 3 minutes you should reach a depth of 12/13m with a drop off down to 20m, this is the start of the main reef.

From here travel in an easterly direction follow the

A diver over the boulders below entry point E3.

base of the drop off, after some 6 minutes you will reach a valley which runs to the top of the reef.

This of course can be your turning point or you can continue until reaching a depth of 35m then ascend to the top of the reef, now head in a westerly direction until reaching the top of the valley. A compass bearing from here of 180' will take you to the coastline reef and a depth of 9m; from here to your exit point keep the reef on your left. Alternatively you could plan your own dive using the same entry/exit points and the coastline reef for your navigation. I found this site to be a place to explore and rummage with a maximum depth of approximately 16m, within this large area there are many gullies, small rocks and boulders to explore. This dive would also be suitable for a second dive or training. A wide variety of marine life can be found here, such as moray octopus, groupers, damselfish, red mullet and shoals of salema fish.

This reef with its drop off down to 30m plus, lies approximately 100 metres from entry point E3.

A cuttlefish (Sepia officinlis) is able to change its colours to match its surroundings.

Local information

There is a small cafe here, which is quite reasonable; they serve hot and cold drinks also snacks. Once again it is advisable not to leave any valuables in your car, unless you have a non-diver with you. Please note that it is a requirement of Maltese law that a Surface Marker Buoy should be used when diving in the harbour.

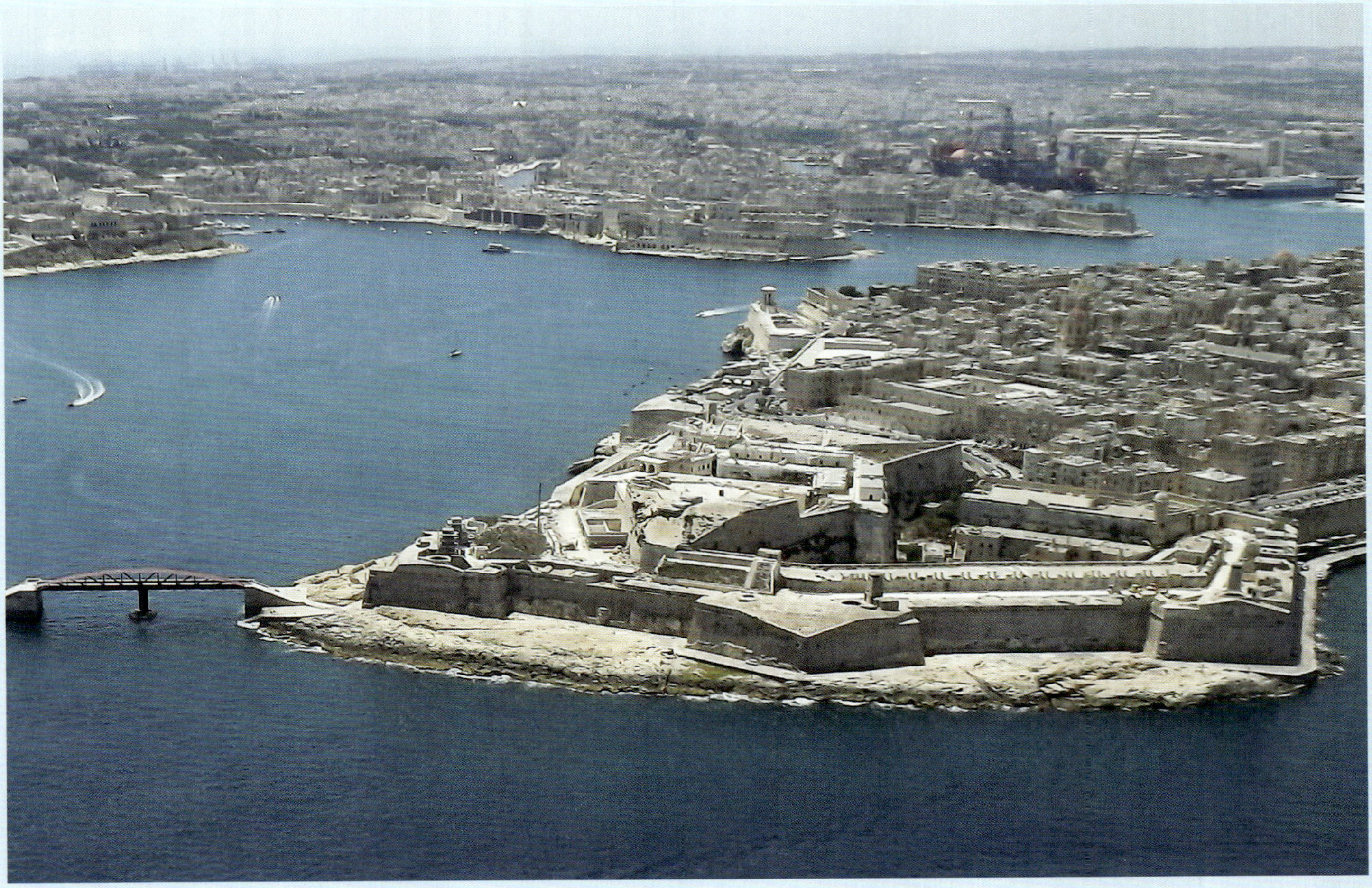

PGL AERIAL PHOTOS

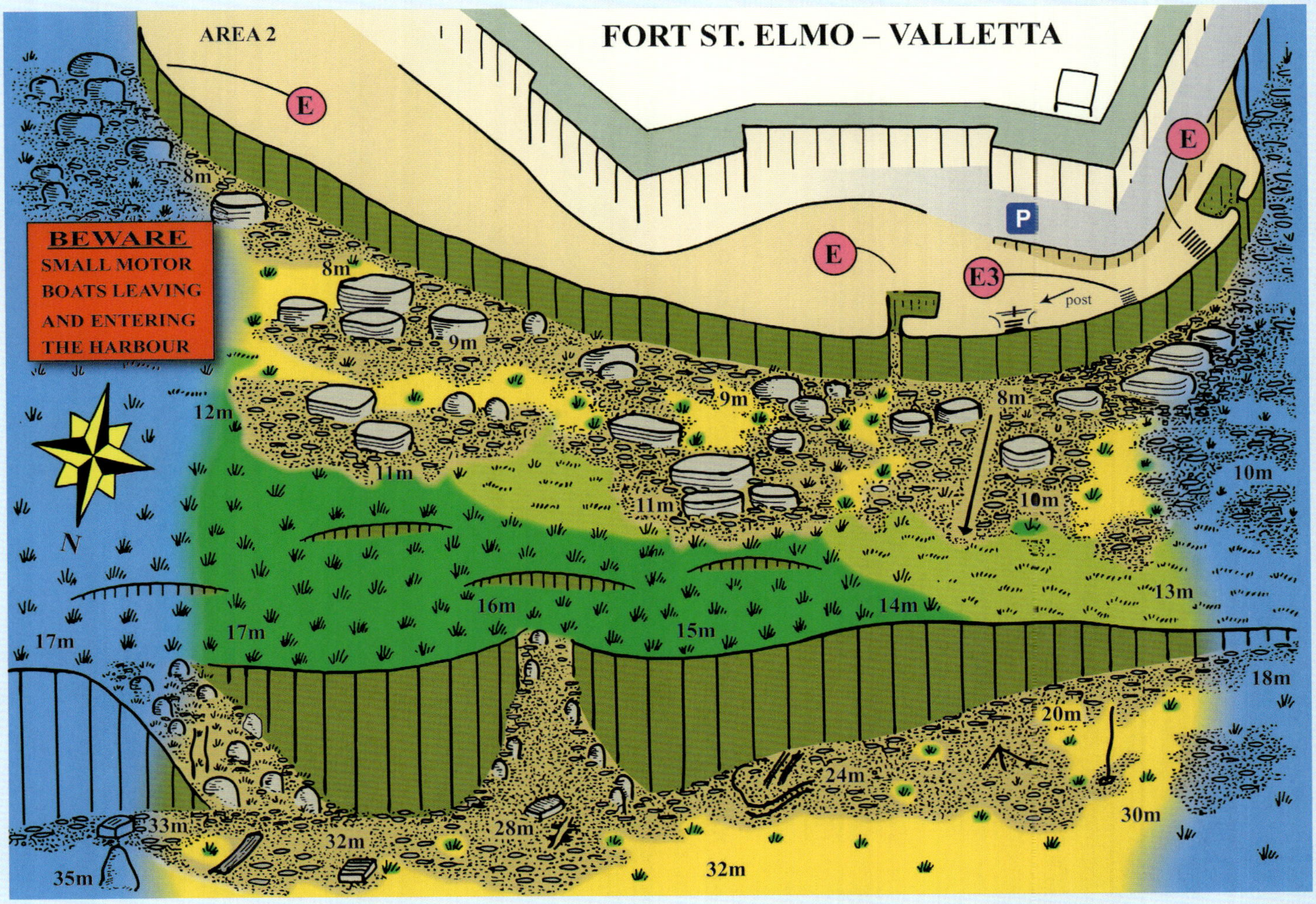
FORT ST. ELMO – VALLETTA
AREA 2
E
E
E
E3
P
post
BEWARE
SMALL MOTOR BOATS LEAVING AND ENTERING THE HARBOUR
N
8m
8m
9m
12m
11m
9m
11m
8m
10m
10m
13m
14m
15m
16m
17m
17m
18m
20m
24m
28m
30m
32m
32m
33m
35m

KALKARA CREEK – SS MARGIT

PGL AERIAL PHOTOS

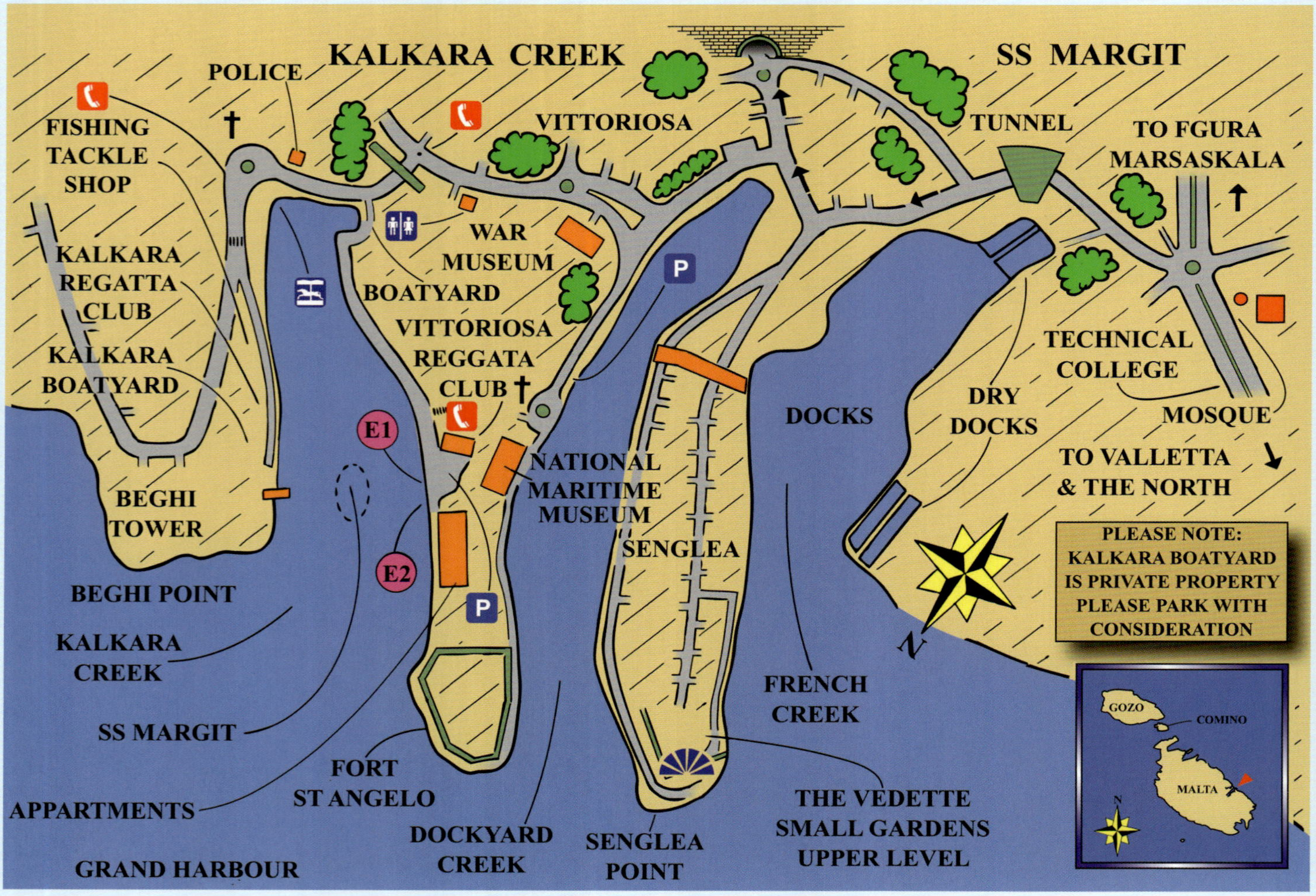

Map Labels

- KALKARA CREEK
- SS MARGIT
- POLICE
- VITTORIOSA
- TUNNEL
- TO FGURA / MARSASKALA
- FISHING TACKLE SHOP
- KALKARA REGATTA CLUB
- KALKARA BOATYARD
- WAR MUSEUM
- BOATYARD
- VITTORIOSA REGGATA CLUB
- TECHNICAL COLLEGE
- MOSQUE
- E1
- E2
- NATIONAL MARITIME MUSEUM
- DOCKS
- DRY DOCKS
- TO VALLETTA & THE NORTH
- BEGHI TOWER
- SENGLEA
- BEGHI POINT
- KALKARA CREEK
- SS MARGIT
- APPARTMENTS
- FORT ST ANGELO
- DOCKYARD CREEK
- SENGLEA POINT
- FRENCH CREEK
- THE VEDETTE SMALL GARDENS UPPER LEVEL
- GRAND HARBOUR

PLEASE NOTE: KALKARA BOATYARD IS PRIVATE PROPERTY PLEASE PARK WITH CONSIDERATION

GOZO – COMINO – MALTA

Kalkara Creek

Kalkara Creek is situated on the eastern side of Grand Harbour on the opposite side of the water to Valletta. On one side of the creek is the city of Vittoriosa and on the lower level road is their Regatta Club, here along the waters edge is a very convenient place to park right next to entry points E1 & E2. On the opposite side of the creek is the old Bighi Hospital (no longer operational) and lift tower, a very busy boatyard and Kalkara Regatta Club, both of these clubs will allow visitors to purchase snacks and drinks when open. The new Marinas' pontoons reach almost halfway across the creek to the buoyed channel which is in the centre of the creek. There is a public right of way along this quayside to the Bighi lift tower; you could of course exit the water here. The SS Margit sits upright at a depth of 22m on a silty seabed and lies almost in the centre of the creek, parallel with the shore line and her bow faces towards the entrance of the creek.

SS *Margit*

This 3496 ton passenger ship, 105.5 metres in length with a 13.7 metre beam, was built in 1912 by Forges & Chantiers de la Mediteranee at La Seyne (Yard No. 1055) and named *Theodore Mante*. Over the next 27 years her name was changed several times, *Mustaapha ll*, *Djebel Antar* and *Gatun*, in 1939 she was re-named *Margit* and arrived in Malta at 1700hrs on April 17th 1939 from Marseilles under a Panamanian flag. She stayed in Malta for the next two years and whilst waiting for a crew, war broke out.

During the early hours of 19th April 1941 while moored to buoy No. 14 at the entrance to Kalkara Creek during an air raid by Ju.87s which took place between 0310-0557hrs, she was hit, set on fire, listed to port and sank. Only her two masts remained sticking out of the water to mark her grave, in 1943 the two masts and her funnel were removed by explosives, this was to make No. 14 berth available for use during the forthcoming invasion of Sicily. Wreck No 37448 Admiralty Chart HN/52.

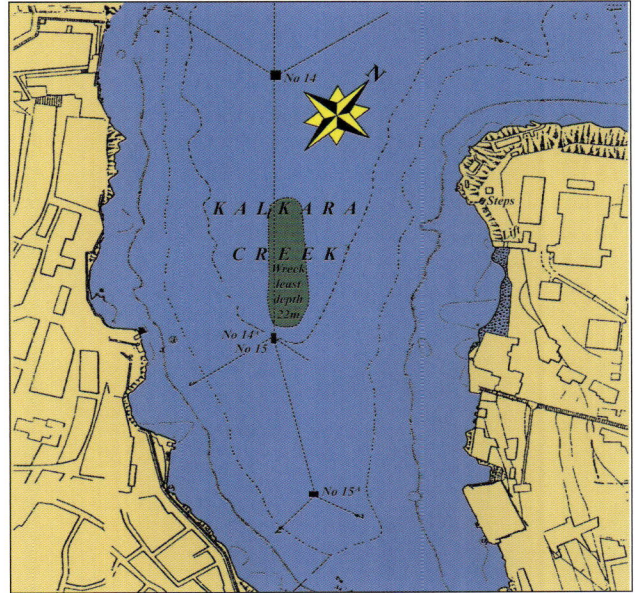

This old chart shows the wreck site of the SS Margit *and the network of massive chains which I am led to believe were moorings for battle ships and aircraft carriers.*

SS Margit *moored on buoys number 14 and 14a in Kalkara Creek, in the background is Fort St. Angelo.*

PHOTO: BY KIND PERMISSION OF JOSEPH CARUANA, THE MALTA MARITIME MUSEUM

Puzzle of names

SS *ODILE* – SS *MARGIT*

Many Maltese in post-war years claimed that the ship sunk at No. 14 buoy on the 19th April 1941 was the ex-Italian *Odile*. In the mid 1980s the National War Museum Association of Malta made an investigation about merchant ships named *Odile* in WW2. There was no Italian ship named *Odile* during the war – indeed there was no ship of that name in WW2. Only one *Odile* could be traced, a 3206 GRT steamer built in 1907 which was re-named *Katvaldis* in 1929 or 1930; as *Katvaldis*, she was torpedoed and sunk in the Atlantic on 24th August 1942.

How did this name *Odile* come about?

On the 9th June 1940 an Italian steamer named *Rodi* arrived in Malta under arrest of the Contraband Control Service. When Italy declared war, on the 10th June she was still in Malta and she was seized. She was moored to No. 14 buoy, when on the 9th July 1940 the Royal Navy took her and other merchant ships to Alexandria so that they were not caught up in the war. The *Rodi* was taken away; she was renamed the *Empire Patrol* and was sunk in 1945. She was replaced at No. 14 buoy by the *Margit*. **Up to here is fact.**

Conger eel (Conger conger. Linnaeus) are experts in finding good hiding places within wrecks.

What follows is conjecture!

Note: *Rodi* has 3 letters in sequence ODI – **R**ODI
Odile has 3 letters in sequence ODI – **ODI**LE

Now in June 1940 the British authorities suspected Malta was a hive of Italian spies. So, perhaps, to mislead these spies, they painted out the R of RODI and added LE, thus making the ship apparently to be named the ODILE and was so seen by the Maltese. Shortly after this time most of the inhabitants of Bighi and Kalkara were evacuated to the country, so that when they returned they failed to realise that the ship which was moored at No. 14 buoy was not the same ex-Italian ship that was there before they were evacuated – one could well imagine that 2 years of rust had made the ships; name unreadable. So they continued to think that the ship was the one they knew as the ex-Italian named RODI.

Remains of the lifeboat on the SS Margit *covered in soft coral.*

The top part of the piston and the driving cogs below.

THE DIVE   Minimum time – 50 mins

This is a great dive although within the harbour, it is still possible to get good visibility but not if there is a strong north easterly wind or you are following a large group of divers. The best time to dive this wreck is when sea conditions are good elsewhere. The normal rule is if you can see the seabed at your entry point then the viz should be reasonable. .

From E1 or E2 surface swim to the starboard buoy (green) do not stray into the channel it can be busy. If there is no starboard buoy use the transit points in the dive plan. You can of course descend at your entry point and swim under the water to the wreck, to do this you will need the following compass bearings: from E1 30° from E2 60° If you get your transit right, you should land some 25m along the wreck from the stern, if the visibility is not too good, the starboard side of the wreck is the easiest to navigate along, and in places it is proud of the seabed by as much as 5 metres.

Beware of boat traffic using the buoyed channel which is almost directly above the wreck.

Points to note or look for are: the stern mooring chain, prop shaft, gangway and supports, engine room with the piston rods, upper structure of the forward

Found an old helmet among the wreckage.

The pretty little nudibranch (Flabellina affinis) comes in varying shades of pink, sometimes found in the most unusual habitats.   PHOTO: JOE FORMOSA

Somehow the massive mooring chain covers some of the wreckage at the bow.

Parts of the engine room are clearly visible.

A diver over the original mooring buoy and the massive mooring chains.

KALKARA CREEK

deck the bow mooring buoy and chain. There are a variety of fish on the wreck including groupers,, but look out for nudebranchs, to see these colourful little creatures on this silt covered wreck is quite remarkable.

Return route to the Vittoriosa side
Once away from the wreck set your compass at 230' it will take you at least five minutes to clear the level silty seabed which will give way to a sandy bottom which gently slopes upwards, it will take you a about five minutes to reach a depth of 9m and less.

Just off the harbour wall around this depth are small areas of wreckage, small rocks also a little reef, lots to explore and the wall itself is alive with marine life, soft corals, cuttlefish, small morays, sea hares and many other small fish, a really good area for macro photography. If your planned exit is E1, a de-kit maybe required or you can exit at the steps at E2. Of course it is possible to exit on the opposite side in front of the Bighi lift tower, if a situation requires you to do so.

Just me taking photographs of the wreckage, fantastic visibility on this particular day. PHOTO: SHARON FORDER

A diver explores inside the hull where some of the wreckage stands 5 metres proud of the seabed.

The Bighi Hospital and lift tower on the opposite side of the creek.

Divers at entry point one.

SS MARGIT – KALKARA CREEK

KALKARA CREEK - SS MARGIT

- BIGHI POINT
- DISUSED LIFT TOWER
- 1m
- KALKARA BOAT YARD
- KALKARA REGATTA CLUB
- HMS ABINGTON SUNK 1942, SOME WRECKAGE REMAINS
- 3m
- MARINA PONTOONS
- "B"
- "A"
- 8m
- 10m
- 12m
- 14m — ENGINE ROOM — 16m
- 18m
- TRANSIT "A"
- 22m
- 21m
- BOW
- 22m
- 20m
- SS MARGIT
- 21m
- SILTY SEABED
- "C"
- STERN
- 12m
- TRANSIT "B"
- KALKARA CREEK
- HARBOUR DIVING REQUIRES SMB
- 12m WRECKAGE
- 9m
- E1
- 9m
- WRECKAGE
- 6m
- E2
- 4m
- 3m
- 2m
- VITTORIOSA REGATTA CLUB
- APARTMENTS
- VITTORIOSA
- TRANSIT "C"
- ST. ANGELO POINT

PGL AERIAL PHOTOS

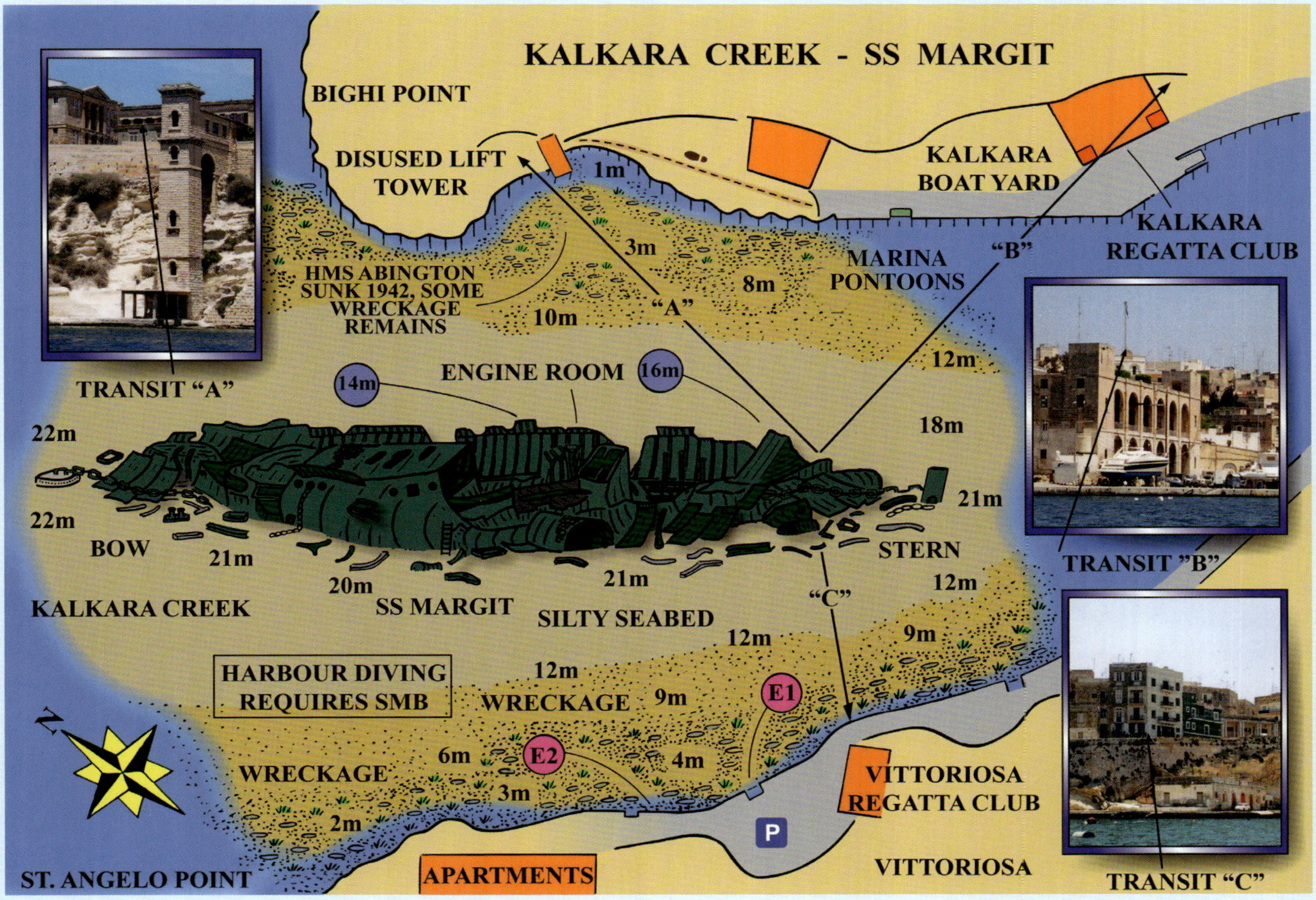

MARSASCALA & ZONQOR POINT

PGL AERIAL PHOTOS

MARSASCALA - ZONQOR POINT

- MINI BLUE HOLE AREA No 2 — E3
- TOWER
- TRACK
- SWIMMING POOL
- ZONQOR POINT
- E2 — TUG BOATS
- E1
- GZIRA POINT
- MARSASCALA
- ONE WAY
- MARSASCALA
- CAFE & BARS
- TO VALLETTA
- PARK OF FRIENDSHIP
- TO ZEJTUN
- MARSASCALA
- ST. THOMAS BAY
- GOZO — COMINO — MALTA

Marsascala – Zonqor Point

Situated on the south east coast of Malta, on the north side of the entrance to Marsascala bay is an area of land jutting out into the sea, this is called Zonqor Point. When driving into Marsascala from Valletta watch out for the central reservation, for then you will need to turn left into a one-way system before you reach the harbour, this route will take you along the north side of Marsascala bay to Zonqor Point. On your return the one-way system takes you past the cafes and little bars on the water front.

At Zonqor Point there is a large swimming pool, often referred to as the National Pool, a new Olympic sized pool and complex is situated between Valletta and Sliema. Within this area there are a number of dive sites, I have selected just two: the two tugboats *St Michael* and tugboat *10* and the Mini Blue Hole. These dives add to the variety of diving on the island, it is an ideal venue, for training, second dive or just want to be away from the crowd. It tends to be more crowded especially when sea conditions are not perfect on the north and west coasts.

Marsascala harbour with many pavement cafes to sit at and pass the time soaking up the sun.

Tugboats – *St. Michael* and tugboat *10*

The two tugboats, *St Michael* and *10* were scuttled on the 16th May 1998 as part of a plan to create an artificial reef at Zonqor Point in Marsascala. At a depth of 21m and 22m they are upright on a flat sandy bottom and have created an oasis for marine life, transforming an ecologically barren area into a shore dive location which is accessible to divers of all levels. The site is particularly well chosen because it is protected from the prevailing north-westerly winds and can therefore be dived when other areas are unreachable due to bad weather conditions. The two tugboats, 20 and 16 meters in length, saw many years of service, towing vessels around Grand Harbour until they were moored at Jetties Wharf and left partially submerged. They underwent a clean up operation to be made environmentally and diver friendly: all glass, doors and hatches were removed and passageways opened to prevent divers who venture within from becoming trapped. The preparation, towing and scuttling operations were funded by Charles and Anthony Cassar Boat and Ship Repair Ltd of Marsa.

The tugboat St Michael *being towed out of Grand Harbour towards its last resting place at Zonqor Point.*
PHOTO: BY KIND PERMISSION OF MARK BALUCI

THE DIVE
Minimum time – 40 mins

Here you have a choice of entry points. Using the nearest entry point E1, turn right after walking through the gap in the wall, when a small ridge appears on your left-hand side, follow it down to the waters edge, from here you will need a compass bearing of 140°. At a slow swim, to reach the sand, will take you some 6/8 minutes, here the depth could be 19/20m you will need to turn left, and from here it could take you up to 2 minutes to reach the wreck. Your second choice E2, is to walk towards the salt pans at the far end, passing between the two little buildings, you will find a distinct cut-out in the shoreline from here your compass bearing is 180°.

Possibly the best way to do this dive is to use the nearest entry point E1, and surface swim out until you can just see the reef below you, then descend and follow the gently sloping reef down to the sand. If your depth is 21m you will be very close to the first tug. If your depth is 17m or less, turn left, more than 22m, turn right following the line where the reef meets the sand. Beware; the first area of sand may be covered by dead sea-grass making it difficult to determine where

the reef ends and the sand start especially in areas where the depth is 17m or less.

The bows of tugboat *10* lie up against the base of the reef, with its stern some 3 metres away from it. The tugboat *St Michael* lies some 60 metres off the bow of the first tugboat, taking a compass bearing of 90°, once moving off the wreck. The second tugboat is situated approximately 15 metres from the reef, which is easy to see when the reef meets the sand, when visibility is good it can be seen from the reef. Sometimes there is a line attached between the two tugs.

When it is time to head for shallower waters, especially from the *St Michael*, take a compass bearing of 330° / 300° and follow the reef up to your required depth. At 9m and 6m below the furthest entry point, E2, the rocks and seabed are covered with marine growth of many colours and this makes an excellent area for photography. This is also an ideal place to test your skills in finding octopus and other marine life. To the west of the nearest entry point, E1, the reef becomes more rugged, but beware of the local fishermen if you travel too far along the reef in this direction before you exit the water.

The shark sucker (Echeneis naucrates) the only one I have ever seen in Maltese waters, didn't see the shark!

The bow of the tugboat 10 *on a sandy seabed at 22m.*

The hull of tugboat 10 *covered in marine life.*

The St Michael, *largest of the two tugboats, sitting upright on a sandy seabed at 22m.*   PHOTO: SHARON FORDER

The propeller and rudder of the tugboat St Michael *a painted comber seems interested in me taking photos.*

TUGBOATS – ZONQOR POINT – MARSASCALA

PHOTO: JOE ABDILLA & PAUL GAUCI

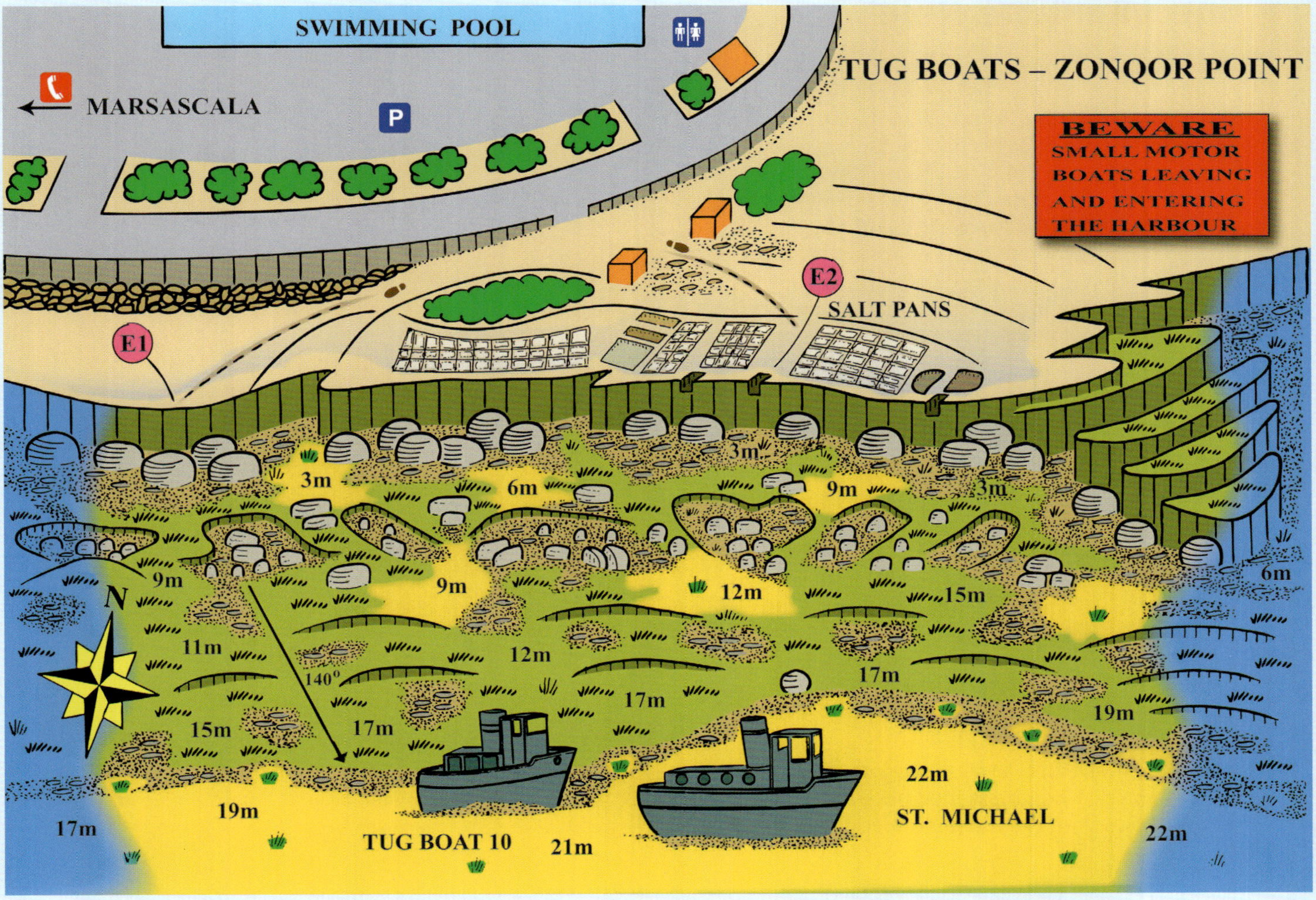

SWIMMING POOL

MARSASCALA

TUG BOATS – ZONQOR POINT

BEWARE SMALL MOTOR BOATS LEAVING AND ENTERING THE HARBOUR

E1
E2
SALT PANS

3m, 3m, 6m, 9m, 3m, 9m, 9m, 12m, 15m, 6m, 11m, 140°, 12m, 15m, 17m, 17m, 17m, 19m, 17m, 19m, 22m, 22m, 21m

TUG BOAT 10
ST. MICHAEL

This unique Mini Blue Hole just north of Zonqor Point has a cave which leads out to the open sea.

The Mini Blue Hole

Area 2

This unique mini blue hole and the tunnel leading to the open sea, has been eroded by the sea over thousands of years. This site is some 700 metres from the entrance of the track and 100 metres south from the tower, the vehicle shown in the photograph is where I suggest you park. It is important that you walk your route to the entry point before you rig, entry point E3, here there is a shallow reef covered in some short reddish marine growth which makes for easy and soft access.

THE DIVE — Minimum time – 30 mins

Once you have entered the water move away from the reef and descend, a short way from the tunnel entrance you will find a depth of 7m. From here I suggest you enter the tunnel and explore, continue to the end, you will then find yourself at the bottom of the Mini Blue Hole at 4m, here you can admire what the sea has created or just take photographs. When you return to the entrance it is your choice which way you decide to go. Immediately along the shoreline in both directions, there are many rocks and boulders giving you interesting areas to explore especially if you have a camera. Here the seabed has a variety of depths, moving away from the shoreline the seabed starts to

A shoal of two-banded seabream (Diplodus vulgaris) live on rocky and sandy seabeds.

flatten out but within this area there are many little gullies with sandy bottoms with small reefs on each side making this a good habitat for hiding octopus and moray. Further out from the shore the seabed is mainly sand. Just bear in mind that your entry point is also your exit.

After your chosen dive you will find there is a small cafe in the car park next to the swimming pool, which is normally only open during the summer months. Alternatively the short journey to Marsascala centre you will find a choice of small bars and cafes, which over look the harbour where you can sit, soak up the sun and enjoy a much-deserved rest.

Spinous spider crab (Maja squinado) can be found on rocky, algae rich seabeds.

Painted comber (Serranus scriba) has a tapered body slightly compressed with a pointed head, the most common fish likely to be seen in Maltese waters. PHOTO: VICTOR FABRI

MINI BLUE HOLE – MARSASCALA

PGL AERIAL PHOTOS

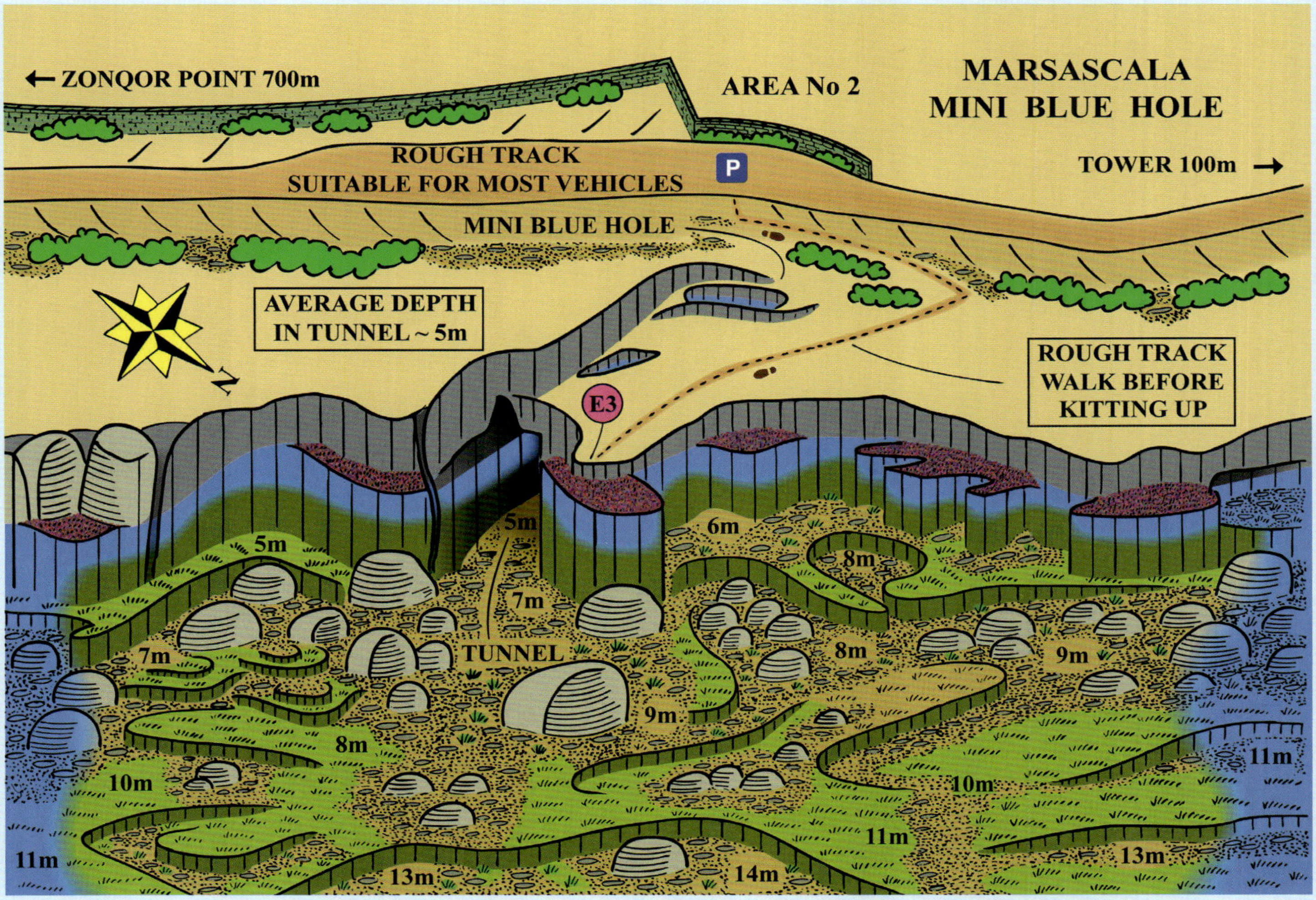

MARSASCALA MINI BLUE HOLE

← ZONQOR POINT 700m

AREA No 2

ROUGH TRACK SUITABLE FOR MOST VEHICLES

TOWER 100m →

MINI BLUE HOLE

AVERAGE DEPTH IN TUNNEL ~ 5m

ROUGH TRACK WALK BEFORE KITTING UP

E3

TUNNEL

5m, 5m, 6m, 8m, 7m, 7m, 8m, 9m, 8m, 9m, 10m, 10m, 11m, 11m, 13m, 14m, 11m, 13m

MARSAXLOKK – DELIMARA POINT

PGL AERIAL PHOTOS

MARSAXLOKK DELIMARA POINT

- TO VALLETTA
- MARSAXLOKK
- CAFES BARS & MARKET AROUND HARBOUR AREA
- MADONNA CONVENT
- HARBOUR
- POWER STATION
- CHIMNEY
- FORT DELIMARA
- LIGHTHOUSE
- ANIMAL SANCTUARY
- ST PETERS POOL
- EAST REEF — E2
- SOUTH REEF — E1
- DELIMARA POINT
- MARSAXLOKK BAY

Inset
- FORT DELIMARA
- LIGHTHOUSE
- DELIMARA POINT
- EAST REEF — E2
- SOUTH REEF — E1

Delimara Point

This dive site is situated on the south of the island, about 4.2km or a 15-minute drive from the town of Marsaxlokk, which is popular with visitors for its fish market, colourful boats and harbour.

Leave the village heading east, at the roundabout head up the hill to the Madonna Convent, here, turn right to Delimara Point, this narrow road passes the rear of the Power Station and keep going until you reach a small cross roads. On your right will be Delimara Fort, the track to your left will lead down to a small bay. Continue straight on, after about 50 metres, fork left down a track, for a distance of approximately 500 metres. On your left you will pass two small brick-built viewing platforms, next a little track off to your right a short distance after this the track you require bears to the right. Follow this along and when you come out into the open with the sea on your left, this is your parking area. See aerial photograph.

There are a number of ways which you can plan and dive this under rated dive site with excellent reefs with depths of 30m plus. There are two main reefs in this area, for easy reference I will refer to them as East or South reef. For the East reef I have three dive plans and one for the South reef. All dives start at entry/exit point E1 which is approximately some 220 metres from the parking area, but in my opinion it is well worth the effort, it was here that my buddy found the largest octopus that I have ever seen in Maltese waters, also a good area to locate the locust lobster.

Depending on your required dive time it may be worth considering using a 15-litre cylinder for this dive site. Alternatively you can plan your own dive, but may I suggest using the reefs for your navigation.

Your route from the parking area to E1, follow the track which leads towards Delimara Point, within metres fork left, when the track reaches the cliff edge (approx. 170 metres) look for the steps down to the lower level, they are slightly hidden by an overhanging rock, see aerial photo

East Reef

THE DIVE   Minimum time – 50 mins

The East reef is shaped like the letter U and runs out from the furthest point of land in an easterly direction. **Dive plan 1.** Once in and under the water follow the top of the reef in an easterly direction all the way along to the corner, where your depth will be 13m, this will take approximately 6 minutes. At this point there are normally large shoals of fish to see or photograph. Here descend to the bottom at 23m passing an interesting ledge at 17m, continue your dive in an easterly direction, following this gently sloping area of grass, rugged boulders and sand. At a depth of approximately 30m

A Locust Lobster (Scyllarides latus) does not swim but spends its time on the seabed.   PHOTO: JOE FORMOSA

Three divers exploring this shallow reef near the entry point.

DELIMARA POINT

Pilot fish (Naucrates doctor) a diver makes eye to eye contact with this energetic, inquisitive fish.

and some 12 minutes into your dive you will find another small reef, turn left follow this reef in a northerly direction for some 50 meters or 4 to 5 minutes.

At this point then a westerly compass bearing will take you back to the East reef, any further and you will require a more south-westerly bearing. Once you reach the East reef, keeping it on your left, the end of this reef runs in a north westerly direction, changing to a westerly direction until it reaches the coastline where you will have to bear right. After a short time the seabed below you will open up to a flat area of sand and small rocks with a depth of 9m, here you will be very close to E2 entry/exit point.

Dive plan 2. Using entry/exit point E1 descend to the seabed at 13m, the choice is now yours, either follow the reef keeping it on your left to The Corner where your depth will be 23m: or move away from the reef for some 2 to 3 minutes and then head east. Take your time to explore this area with its large boulders,

Diver lets his DPV take the strain!

overhangs, grass and small sandy patches; this is a good area for locating the locust lobster. Once you reach a depth of about 20/22m, or the Lone Boulder at 25m, now head north to The Corner at 23m This is an excellent area where you normally find large shoals of fish, bring your camera.

Now follow the reef keeping it on your left, in a northerly direction, either at its base or on the top, after a short time the bearing of the reef will change to north-westerly then westerly towards the coastline, where the reef bears to the right towards entry /exit point E2.

Divers below entry/exit point E2 at 6m. Here the reef seems to have formed steps.

Dive plan 3. Using the same entry/exit point E1, descend to the seabed at 13m, leaving the main reef behind you, swim in a southerly direction and within 5 minutes another reef will appear in front of you, here your depth will be 16m. If you turn right the reef will take you to the little island just off Delimara Point, but you need to turn left. Now the dive will take an easterly direction until you reach the end of the reef, where the depth is 20m; to reach this point will take approximately 10/12 minutes. Continue in the same direction down over the grass and small rocks to an area of sand and a number of small boulders at 34m. Here the reef will be on your left it is quite steep and rises up to 25m and to assist you with your bearings keep it in view.

When it is time to return, ascend the reef to the top, follow it in a westerly direction along its ridge, until you reach the single boulder at 25m. When the visibility is good, from this point you will be able to see the corner on the East reef, if not, take a northerly bearing and within 3 minutes you will reach the corner of the reef. At this point I would ascend to 13m at the top of the reef, then follow the ridge, on the south side of the East reef, in a westerly direction to my entry/exit point E1.

> **It must be noted that there is a possibility of strong currents in this area or swell following a storm, which also may affect the visibility, making navigation more difficult. A good guide for visibility is that you should be able to see the seabed from your entry point.**

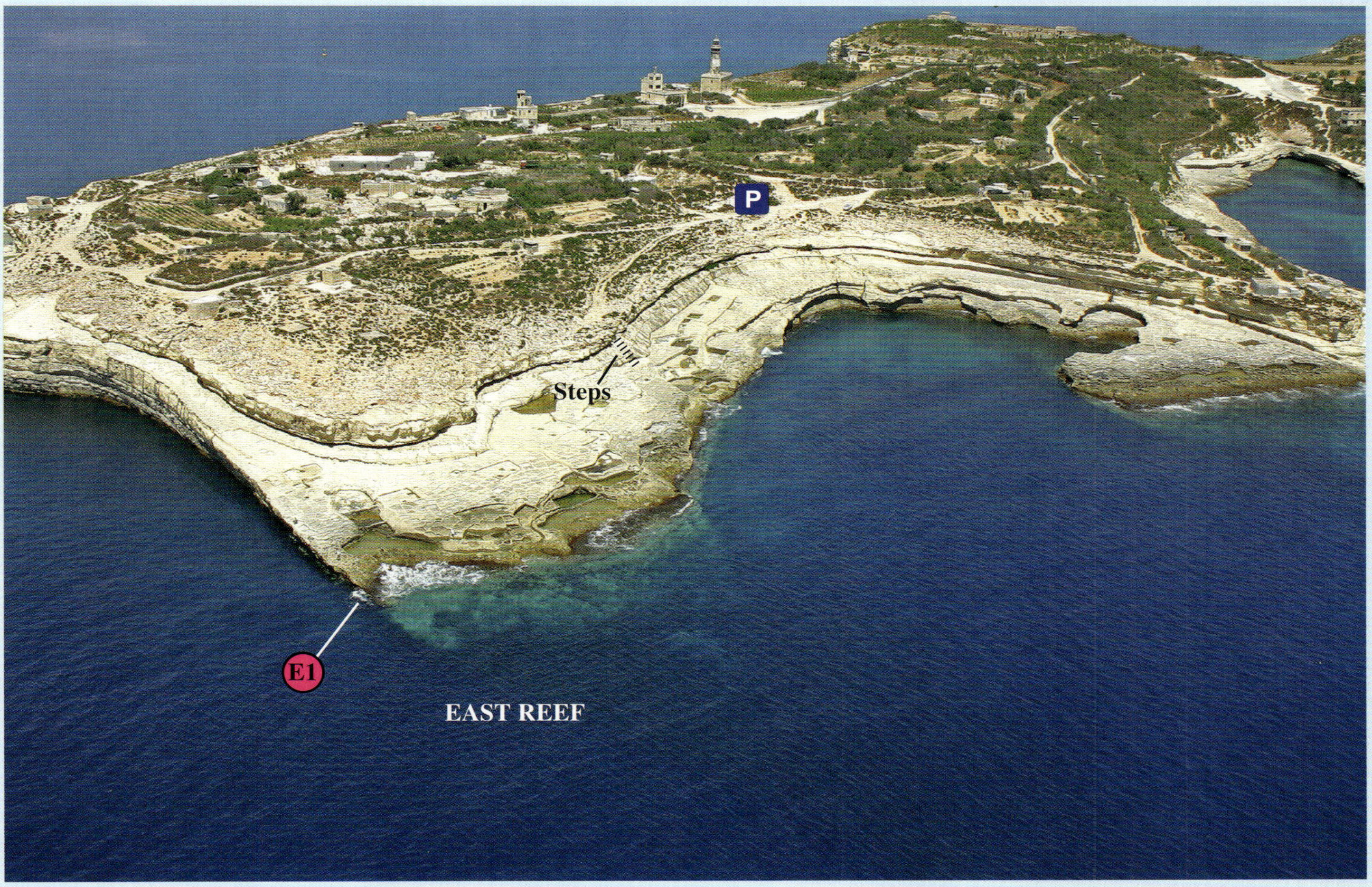
P
Steps
E1
EAST REEF

PGL AERIAL PHOTOS

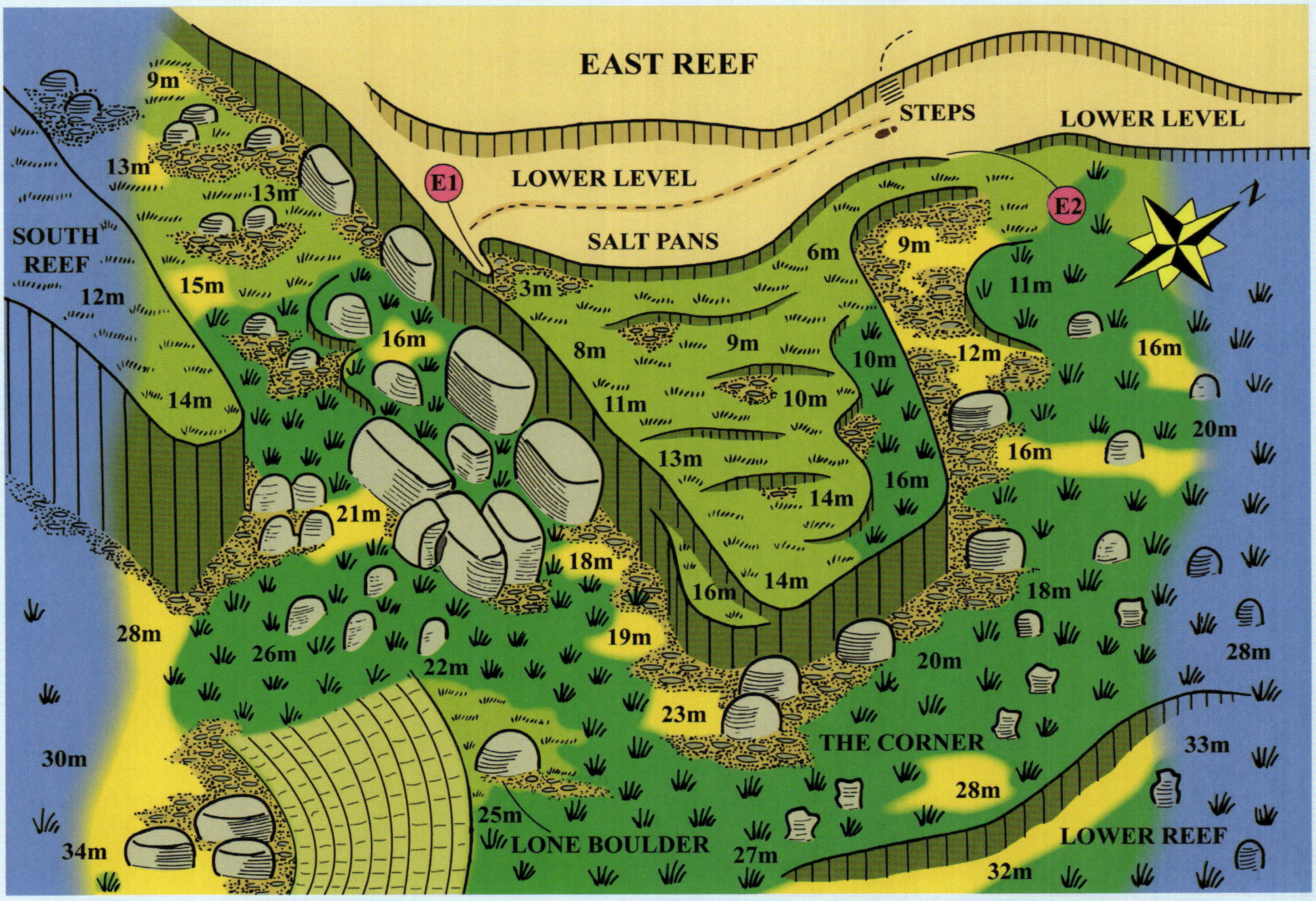
EAST REEF
STEPS
LOWER LEVEL
LOWER LEVEL
E1
E2
SALT PANS
SOUTH REEF
N
9m
13m
13m
12m
15m
14m
16m
3m
6m
8m
9m
9m
11m
11m
10m
10m
12m
16m
20m
13m
14m
16m
16m
21m
18m
14m
16m
18m
28m
26m
22m
19m
20m
28m
23m
THE CORNER
30m
33m
28m
25m
LONE BOULDER
27m
LOWER REEF
34m
32m

DELIMARA POINT

South Reef

THE DIVE — Minimum time – 55 mins

In my opinion this dive is for the experienced diver and should not be attempted from the shore in strong currents and /or bad visibility. For this dive the entry / exit point will be E1, once in the water, surface swim in a southerly direction for some 3 minutes, then below you, you should be able to see the South Reef at 12m, if the visibility is reasonable. If you cannot see the seabed when entering the water, drop down to a depth of where you can and then continue in a southerly direction until you reach the reef. Continue over the top of the reef in the same direction until you can see the drop-off, which goes down to 26m.

Descend onto the top of the reef, from here head in a westerly direction, slowly descending the reef and in this area you will find three large boulders which I have called the Three Peaks. Now continue along the base of the reef to the end, depth 22m: from here when the visibility is good you will be able to see Arrow Head Rock, otherwise a southerly compass bearing will take you across the valley to its base at 24m. The next reef is shaped like a U, follow it all the way round until the reef turns to a southerly direction, keeping it on your right hand side, your average depth here will be 22m, within in a short distance you will see two large boulders on your right, they will be slightly obscuring the entrance to Abigails Cave at 18m.

The end of the third reef from your entry point and at the top Arrowhead Rock can clearly be seen.

Nudibranch (Peltodoris atromaculata) with distinctive brown and white colours, feeds on sponges. PHOTO: JOE FORMOSA

At this point your dive time is possibly 35 minutes, bearing in mind you are at least 20 minutes from your exit point.

Once inside, the cave it is quite light due to two openings in the roof, of which you will be able to exit easily onto the top of the reef at 16m. Your choice of return route depends on the time and air you have remaining, you can either reef hop from one to the other taking a north to north-easterly bearing which would be the most direct route to your exit point or you can navigate the tops of the reefs, only crossing at their narrowest parts back to your exit point. Of course at any time during your dive, if you wish, you could ascend to the top of the reef and return to your exit point.

This is not a welcoming gesture from a grouper (Epinephelus guaza). PHOTO: VICTOR FABRI

Remember that this site is well away from any amenities and the nearest telephone is in Marsaxlokk, if you require refreshments it is advisable to take them with you. If you do not have any non-divers with you do not leave any valuables in the car. You can of course after your dive, drive into Marsaxlokk, where there are a wide variety of cafes and bars situated along the harbour front. The market is a daily event, but the Sunday fish market is very popular, with not only the local people but also tourists, so you can expect heavy traffic and crowds of people in Marsaxlokk.

SOUTH REEF – DELIMARA POINT

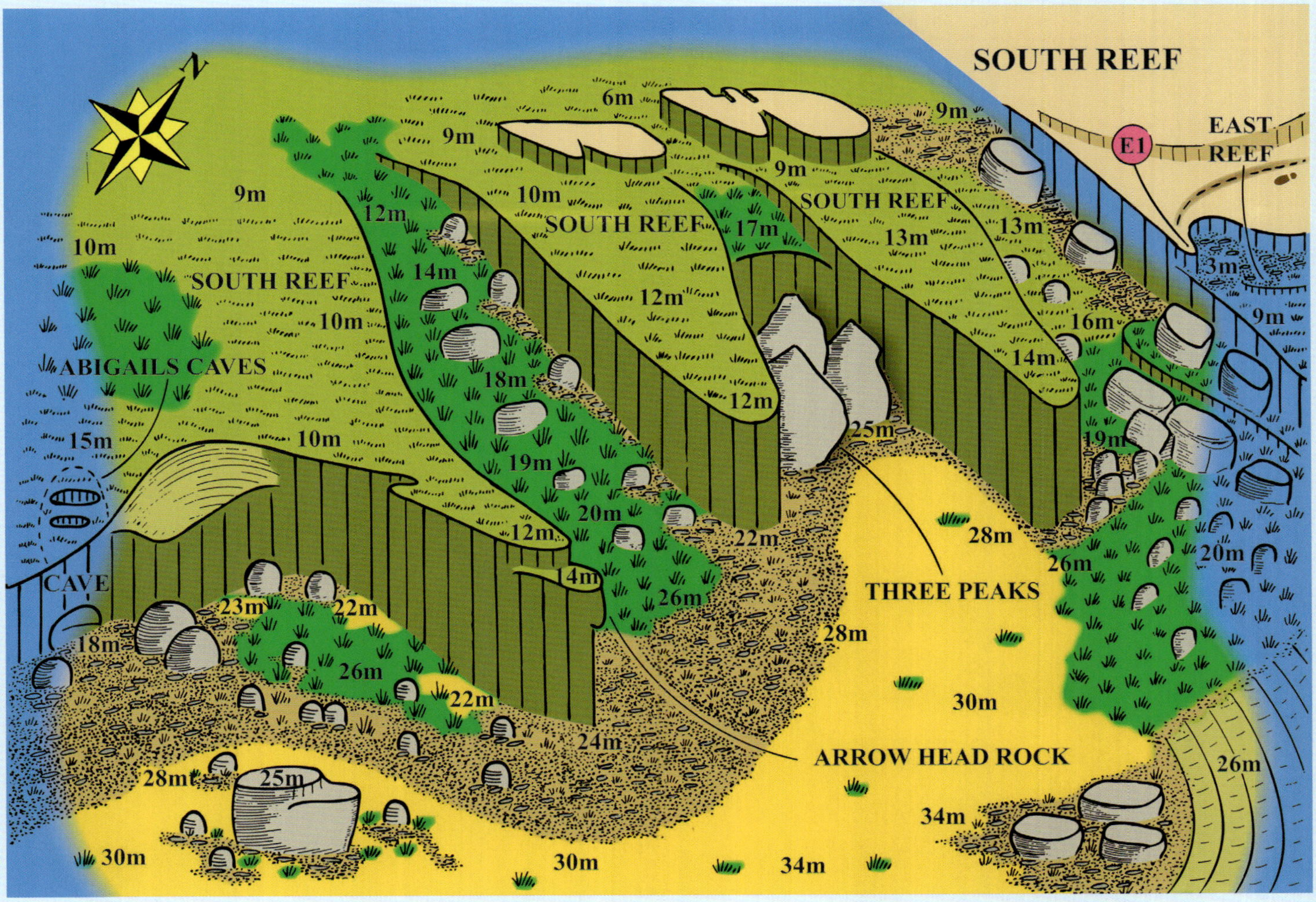

WIED IZ-ZURRIEQ (BLUE GROTTO)

Wied iz-Zurrieq (Blue Grotto)

Wied iz-Zurrieq is a small village situated on the south coast, there are two main routes to this site, one from Rabat 10km along a country road, or from Luqa 7km taking the road which passes under the airport runway. The village is very popular, with divers for the *Um El Faroud*, possibly the best wreck dive in the Mediterranean, and with tourists' for the beauty of the Blue Grotto.

One of the entry/exit points at the inlet.   PHOTO: SUE LEMON

This dive site is normally referred to as the Blue Grotto, but the Grotto is approximately half a mile to the west of the inlet and can only be reached by sea, there is a viewing area up on the main road above the Grotto, see plan. Parking for divers is at the bottom of the hill where the road ends, here it is close to your entry / exit points please note it can be extremely busy at peak times. The sea conditions must be checked here, for although there is virtually no tide, sometimes there are currents even when sea conditions are calm. Maybe if there are divers leaving the water you could ask them if they have experienced any currents during their dive. Remember the small inlet is your only exit area, and depending on the sea conditions you might have to consider use of the slipway, E2, which is sheltered from the open sea.

Beware of the boats taking tourists to the Blue Grotto, they travel quite fast so if you intend to surface swim across the inlet be careful, stay together and keep a look out. There will normally be fishermen here so take care and enter the water away from their lines. There are three diving areas here, but the dive plan can be varied depending on experience and depth required. Please note that due to weather conditions or the possible removal of stepladders, near E1 entry point during the winter period, the slipway is the only exit point, E2 but be careful for this is where the boats leave from.

A diver on the bows of the Um el Faroud *which was scuttled in September 1998.*

Um el Faroud

The ill fated tanker *Um el Faroud* was scuttled on Wednesday 2nd September 1998. three and a half years after the explosion that killed nine dockyard workers in Grand Harbour Valletta, this tragic event shocked the people of Malta. Her final voyage started in the early hours of the morning, arriving off Wied iz-Zurrieq around 9.30am. It then took over three hours to get her into position, due to a moderate south-easterly swell. At about 12.30pm the special valves that were fitted for the scuttling were opened and the ship started to take in water, then around 3.30pm she sank quietly beneath the surface, down onto the sand at 35m. At this moment in time she is upright on the seabed in two sections with the bow separated from the bridge. In the centre of the bridge at the front, just below the remaining top floor, is a brass plaque in memory of the workers killed in the explosion

The 3,147 gross ton vessel is a single screw motor tanker, built by Smith Dock Co. Ltd., Middlesborough England in 1969. The port of registry was Tripoli and owned by General National Maritime Transport. The engine room, bridge and accommodation are arranged aft. The cargo section is sub-divided into four centre tanks and four wing tanks on each side. The overall length is 110 metres and the breadth is 16 metres, still in place are the propeller and rudder.

WIED IZ-ZURRIEQ (BLUE GROTTO)

A diver with a torpedo DPV above the Um el Faroud.

A diver above the stern of this massive wreck.

The Um el Faroud *being manoeuvred into position prior to sinking on the 2nd September 1998 at 1530 hours, in the background the village of Wied iz-Zurrieq (Blue Grotto).*

CUSTOM AERIAL PHOTOS

WIED IZ-ZURRIEQ (BLUE GROTTO)

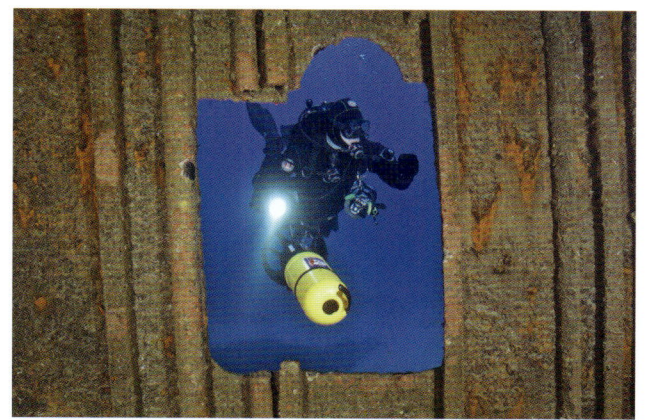

A diver looks into one of the exits which have been cut in this wreck.   PHOTO: MAX VALLI, ORANGE SHARK H2O

The ships' chimney is a good place to take a souvenir photograph.

The bridge of the Um el Faroud *after a storm.*

A plaque in the centre of the bridge placed in memory of the dock workers who sadly lost their lives in the explosion.

From stern to bridge the starboard side of the gangway.

The port side of the bridge and stern.

49

THE DIVE

Minimum time – 50 mins

There are number of ways to reach the *Um el Faroud*, you could of course go by boat, for if they are not too busy the fishermen or the pleasure boatmen will take you out, drop you off over the wreck but they will not wait for you. I personally have two different routes for reaching the *Um el Faroud*, and for both, my entry point is the same, E1 just to the left at the bottom of the steps, they are as follows:

Amberjacks (Serola dumerili) possibly looking for prey around the wreck, could also indicate there is a current.

PHOTO: JOE FORMOSA

Route 1 If sea conditions are perfect, surface swim taking a compass bearing of 240° until you have a 20° compass bearing on the flat faced sandy coloured rock, which can clearly be seen in the aerial photograph. The surface swim is approximately 200 metres from your entry point, E1 and will take some 8/15 minutes, do not attempt this route if there are any currents

Route 2 In my opinion the best way to dive this wreck is to surface swim across the inlet entrance, west along coast for approximately 100 meters until you reach a little cove, even at a slow swim, this will take no more than 8/10 minutes. If you are facing out to sea, behind you will be a large sandy coloured flat faced rock and below you a 10m ledge. From this ledge, take a compass bearing of 200°. Your distance from here to the wreck is about 70 metres and takes about 3/4 minutes.

The bow and the anchor chain.

A diver poses for a photograph above the huge propeller and rudder of the Um el Faroud.

For the depths on this ship, see plan. If penetration is in your dive plan ensure that all diving safety procedures are carried out. For your safety all doors and windows have been removed also holes have been cut in the hull for entry and exit. Do not be tempted to stay too long, I recommend that you leave the wreck with a minimum of 100 bar which will give you time to explore the reef on your return journey. When it is time to return, leaving from the bridge and once away from the wreck, take a compass bearing of 330°. This compass bearing will not lead you directly back towards the inlet, but to the closest reef to the wreck, which is approximately 50 metres here the depth will be 18m. To ascend this reef to a depth of 6m will take approximately 5/6 minutes from the bridge of the wreck.

Once you have reached your required depth, bear right heading in an easterly direction; follow the reef all the way round back to the inlet and your planned exit point. You should allow for this return journey some 20/25 minutes, but can be done quicker if you do not explore the reef on the way. If you do not have sufficient air when leaving the wreck, take a compass bearing of 60° this will lead you directly back to your exit point, do not miss the inlet entrance. In my opinion unless you have boat cover, this dive is for experienced divers only and a 15 litre cylinder should be used.

UM EL FAROUD – WIED IZ-ZURRIEQ

PGL AERIAL PHOTOS

UM EL FAROUD
AREA 1

FLAT FACED ROCK

BEWARE OF BOATS USING THE INLET

8m
6m
10m LEDGE
14m
12m
6m
E2
7m
10m
E1
12m
15m
14m
20m
22m
12m
9m
24m
24m
28m
28m
PLAQUE
26m
CAVES
24m
24m
25m
31m
30m
28m
31m
UM EL FAROUD
27m
31m
26m
28m
26m
25m 26m
31m 26m
32m
35m
33m
32m 29m 27m
20m
32m 28m

UM EL FAROUD

WIED IZ-ZURRIEQ (BLUE GROTTO)

Wied iz-Zurrieq – West Reef

Area 2

This dive site is situated on the western side of the inlet and there are a number of different areas to explore. There are drop offs, ledges, gullies and boulders surrounded by sea grass and sandy areas. There are also two caves, the walls of which are covered in a wide variety of brightly coloured corals and inside many cardinal fish using them as their home.

A diver checks out the small entrance to Bell Cave.

Divers admiring the plaque which has been placed by 'Atlam Divers' marking fifty years of their diving club. A good pilotage mark for the Um el Faroud.

THE DIVE Minimum time – 40 mins

Enter the water at E1 and down to 10m cross the inlet to the western side, down over the rocky slope onto the small area of sand at 24m. Follow the reef around to the right heading west; over the sea grass, the first of the two caves is at 24m, further round you will find a small area of sand where you will find the entrance to Bell Tower cave at 26m, the cave has enough room for two divers, when entering the cave be careful not to kick up the sand. You can exit the cave at 21m. On the left hand side of the cave is a large rock, from this point follow a line where the grass, rocks and boulders meet the sand at an average compass bearing of 240' this will lead you to the divers helmet plaque at 30m, placed there by BS-AC Atlam Dive Club to commemorate fifty years of their club. When it is time to return ascend the reef to your required depth. Follow it along and on the ridge, just before the inlet you will find a fissure, which runs from 16m to the top, another good place to explore. If you intend to cross the inlet underwater, remember the pleasure boats using the inlet, so leave enough depth to be safe.

Cardinal fish (Apogon imberbis) usually found in shoals below 10m, in crevices and overhangs, which act as a refuge when a predator passes by.

The moray (Muraena Helena) hides in holes and fissures in the reefs and wrecks. PHOTO: JOE FORMOSA

WEST REEF & CAVES – WIED IZ-ZURRIEQ

PGL AERIAL PHOTOS

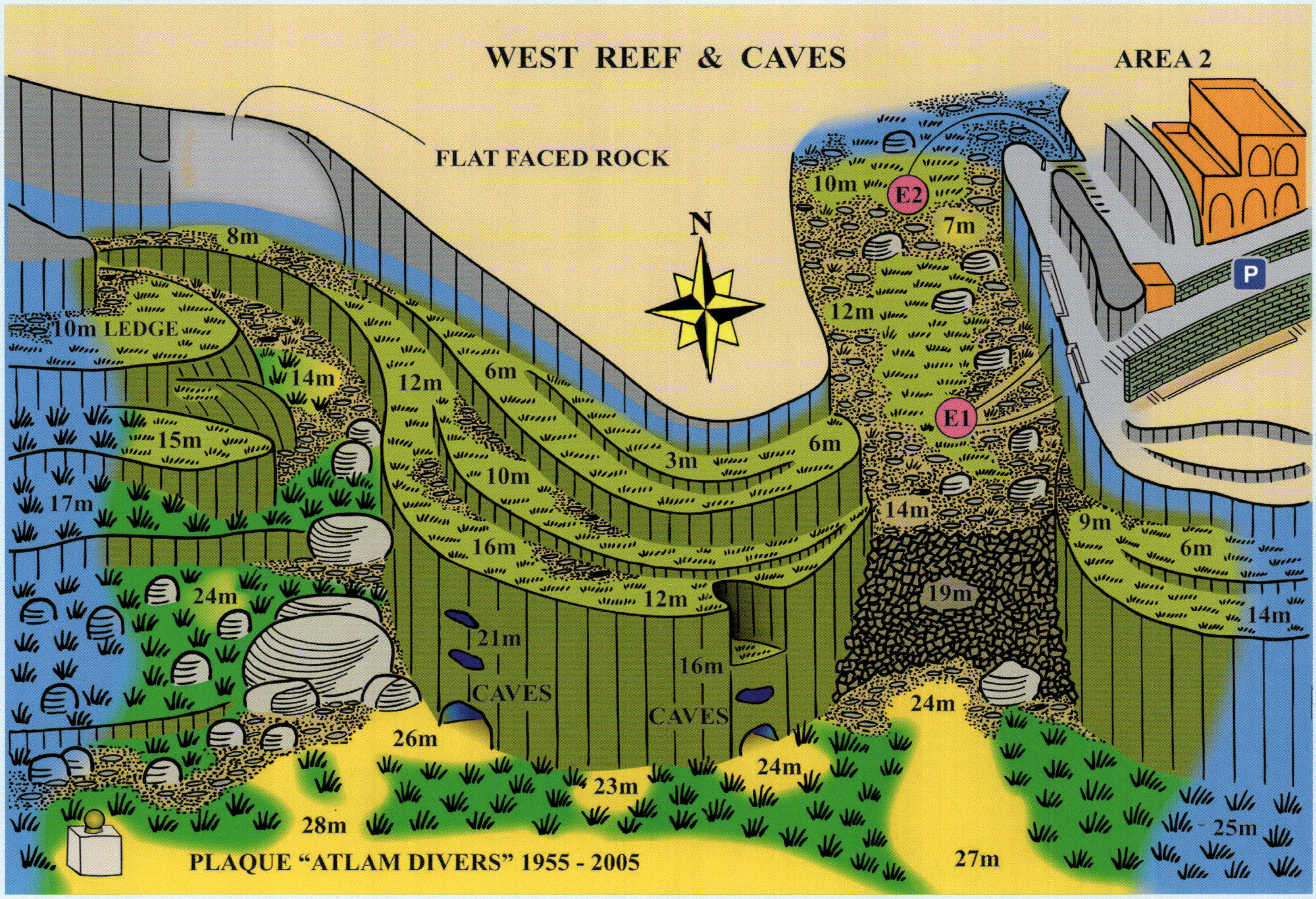

WEST REEF & CAVES — AREA 2

FLAT FACED ROCK

N

- 8m
- 10m LEDGE
- 14m
- 15m
- 17m
- 24m
- 12m
- 6m
- 10m
- 3m
- 16m
- 12m
- 21m
- CAVES
- 26m
- 28m
- 23m
- 10m
- E2
- 7m
- 12m
- 6m
- E1
- 14m
- 19m
- 16m
- CAVES
- 24m
- 9m
- 6m
- 14m
- 24m
- 25m
- 27m

PLAQUE "ATLAM DIVERS" 1955 - 2005

Wied iz-Zurrieq – East Reef

Area 3

This single line reef continues in an easterly direction for 300/400 metres. At the start of this reef is a large ledge with depths from 9m to 16m, the maximum depth to the seabed is 36m. Of course on moving away from the reef the depth will increase, but this area is mostly sand and sea grass. The visibility here can be excellent, with clear water up to 40 metres plus. Usually large shoals of small fish can be seen on the reef, so keep an eye out into the blue for those larger fish that may be coming in to feed.

THE DIVE — Minimum time – 40-50 mins

Entry for this dive can be made directly below the steps E1, or further round to the east there is another entry point, E3, bearing in mind that exit is not possible from the latter. Once under the water you can follow the ledge along for some 60 meters and at varying depths of 9m to 16m. at the end of the ledge descend the drop-off down to 28m plus, if you have decided to use entry point E1 descend to 9m then down over the rocky slope to 24m. and out of the inlet bearing left and heading east, follow the bottom of the reef at 28m – **here both routes meet.**

Continue to follow the line where the bottom of the reef meets the sand past the small overhang, staying close to the base of the drop off the seabed in front of you will begin to rise, passing a number of large boulders on the seaward side until you reach a depth of 9m you are now immediately beneath the overhang on the surface, This could be your turning point from here return to the ledge at your required depth. Follow the reef all the way along heading west, round into the inlet and your planned exit point.

Alternatively if you wish to be a little more adventurous, the best way to dive the reef is to surface swim to the overhang (see aerial photograph) be sure to check for currents and keep to the shoreline, as the pleasure boats also use this route to the Blue Grotto. Once you have reached the surface overhang, which should take you 6 to 8 minutes from E3, descend to 8m on eastern side of the reef, from here you will be able to descend a drop off to 35m. Follow the line of the reef staying at a depth of 30m keeping the reef on your right and heading in a westerly direction, once you meet the main reef ascend to your required depth until you return to the inlet and your exit point.

This vertical reef only meters from the village of Zurrieq.

A John Dory (Zeus faber) can be spotted inshore among the rocks during the summer months. PHOTO: JOE FORMOSA

Night diving

Wied iz-Zurrieq is an excellent venue for a night dive, for there is an abundance of marine life to see around the small overhangs and rocks within the inlet. There are reef walls to navigate by, safe exits, lighting and footpaths, and if you are very lucky a full moon will shine down and glisten over the sea while you sit and enjoy a drink of your choice after the dive.

There are many fish to see here during the day or night, just to name a few, damselfish, red mullet, cardinalfish within the caves, painted combers, scorpionfish, moray-eels, cuttlefish, wrasse, john dory and it was here at 6m in the inlet, I saw my first seahorse in Malta.

Restaurants, café's and gift shops are open during the day and evening over the summer period but close earlier in winter.

EAST REEF – WIED IZ-ZURRIEQ

BEWARE
PLEASURE BOATS GOING TO AND FROM THE BLUE GROTTO

EAST REEF

CAFE BARS & SHOPS

TOWER

E1, E2, E3

OVERHANG

7m, 9m, 16m, 25m, 27m, 9m, 6m, 14m, 16m, 28m, 34m, 30m, 34m, 36m, 9m, 8m, 12m, 24m, 25m, 23m, 36m, 30m, 34m, 30m, 38m, 38m

PGL AERIAL PHOTOS

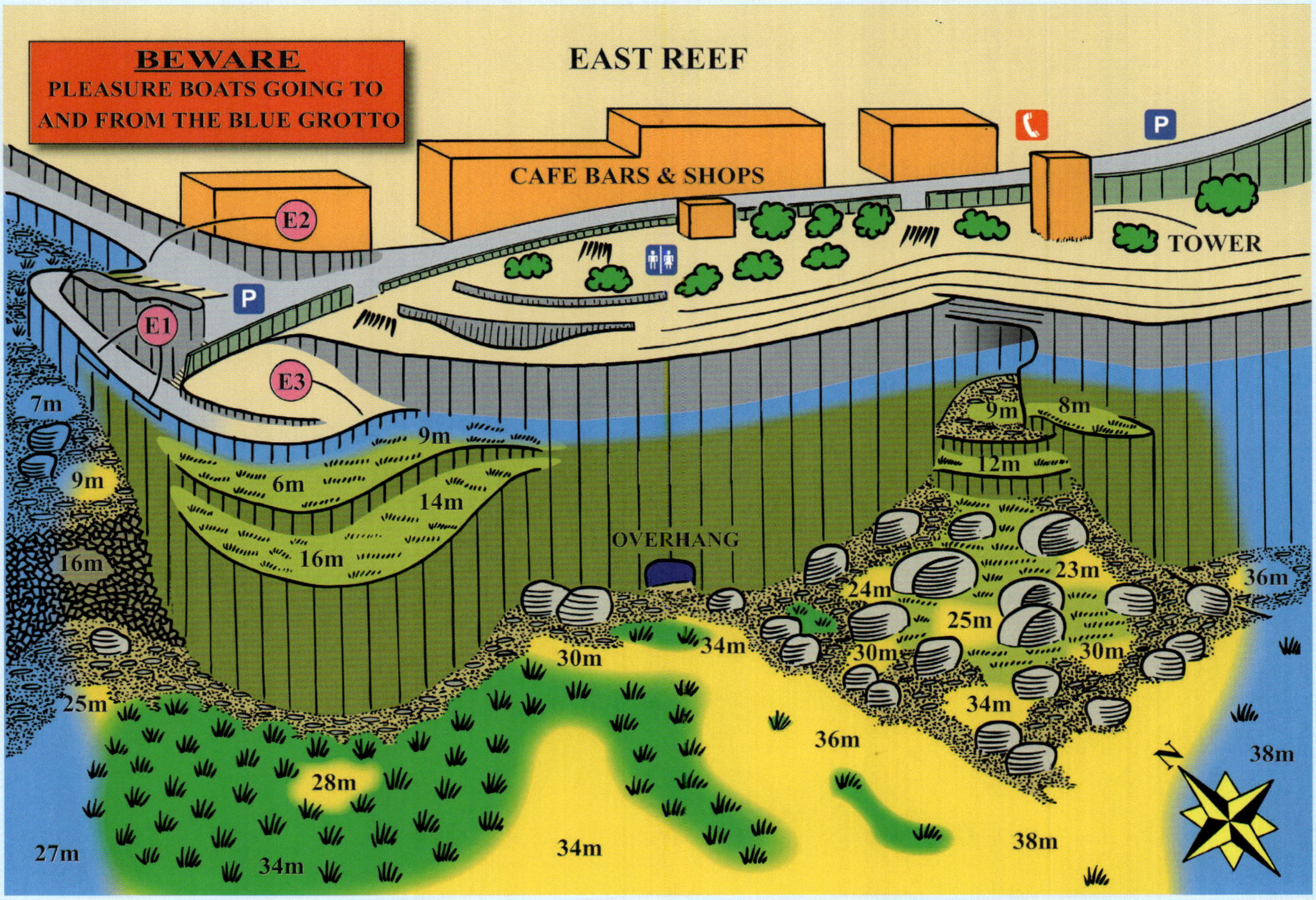

GHAR LAPSI

PGL AERIAL PHOTOS

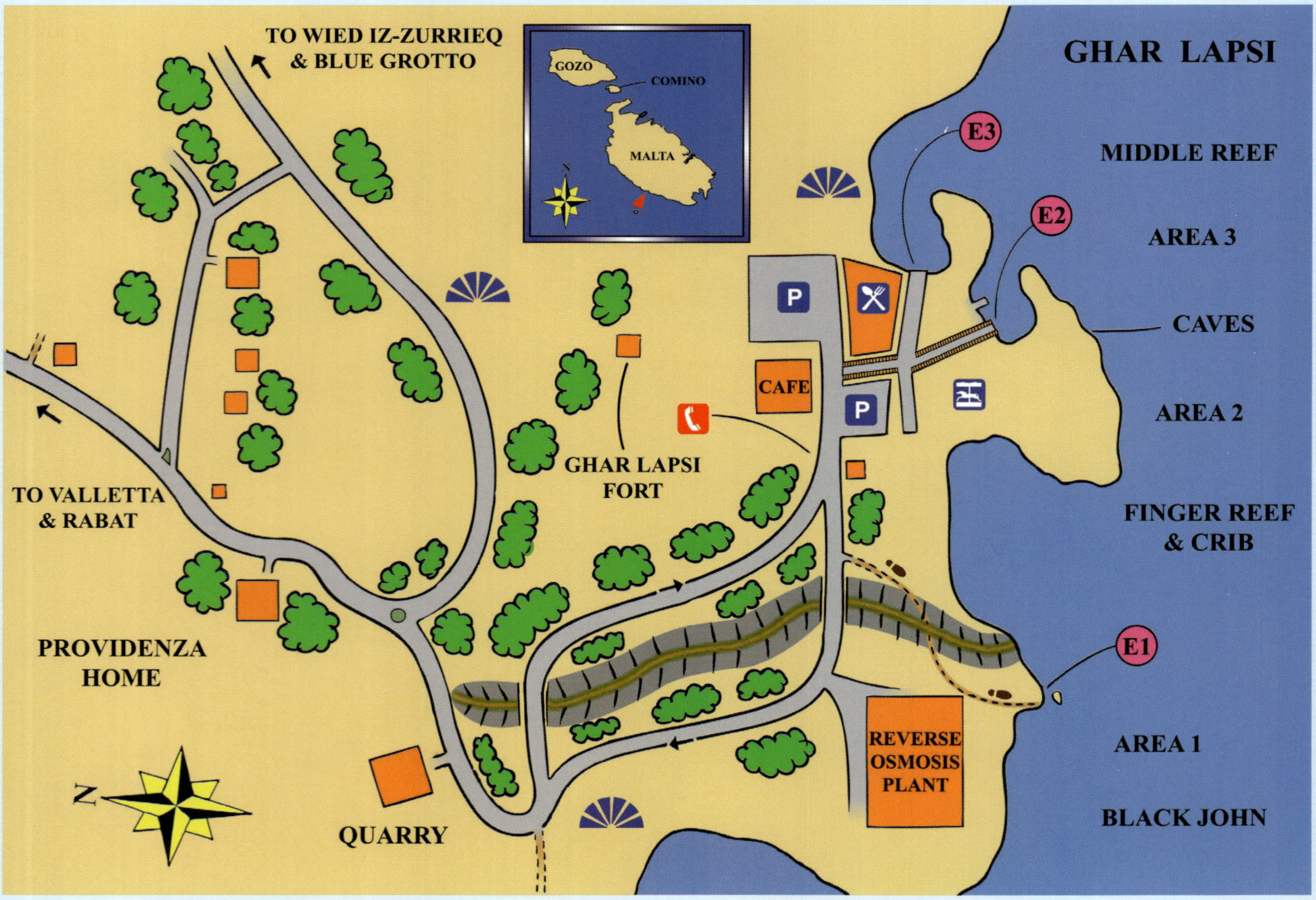

GHAR LAPSI

TO WIED IZ-ZURRIEQ & BLUE GROTTO

GOZO • COMINO • MALTA

E3 — MIDDLE REEF

E2 — AREA 3

CAVES

CAFE

GHAR LAPSI FORT

AREA 2

TO VALLETTA & RABAT

FINGER REEF & CRIB

PROVIDENZA HOME

E1

REVERSE OSMOSIS PLANT

AREA 1

QUARRY

BLACK JOHN

Ghar Lapsi

Ghar Lapsi is a very small hamlet which has a pretty little cove and is situated in the south of the island and is one of the few places where the sea can be entered along this coastline. To reach Ghar Lapsi from the north you will probably travel from Rabat/Mdina 9km in distance along single lane country road. From the village of Wied iz-Zurrieq, famous for its Blue Grotto and travelling from the south continue along the coast road to Ghar Lapsi, 5km passing the Prehistoric Temples (Haga Qinn). At the roundabout turn down the hill and past the quarry to where the road splits in two and a one-way system is operated, where you are almost at your destination. Here you will find two car parks, ideal for dive areas 2 & 3. Next to the small car park is a steep road with steps either side leading down to the cove where your entry/exit points E1 & E2 are. Parking for dive area 1 is near the Osmosis Plant, see plan.

Black John

Area 1

The dive at Black John takes you away from the popular dive sites and it is almost a certainty that you will be the only divers here. The dive site is situated at the rear of the Osmosis Plant; this involves a 200 metre walk over uneven ground.

Follow the rough track down to a small concrete hut then follow the pathway into a little valley, a short climb up the other side, turn left, follow the fence around the Osmosis Plant going under the water outlet. Keep following the fence until you find steps cut into the rock. This leads down to a small concrete platform, which is your entry point and to the right is your exit point E1.

Check this route before you rig. Remember it is not possible, with safety in mind, to dive this site during rough sea conditions for there is only one entry/exit point. The next nearest exit point is the cove at Ghar Lapsi, which is some 400 metres away.

There are two ways to dive this offshore reef; you can plan your dive with a maximum depth of 25m. At E1 descend to the seabed directly below your entry

The entry point E2 at the bottom of the steep hill and steps.

point. Alternatively, you can surface swim to the far side of Black John; this is the small part of the reef that is visible from the shore. This will give you an opportunity to reach depths of 38m. You must bear in mind that at times in this area there are offshore currents, in my opinion this is a dive for the more experienced diver.

From the parked vehicle on the road to the entry point is quite a difficult walk, I strongly suggest that this route is walked before kitting up.

GHAR LAPSI

A diver poses behind a shoal of salema fish (Sarpa sarpa).
PHOTO: JOE FORMOSA

Golden zoanthid (Parazoanthus axinellae) lives on rocky bottoms and on other organisms: e.g. sponges, colonies can cover broad surfaces.

THE DIVE Minimum time – 40 mins

Entry is a 2m drop to the water and below you a depth of 10m, once on the seabed move away from this area, with the reef on your left heading east past a large rock and under an arch/overhang. Coming through the

Lots of marine life to photograph on these shallow reefs.

other side do a part U-turn and take a compass bearing of 200° to the main reef. On reaching the reef keep it on your left; follow it all the way round until it is heading east.

If you stay reasonably close to the reef your maximum depth will not exceed 25m, but further away from the reef, depths of 30m or more are possible around the large rocks, grass and sandy areas. After some 25 minutes into your dive, depending on the time you have taken to explore and you are close to the base of the reef you will find what appears to be a large crack which leads diagonally upwards to the top of the reef.

Once at the top of the reef head in a westerly direction along the ridge, it will take you no more than 6 minutes to reach the base of the reef at 10m that leads up to Black John itself. Now a northerly compass bearing will take you towards the coastline, first over the reef to Propeller rock and then over the sand where the water from the Osmosis Plant falls into the sea, here there is normally an abundance of marine life.

To find your exit point head west and you will pass over the large rock and overhang where your dive began, then ascend to the 6m ledge where you can do your safety stops and explore at the same time, bear round to the for right for the exit point.

The alternative way to do this dive with a depth of 38m is to surface swim to the far side of Black John continue on until you are clear of the shallow reef. Now descend keeping clear of the boulders, once on the seabed head in an easterly direction with the large boulders and grass on your left and the sandy area on your right, depth 38m. Keeping to this route and in approximately 9 minutes you should reach a depth of 32m.

Turn to your left and facing in a northerly direction you should be able to see in front of you, a very large boulder, which has its base at 30m. Ascend to the top of this boulder and then on to the main reef, now follow the ridge in a westerly direction, it should take you no more than 10 minutes to reach the base of the reef at 10m that leads up to Black John itself. **From this point of your dive to your exit, is as the same as the first alternative, E1.**

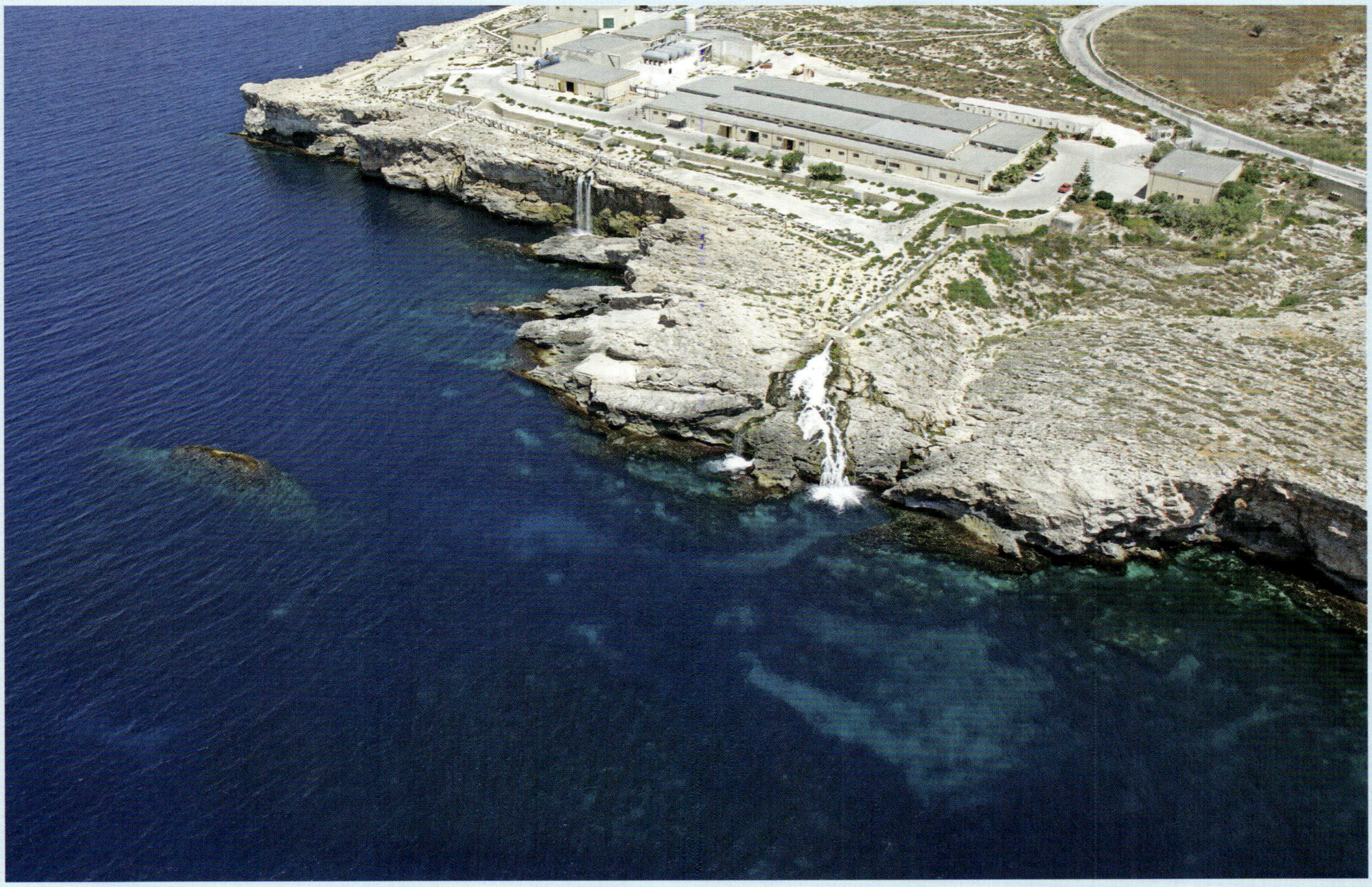

PGL AERIAL PHOTOS

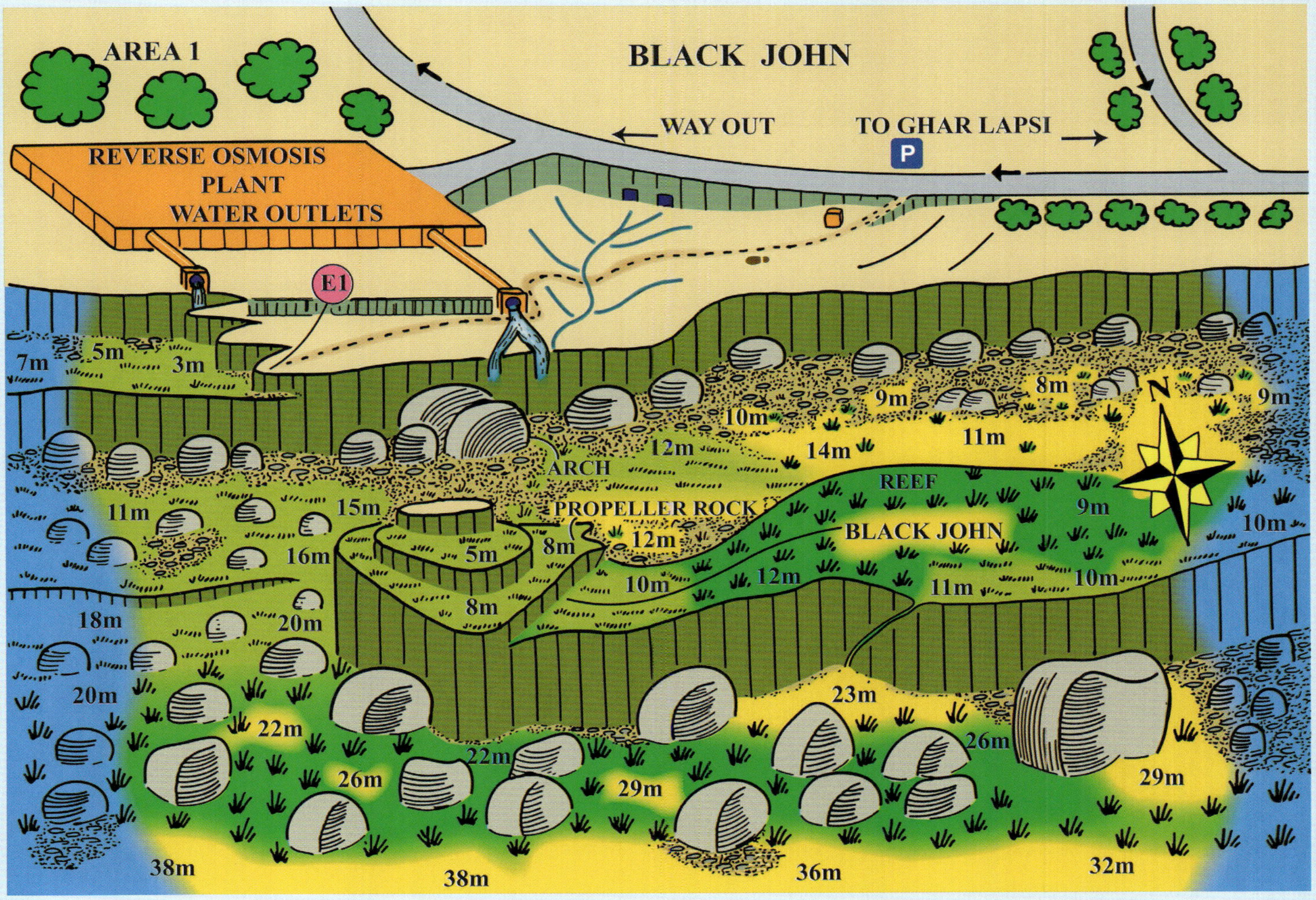

BLACK JOHN
AREA 1
WAY OUT
TO GHAR LAPSI
P
REVERSE OSMOSIS PLANT WATER OUTLETS
E1
7m
5m
3m
10m
9m
8m
9m
12m
14m
11m
ARCH
N
REEF
PROPELLER ROCK
11m
15m
9m
10m
BLACK JOHN
16m
5m
8m
12m
12m
10m
11m
10m
8m
18m
20m
20m
23m
22m
26m
22m
26m
29m
29m
38m
38m
36m
32m

GHAR LAPSI

Divers swim across the cove to the little pool where the entrance to the cave system is to be found.

Inside the cave system near the exit to the open sea at 8m.
PHOTO: SERGEY MARKOV, DIVE SYSTEMS

Finger Reef and Crib
Area 2

Before diving this area you will have to decide which route you are going to take to the cave at 19m with a hole in its roof. Route one via Finger Reef, the shorter distance of the two, or Route 2 via the Crib at 22m, if during your dive you stay in close proximity to either of these reefs this will be your maximum depth. Basically there are two main reefs, one is shaped like a finger, hence its name, the second twists and turns until it reaches the cave via the Crib. The Crib, a nativity scene, is of almost life sized figures cut from plate metal, welded to a tubular frame, placed under the water within an overhang, by the Calypso Diving Team. Around these reefs are areas of boulders, rocks, sea grass and sand. Of course within this area there are many permutations of dives giving you the opportunity to create your own dive plan.

Opposite the entry/exit point, E2, within the cove, there is an entrance to a cave system, the entrance is just large enough for a diver, but there is plenty of room inside. There is a larger exit into the open sea at 8m a gulley will then lead you down on to the sand at 11m. A little further along from the first exit there is second exit to the open sea at 6m. Within the cave there are many small openings, which allow bright rays of sunlight to shine through, illuminating parts of the cave.

Fireworm (Hermodice carunculata) please do handle this pretty little creature. PHOTO: JOE FORMOSA

These two unusual boulders mark the north easterly end of Finger Reef.

The author is hoping for some good photographs.
PHOTO: SHARON FORDER

THE DIVE
Minimum time – 55 mins

Your entry point, E2, is immediately below the small car park at the bottom of the steep hill. Surface swim to the centre of the cove and descend, once on the bottom swim out of the cove following the reef around to your right, when out of the cove. Continue down over the reef heading in a westerly direction, until you reach the sand at 11m.

Alternatively if the weather conditions permit and there is no surge in the cave it could be used for the start of the dive, or if you prefer at the end. Surface swim directly across the cove, submerge and pass through a small hole in a rock wall, depth 1m into a little pool. The entrance to the cave is on your right, which is small, but once inside there is sufficient room for a diver to move around. Whilst descending through the cave you will see the underwater exit at 8m follow the gulley out of the cave and down onto the sand at 11m. **Here the two dives meet.** From here follow the line where the sand meets the reef in a westerly direction for approximately 2 minutes where you will see a mound covered in sea grass on your left, this is the point where the two dives separate at a depth of 12m. **See route 1 or route 2.**

Route 1. To go to the cave with the hole in the roof via Finger reef, continue in a westerly direction over the sand into an area where there are many small boulders, the depth here is 12m. Now bear slightly to your left and the reef will start to rise beside you, here your depth will decrease to around 9m and you will be about 10 minutes into your dive.

Dropping over a small ridge to a depth of approximately 11m, on your left you will see the start of what I call Finger Reef. Here it is easy to follow this reef all the way to the end, but take your time to explore the many little over-hangs filled with colourful marine life. When you reach the end of the reef you will possibly be 20/25 minutes into your dive, here the depth will be 20m.

From the end of the reef take a compass bearing of 60°, this will lead you in an easterly direction over the sea grass to a ridge at 16m. Drop over this ridge down to 18m, turn left and the cave entrance at 19m; will be just in front of you. When entering take great care, for you may be lucky to see the groupers that are sometimes here. After you have explored the cave, leave through the hole in the roof emerging on the top of the reef 12m. At this point you will be some 30/35 minutes into your dive and from here to your exit point, E2, is a minimum time of 15 minutes. **See return route.**

With the digital camera it is easy to check your results.

Diver at the entrance to the cave, with the hole in the roof, on the outer reef.

Leaving the cove heading for Finger Reef.

GHAR LAPSI

Route 2. To go to the cave with the hole in the roof via the Crib take a compass bearing of 210° this will lead you in a southerly direction and over the mound covered in sea grass which is surrounded by sand. For the next 7/8 minutes the area on your left will be mostly sand and on your right is mainly sea grass with two or three patches of sand.

Common stingray (Dasyatis pastinaca) sometimes found partly buried and often in shelted places. PHOTO: JOE FORMOSA

The Crib, which are almost life-sized figures cut from plate metal.

On reaching a depth of 14m on the sand in front of you will be an area of sea grass, continue straight on over the sea grass and within 2 minutes, at a depth of 12m you will be on top of the reef. Descend to the bottom at 16m and turn right, follow the base of the reef along for approximately 5 minutes when you should reach a depth of 22m, this is the deepest part of your dive and the Crib is in an overhang on your right hand side. Make sure that you stay close to the reef at this point or you may miss it altogether. When it is time to move on, almost immediately the reef starts to head in a northerly direction and from here it will take you around 5 minutes to reach the Double Hooks.

Cutting the corner continue over to the reef on the opposite side and from here it will take you some 5 minutes to reach the Elephant Rock, be careful for his trunk almost reaches the seabed. Once more cut the corner and continue to the reef on the other side, from here to the cave will take you no more than 4 minutes. When you have explored the cave ascend through the hole in the roof to the top of the reef at 12m. At this point you will possibly be 40/45 minutes into your dive. Of course you can at any time go up on top of the reef take a northerly compass bearing and return to the main coastline.

Flying gurnard (Dactylpterus volitans) hovers above the sand approach with care and you will be treated to a fine display.

Return Route. From the hole in the roof of the cave follow a compass bearing of 70° until you reach a 9m drop-off to an area of small boulders at 12m. Alternatively once out of the hole head north to the ridge of Finger Reef, then in a north easterly direction follow it all the way along, then down to the area of small boulders at 12m. Now head in an easterly direction and in a very short time the main coastline will be on your left. Continue along this reef at your required depth. Normally the entrance to the cave is marked with a small heap of stones; at this point your maximum depth should be 6m this will enable you find the reef and follow it into the cove and your exit point. If you wish you can use the route through the cave, into the cove and your exit point, E2.

LEFT: *A diver enters the area where to his right is the rock which resembles an elephants head and trunk.*

FINGER REEF & CRIB – GHAR LAPSI

PGL AERIAL PHOTOS

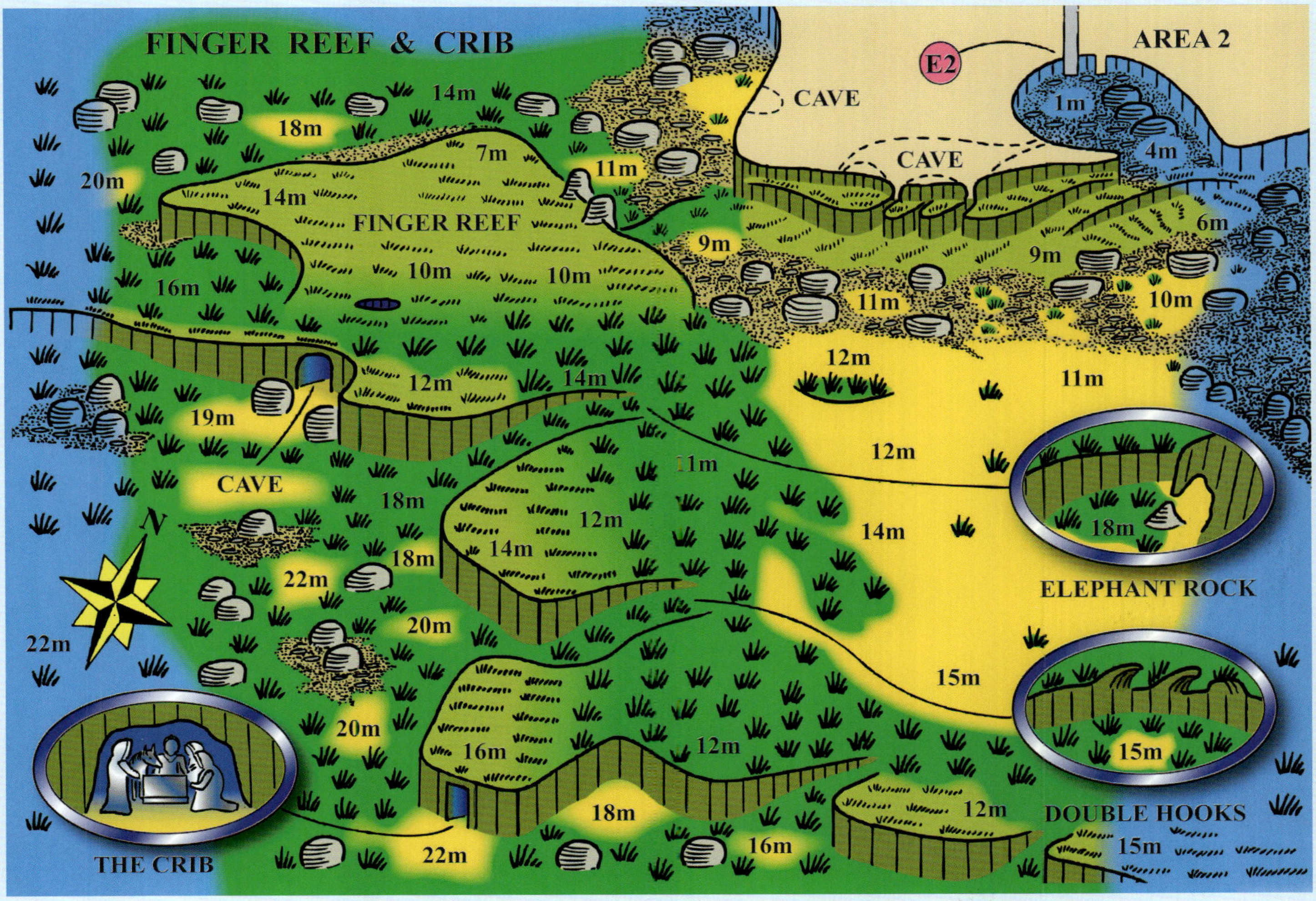

FINGER REEF & CRIB

- 14m
- 18m
- 7m
- 11m
- 20m
- 14m
- FINGER REEF
- 16m
- 10m
- 10m
- 9m
- 12m
- 19m
- CAVE
- 18m
- 18m
- 14m
- 11m
- 12m
- 22m
- 20m
- 22m
- 20m
- 16m
- 12m
- 15m
- 18m
- 22m
- 16m
- THE CRIB

AREA 2

- E2
- CAVE
- CAVE
- 1m
- 4m
- 6m
- 9m
- 10m
- 11m
- 12m
- 14m
- 18m — ELEPHANT ROCK
- 15m
- 12m — DOUBLE HOOKS
- 15m

Middle Reef
Area 3

This site makes an interesting second dive, you have a choice of entry/exit points, E2 / E3 – I favour E2. Here, there are a number of small reefs to explore, which are surrounded by areas of sand, sea grass and small boulders, with a maximum depth of 16m. This dive will test your navigational skills, both with a compass and underwater pilotage; remember to take your slate and pencil.

THE DIVE — Minimum time – 50 mins

From the entry point, E2, surface swim to the middle of the cove and descend, head out of the cove and over a small ridge, then take a compass bearing of 120° continue down onto the sand at 10m. Once here place a stone marker and continue directly over the sand to the opposite reef, then follow the line were the grass meets the sand with a compass bearing of 220°. When you have rounded the first corner, your compass bearing will be 160° you will be able to see, if the visibility is good, Middle Reef on your left-hand side with its two prominent rocks on top. This reef can be explored on your return journey. Continue on following the line where the grass meets the sand until you reach a depth of 14m. Here out on the sand, it is possible to see flying gurnards and small rays.

When it is time for you return, proceed back to the

Good buoyancy skills makes diving a pleasure!

Red gurnard (Aspitrigla cuculus) found mainly in deep waters, but often seen near shore. Feeds on crabs, cuttlefish and small fish. PHOTO: SHARON FORDER

reef with the prominent rocks. Explore this reef and on its north east corner there is an area of sand, from here take a compass bearing of 50°, this will lead you to an area where there are two long reefs which run from east to west. Use these for your navigation and when it is time to return head in an easterly direction. When you reach the overhang Lizard Head, at the easterly end of the largest reef, continue for a short distance over the grass and you will come to a patch of sand.

Follow this around to your right, locate your stone marker and take a compass bearing of 300°, which will hopefully lead you back over the small ridge and into the cove and your exit point, E1. Marine life to be found on these dives are octopus, cuttlefish, shoals of salema fish, the occasional barracudas, out on the sand eagle sting rays and red mullet digging in the sand also of course many other species.

The Lizards Head, one of the only reefs I have named in this dive.

Situated next to the car parks are two nice restaurants, which are very popular with the Maltese and at weekends can be quite busy. In the late autumn and winter they are not always open. Ghar Lapsi is a very pleasant place for non-divers to visit, ideal for snorkelling, swimming or sunbathing within the cove, there is a children's playground, also public toilets. A whole day could be spent in this area maybe diving at Wied iz-Zurrieq as a first dive and then on to Ghar Lapsi for a second dive, but remember that you will need to take two cylinders with you.

MIDDLE REEF – GHAR LAPSI

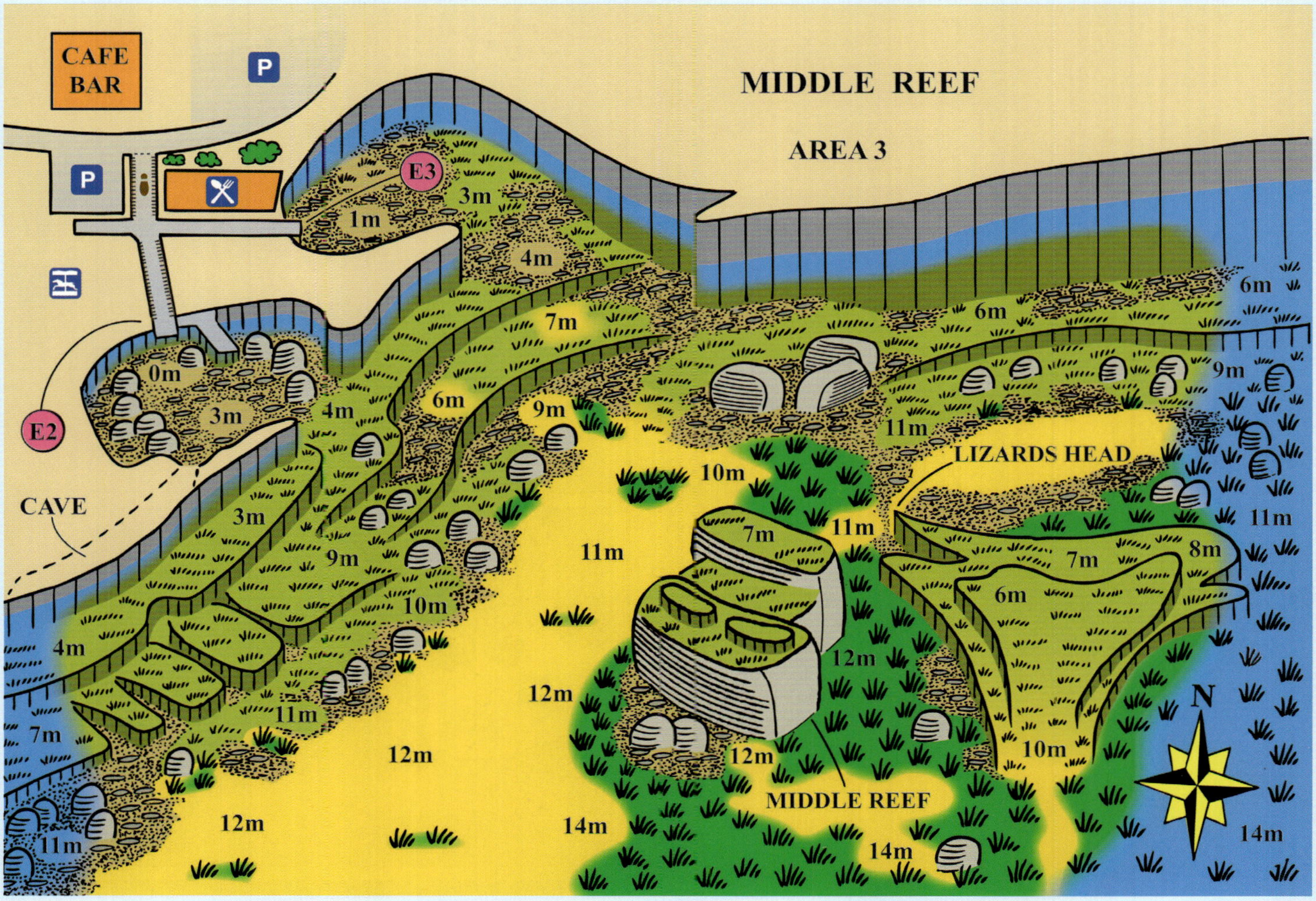

RABAT TO MIGRA FERHA

PGL AERIAL PHOTOS

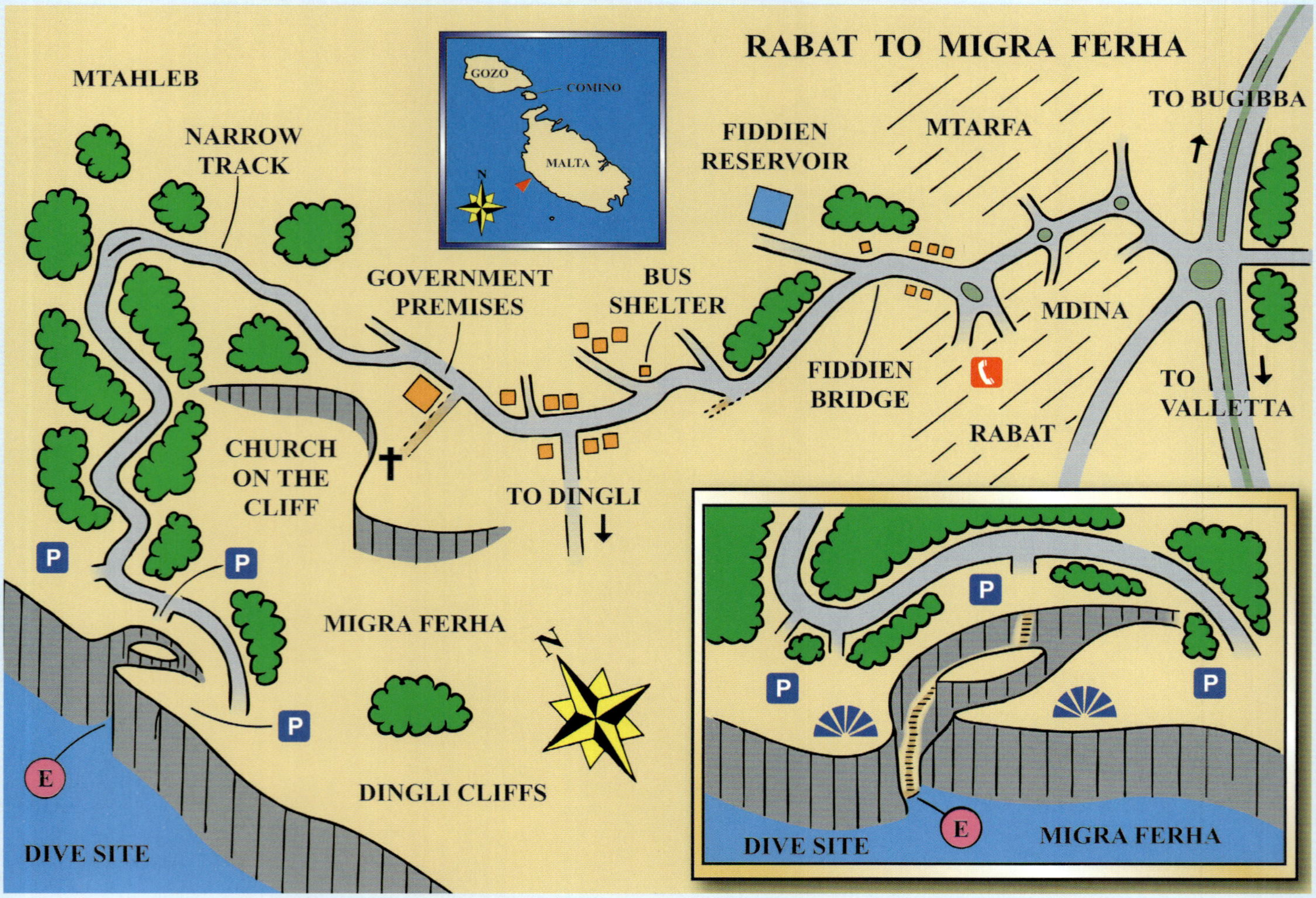

RABAT TO MIGRA FERHA

- MTAHLEB
- NARROW TRACK
- GOZO, COMINO, MALTA
- FIDDIEN RESERVOIR
- MTARFA
- TO BUGIBBA
- GOVERNMENT PREMISES
- BUS SHELTER
- MDINA
- FIDDIEN BRIDGE
- RABAT
- TO VALLETTA
- CHURCH ON THE CLIFF
- TO DINGLI
- MIGRA FERHA
- DINGLI CLIFFS
- DIVE SITE
- DIVE SITE
- MIGRA FERHA

Migra Ferha

The route to this dive site will take you some twenty minutes and starts by going through a valley. On one side is Mdina, known as the Silent City, this was once the ancient capital of Malta, on the other side, the village of Mtarfa, famous for its clock tower. Leaving Rabat you will pass Fiddien Bridge, a bus shelter and a Government premises Now bear left on to a very narrow road/track, looking to your left over the valley you will see a Church which is built in the rock face.

After a short distance the road gets better and this will lead you down to Migra Ferha. There are two car parks here; it is better to go to the first one for it is less distance to walk. Beware of surface conditions in the car park.

A family enjoy the calm sea conditions at the entry point for this dive. There is a nice entry step to the left at the bottom of the steps.

This unique and unspoilt dive site should only be attempted by experienced and very fit divers, due to the fact that there are approximately 150 steps to be negotiated to reach the entry/exit point below the Dingli Cliffs, which run along this westerly coastline in each direction. Please do not upset the fishermen for they made the steps that enable us to reach sea level and they also have to replace them after heavy rain, as the gully becomes a river. Before you dive this site you must check the sea conditions, as this is your only exit for a number of kilometres. Once in the water be aware that there are some offshore currents.

There are two dive area's here, to the north a large reef with depths of 16m to 9m and over the drop-off 30m plus. To the south a large area of boulders to explore, depths to 25m, once you move away from the reef or the boulders, within 30 metres distance your depth will be at least 36m, from this point the bottom drops away very quickly. If you decide to dive this site take a 15 litre cylinder and make the most of one good dive. It is always a good idea, even for the very fit diver, to sit down for 20/30 minutes after your dive before attempting the climb back up the 150 steps! As this would be considered heavy exercise, the rest would give time for the slow release of nitrogen and help to prevent exercise related DCI.

Diving the Reef

THE DIVE   Minimum time – 50 mins

Once on the ledge that you will be using for your entry/exit turn to your left and you will find a nice little stepping area to assist you especially with your exit. Into the water, depth below you is 16m, when on the bottom head in a westerly direction keeping the reef on your right hand side, within 8 minutes you will reach the corner of the reef, depth 29m. Continuing straight out the reef gently slopes away to where it reaches a depth of 40m plus before dropping away sharply.

Divers below entry point E1

Of course you can do this dive the easy way, just organise a boat!

Now, keeping the reef on your right hand side, head in a northerly direction. Within 10 minutes, you will come to an area where you will see cars littered on the bottom at 36m and deeper, from this point ascend the cliff face to a ledge at 15m, here you will also find a number of cars, they have all been pushed over the cliff top. This should be your turning point; from here you will be able to see the shoreline and the base of the cliffs, which will enable you to go to your required depth. Keeping the reef on your left, head in a southerly direction and you will find two small caves

A diver explores one of the small caves on the plateau to the north-west of entry point E1.

and a large over-hang, almost immediately you will have to bear round to your left, you should now be above your outward route and almost at your exit point. The return journey should not have taken more than 10/15 minutes, plus exploring time.

Diving the boulder area

THE DIVE   Minimum time – 50 mins

Once on the bottom follow the cliff wall in a southerly direction, almost immediately you will come to a large over-hang, this is worth a look inside, continue on the same course keeping the reef on your left. This area is littered with large boulders and between them small rocks, a haven for marine life with many places to explore. Within 15 minutes, depending on the time spent exploring, on your left you will see a very large rock that seems to be leaning up against the cliff wall, it is also a corner where the reef changes direction, depth 25m.

At this point you should turn and swim in a northerly direction, keeping the boulders on your right and the flatish area on your left staying at a depth of around 25m, remember this is a good area for finding octopus and moray. In approximately 15/20 minutes you should reach the reef wall, depth 25m, if you turn to your right follow it in an easterly direction, this will lead you into a corner below the ledge at your exit point. Alternatively you can explore the area on top of the reef before returning to your exit point. Of course you can plan your own dive, but to fully complete both areas in one dive is really just too much and will give you no time to explore. In my opinion, the reef is the best dive.

It is very important to remember that there are no amenities here, so bring refreshments. **The reception here for mobile phones is very poor and the nearest public phone is in Rabat.** Do not leave valuables on display in your vehicle. If you happen to be here in the evening some beautiful sunsets can be seen over the sea.

The vehicles which have been pushed over the cliff top to their graveyard below, these have now become home to the local marine life.

MIGRA FERHA

PGL AERIAL PHOTOS

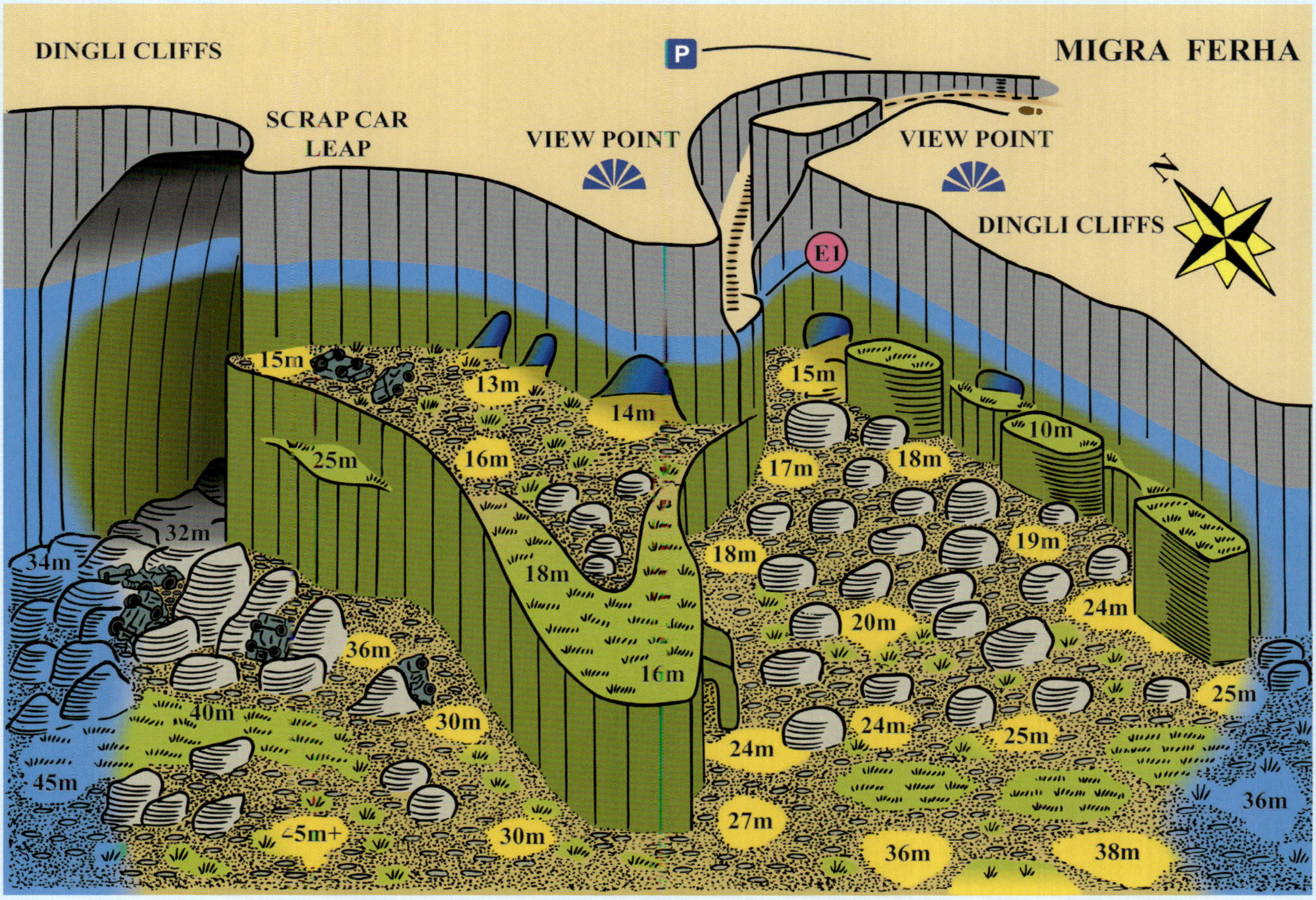

DINGLI CLIFFS

SCRAP CAR LEAP

VIEW POINT

MIGRA FERHA

VIEW POINT

DINGLI CLIFFS

E1

15m, 13m, 14m, 15m, 10m, 25m, 16m, 17m, 18m, 32m, 18m, 19m, 34m, 36m, 18m, 20m, 24m, 40m, 30m, 16m, 24m, 25m, 45m, 5m+, 30m, 24m, 25m, 36m, 27m, 36m, 38m

MELLIEHA TO ANCHOR BAY

PGL AERIAL PHOTOS

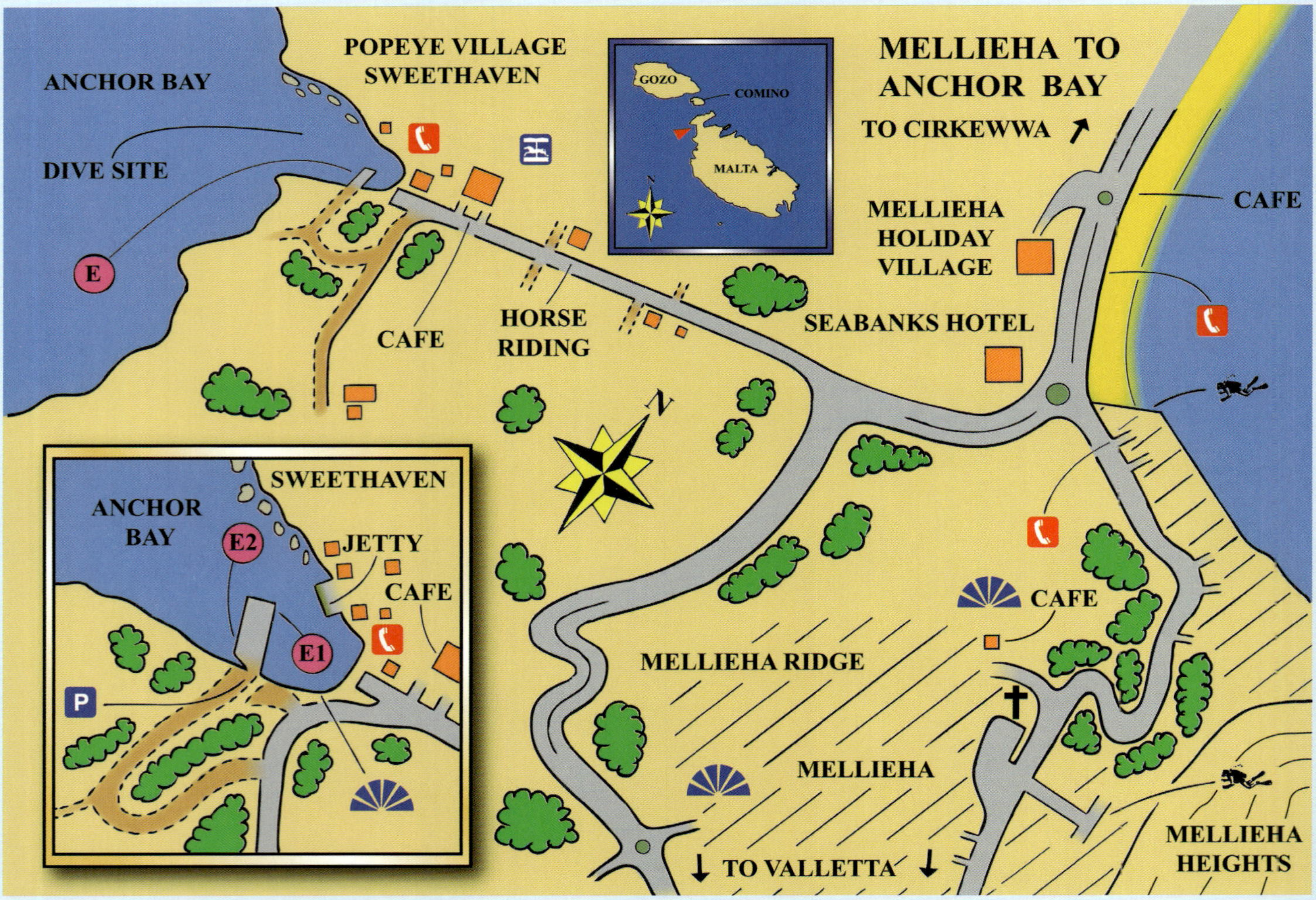

MELLIEHA TO ANCHOR BAY

- ANCHOR BAY
- DIVE SITE (E)
- POPEYE VILLAGE SWEETHAVEN
- CAFE
- HORSE RIDING
- TO CIRKEWWA
- MELLIEHA HOLIDAY VILLAGE
- SEABANKS HOTEL
- CAFE
- MELLIEHA RIDGE
- MELLIEHA
- MELLIEHA HEIGHTS
- TO VALLETTA

Inset: GOZO, COMINO, MALTA

Inset detail:
- ANCHOR BAY
- SWEETHAVEN
- E1, E2
- JETTY
- CAFE
- P (parking)

Anchor Bay

Anchor bay is a small inlet situated on the north west coast of Malta, only a short drive from Mellieha. The view from the main road going down the hill towards Mellieha Bay, before turning left to Anchor Bay, is quite breathtaking and the 'Popeye' village can be seen quite clearly from here and this is one of the only places on the island where you can see both coastlines.

This site is usually used as a second dive or when there are strong north to north east winds. Depth ranges are from 2m to 12m within the bay.

The village of Sweethaven or Popeye village was originally built for the making of the film Popeye; *it is now a very popular tourist attraction.*

This bay was made famous by the building of the timber village called Sweethaven, which was the film set for the production of the film *Popeye* with Robin Williams. A jetty was constructed to enable boats to unload materials at this isolated bay when they constructed the village, one of these being the *Scotscraig* which is now a boat dive and lies just around the headland. The name Anchor Bay came from the anchor which was used as a mooring, it is still here and attached to it is a long heavy chain. (See plan)

> Please note the jetty has been severely damaged by storms and is no longer nicely attached to the shore line. Check your entry/exit point before kitting up, a de-kit exit may be required.
> Beware, for there are boats bringing parties of tourists and they land and embark from the little jetty in front of the Popeye village.
> Leave nothing of value in your vehicle.

RIGHT: *The storm damaged jetty. Check it out!*

THE DIVE Minimum time – 50 mins

From the entry point E1 proceed to the end of the jetty continue over the sand you will reach a bank with sea grass on the top of it. Now head about 320° but do not miss the very large anchor chain, for in places it is covered in marine growth. Once you have found it turn left and follow it, at the end you will find a very large anchor, 8m. From here head 210° to start off with there is a small reef on your left, it helps with navigation.

Eventually you will pass an area of small rocks on your left, here leave this small reef but remain on your present compass bearing until you reach the base of the shoreline cliff face on the south side of the bay, if your depth is less than 8m turn right, if more than 11m turn left. The entrance to the cave is on the seaward side of the very large boulder, which allows no access between it and the cliff face. From your entry point to the cave, allowing for time to look around, will take you some 24 minutes. The depth at the entrance of the cave is 10m, inside the cave the depth ranges from 8m to 2m. There is a large cavern above water level in which you may surface and admire this impressive dome shaped ceiling.

ANCHOR BAY

The anchor which gave the bay its name.
PHOTO: MAX VALLI – ORANGE SHARK H2O

A diver surfaces in the cave, remember you should check that fresh air is entering cave before removing regulator.
PHOTO: SERGEY MARKOV – DIVE SYSTEMS

The area on the westerly side of the cave entrance is quite rugged and if you have the time and air, is worth exploring. When it is time to return, head 60° east keeping the cliff face on your right, from the cave to your exit point it will take you approximately 15 minutes, longer if you wish to explore. You can of course complete this dive in reverse, by going directly to the cave from your entry point. On the north shore of Anchor Bay, not far from the anchor is an area of large boulders surrounded by a sandy seabed, often to be found here is the Tun Shell. You can of course plan your own dive but remember, the swim from the cave to your exit point will take you approximately 15 minutes, with no time spent exploring. The nearest public telephone boxes are situated at Mellieha Bay, but in an emergency the proprietors of the Popeye Village will allow you to use their private phone in the entrance kiosk, which is manned 24 hours a day, 365 days a year either by employees or security personnel.

On to the approach road to the bay there are some riding stables where horses can be hired for visitors, obviously the 'Popeye' village itself is worth a visit. As you leave the road and go on to the track, stop at the top of the cliffs, this viewpoint is a good position to take photographs of the village and bay. There is a restaurant and gift shop next to the car park above the village.

Mellieha

Mellieha has a busy shopping centre and the steep main street is lined with a variety of shops, small bars and restaurants. Perched on the hill side in front of the church with fantastic views over the north coast of Malta with Gozo in the distance is a small family run café / bar and a children's playground, a great place to relax after a dive. In an effort to preserve both local and migratory birds, the wetland inland from Mellieha Bay has been turned into a bird sanctuary.

Divers enter the Anchor Bay Cave.
PHOTO: MAX VALLI – ORANGE SHARK H2O

The end of the cave just below the surface at a depth of 2m.
PHOTO: MAX VALLI – ORANGE SHARK H2O

ANCHOR BAY

PGL AERIAL PHOTOS

CIRKEWWA – MARFA POINT

The Ferry Terminal at Cirkewwa where the boats leave for Gozo. On the North-West side are some of Malta's most popular dive sites.

PGL AERIAL PHOTOS

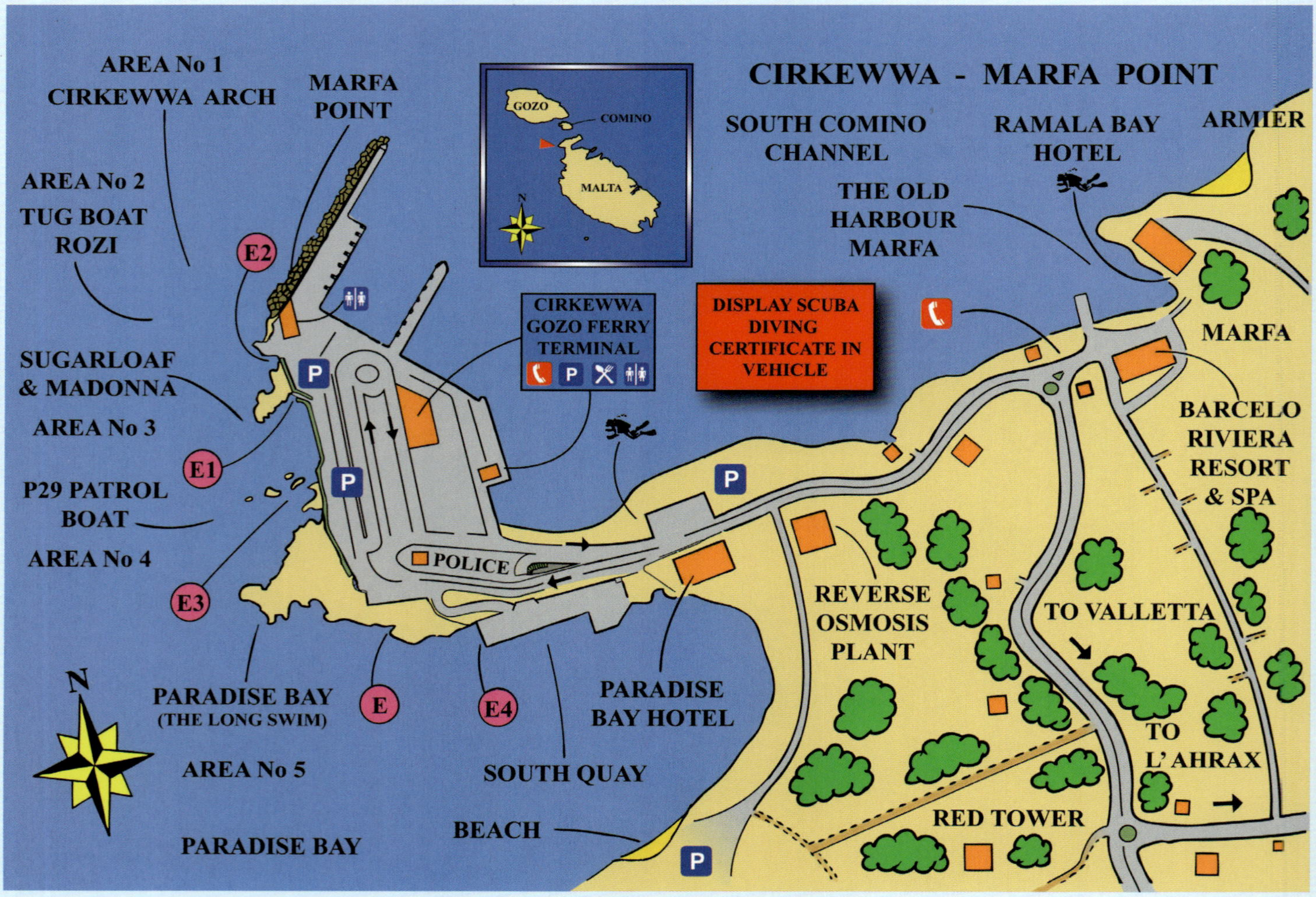

CIRKEWWA - MARFA POINT

- AREA No 1 – CIRKEWWA ARCH
- MARFA POINT
- AREA No 2 – TUG BOAT ROZI
- SUGARLOAF & MADONNA
- AREA No 3
- P29 PATROL BOAT
- AREA No 4
- PARADISE BAY (THE LONG SWIM)
- AREA No 5
- PARADISE BAY

- SOUTH COMINO CHANNEL
- THE OLD HARBOUR MARFA
- CIRKEWWA GOZO FERRY TERMINAL
- **DISPLAY SCUBA DIVING CERTIFICATE IN VEHICLE**
- RAMALA BAY HOTEL
- ARMIER
- MARFA
- BARCELO RIVIERA RESORT & SPA
- POLICE
- REVERSE OSMOSIS PLANT
- PARADISE BAY HOTEL
- SOUTH QUAY BEACH
- RED TOWER
- TO VALLETTA
- TO L'AHRAX

GOZO – COMINO – MALTA

Cirkewwa (Marfa Point)

Cirkewwa is situated at the north west coast of the island and is the main terminal for the car and passenger ferries to Gozo. Most divers refer to this area as Marfa and is the most popular dive location on the island, a divers parking permit is required here. The actual hamlet of Marfa itself is approximately 1km along the coast where there is a small harbour.

Before the terminal was built, the rocks below the lighthouse were not part of the mainland, these outcrops of rocks were known as Marfa Point. There are two quays at the Cirkewwa terminal, the north quay, which is the normal one used; the south quay is used when weather conditions dictate otherwise. The car ferries are not a problem for divers unless you leave the main dive areas and surface well out to sea. It is the small craft, fishing and pleasure boats that can be a problem; they tend to cut the corner when rounding the headland, occasionally dive boats visit this area, so beware of anchors and shot lines. Due to the fact that it is so popular it can become really busy at times. There are five dives here which of course can be interchanged to suit your qualifications and dive plan requirements, with depths down to 36m.

The parking area for entry points for E1 and E2.

Cirkewwa Ferry Terminal (Marfa Point), showing both North and South Quays.

PHOTO: JOE ABDILLA & PAUL GAUCI

CIRKEWWA (MARFA POINT)

Cirkewwa Arch
Area 1

This unusual arch some 12m below the surface and 8m above the sea bed has a compass bearing from the lighthouse directly over the reef of 320°. Your route is not direct but will take you along the side of the reef, which can be used, for navigation; the approximate distance for this route is 180 metres. Most of the sea bed area of this dive site is covered in sea grass with large boulders and small areas of sand. On your outward journey you will find a small cave, which can be explored, while returning along the shallow depths of the reef, where the marine growth is short, there are many nooks and crannies which make good hiding places for marine life.

▌THE DIVE   Minimum time – 40 mins

Entry point E2 is just below the lighthouse. From the entry point surface swim around to the end of the reef, once on the north west side of the lighthouse descend to 6/7m, now swim in an easterly direction past a large reef/boulder when the next reef appears in front of you, descend bearing to your left continue down to a depth of 14m, here the bottom is covered

The Arch at Cirkewwa is a really good place for some unusual photography.   PHOTO: SHARON FORDER

A diver in the tunnel/cave en route midway between Cirkewwa Arch and the entry point.

in sea grass and the main reef will be on your right hand side.

Continue along the reef until you come to an area of sand, be sure not to miss the little cut out in the reef, for on the left-hand side of this cut out is the entrance to the cave. Once you have entered the cave leave by the first exit on your left, as the other exit is too small for divers, continue to follow the reef on your right. Within a short distance the reef bears sharply to the right, at this point you can either follow the reef to the Arch or take a compass bearing of 350°

Take your time and explore this area while admiring the breath taking view of the reef formation. If you are lucky, under the Arch there are sometimes large shoals of amberjacks, especially if there is a slight current, if you are really careful you can get very close to them, which makes a great photographic opportunity. When on the seabed below the Arch take care not to stir up the sand, moving under the Arch towards the reef wall at the far end, where there are a number of hiding places for groupers and moray eels.

On your return route follow the reef until you are above the cave; if there are divers inside the bubbles form a curtain, again another chance for an unusual photograph. After you have passed the cave bear right past the first boulder/ reef then cross over to the main reef, you will now be below the lighthouse where you can exit at E2 or if the sea is choppy and you have the air then continue to Susie's pool E1, at your chosen depth.

CIRKEWWA ARCH – CIRKEWWA

PGL AERIAL PHOTOS

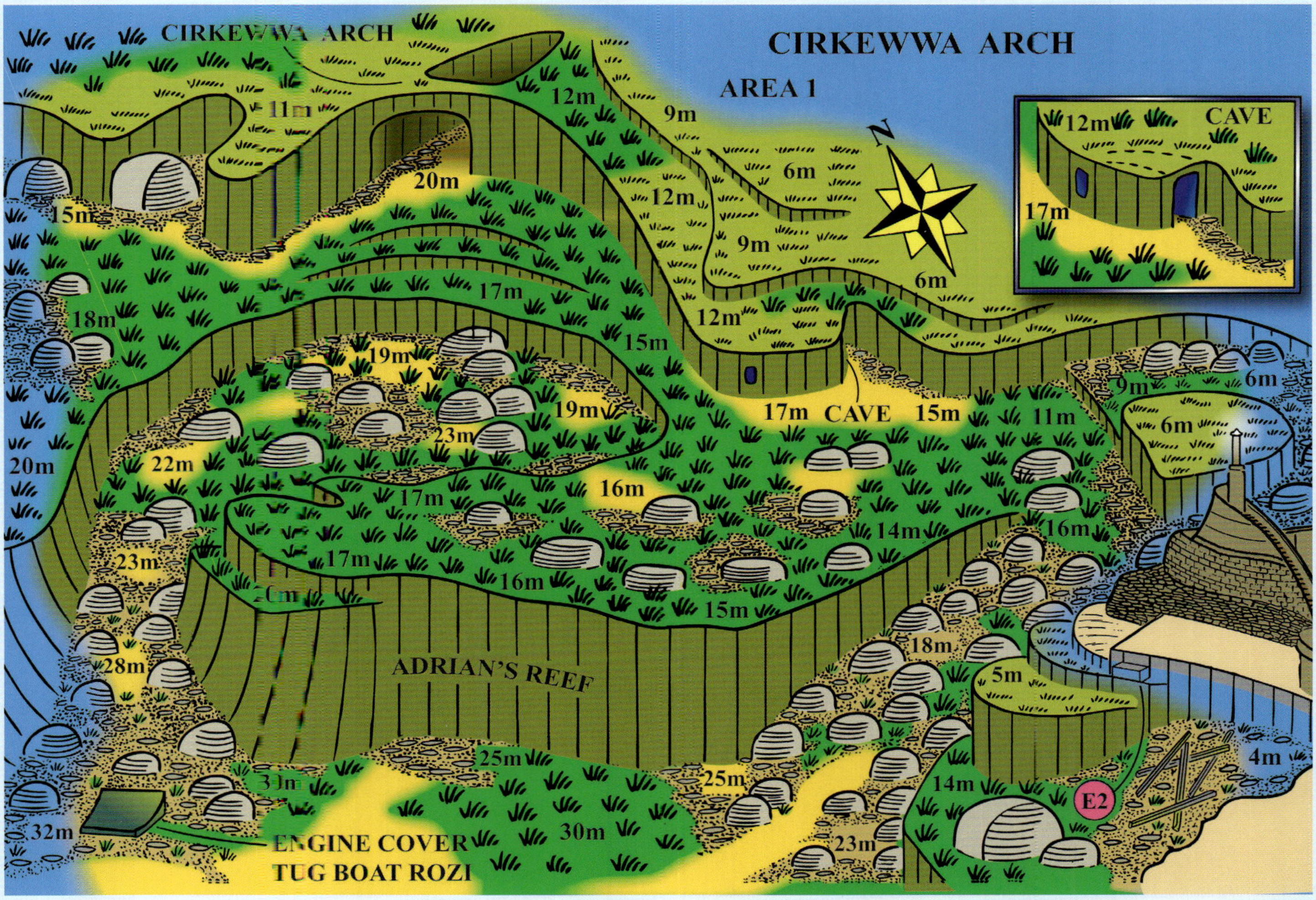

CIRKEWWA ARCH
AREA 1

CIRKEWWA ARCH

CAVE

17m CAVE

ADRIAN'S REEF

ENGINE COVER
TUG BOAT ROZI

A look around Cirkewwa (Marfa Point)

The Brief.

Entry Point E2.

Susie's Pool.

Swimthrough.

Cirkewwa anchor.

P29 – grouper and bream.

The Overhang.

Sugarloaf.

Rozi below.

The Tugboat *Rozi*

The tugboat Rossgarth *working in Grand Harbour, later sold to Tug Malta and re-named* Rozi.

PHOTO: BY KIND PERMISSION OF BETTINA ROHBRECHT, HAMBURG

The Rozi *Grand Harbour.* PHOTO: COURTESY OF TUG MALTA

This 30m tugboat named *Rozi*, built in Bristol, England in 1958 by Charles Hill & Sons Ltd, for Johnston Warren Lines Ltd, of Liverpool and launched as *Rossmore*. She was renamed *Rossgarth* in 1969 and in 1972 was sold to Mifsud Brothers (Malta Ship Towage) Ltd, Malta, retaining her name. In the same year she sailed from Liverpool for Malta where in 1973 she was registered. She was sold to Tug Malta in 1981 and renamed *Rozi* and then sold to Captain Morgan Cruises, Malta who scuttled her as an artificial reef off Cirkewwa in 1992 as an attraction for a tourist submarine. Buoyed some 130 metres west of the lighthouse at a depth of 36m she sits upright on a sandy seabed. There was a time when tourists enjoyed seeing divers on the *Rozi*, but the submarine has long since gone. During the intervening years thousands of divers from all over the world have enjoyed diving on her, and seeing the marine life that have made the *Rozi* their home.

A variety of bream above the bridge of the Rozi.

Two divers at the bow of the tugboat Rozi.

A diver hovers above the stern of the Rozi.

The Tugboat *Rozi*

Area 2

THE DIVE Minimum time – 50 mins

There are a number of permutations for this dive; your entry point E2 is from the south side of the lighthouse. Your dive plan will either be to surface swim to the end of the reef, and then down to the first level at 14m, pass directly over the rocky valley to the reef on the other side, depth 15m. Follow the edge of the reef for about 70 metres, on your left down on the bottom you will see a path of sand shaped like a banana which separates the sea grass. The Rozi's bows lie just to the right of this path; dive time to the wreck is approximately 6 minutes.

The alternative is a surface swim, she is buoyed and the compass bearing is 300° from entry point E2. You will have to take great care and keep an eye out for small boats cutting the corner. Also the currents that occur here from time to time are inclined to push you off course without you realising it. I think the best plan is to descend to a minimum depth where you can use the reef for navigation. For your return journey you have three choices, most divers plan to return to Susie's Pool E1, but of course you can exit at E2.

A diver using a rebreather visits the Rozi.

Return route 1. Mid-way port side of the wreck follow a compass bearing of 150°, to the anchor, which is 50 metres away at a depth of 32m. From this point continue on a compass bearing of 120°, this will lead you back on to the reef, when you have reached it, ascend to your required depth then head in a southerly direction keeping the main reef on your left. Once you have reached the swim-through cave at 11m and either passed through it or taken the short trip round, then continue to follow the reef wall. Within approximately 2 minutes at a depth of 11m you will find a ledge that will lead you up into the training area and Susie's Pool.

This moray (Muraen Helena) has found a home on the Rozi.

Return route 2. Leave the stern of the *Rozi* behind you and following a compass bearing of approximately 60° until you reach the top of the reef, at approximately 17m. At this point turn right; continue along the edge of the reef until you reach the rocky valley cross over to the other side. Here the reef rises to the surface, near E2, bearing in mind to reach this point from the wreck, will take you some 5/6 minutes. Once you have reached your required depth bear to the right, keeping the main reef on your left and you will pass the small arches in the reef; continue on to the swim-through cave. Follow the reef at 5m to exit at the stony path or at 11m to find the ledge and overhang that will lead you into the training area and exit at Susie's Pool.

Return route 3. This I consider to be my favourite return route. Leave the bows of the *Rozi* passing over the engine cover, which lies on the sand, and follow a compass bearing of 30°. Continue in this direction following the gently sloping reef to higher ground. At a depth of around 20m you will find a small drop-off on your right, follow its edge until you have a reef in front of you, continue to the top of this reef, depth 11m. Taking a southerly compass bearing will lead you directly over the Arch and on to a reef where you can select your own depth; the minimum time from the wreck to this point will take you 6 minutes. Follow the reef all the way to your exit point E2, on the south side of the lighthouse.

TUGBOAT *ROZI* – CIRKEWWA

PGL AERIAL PHOTOS

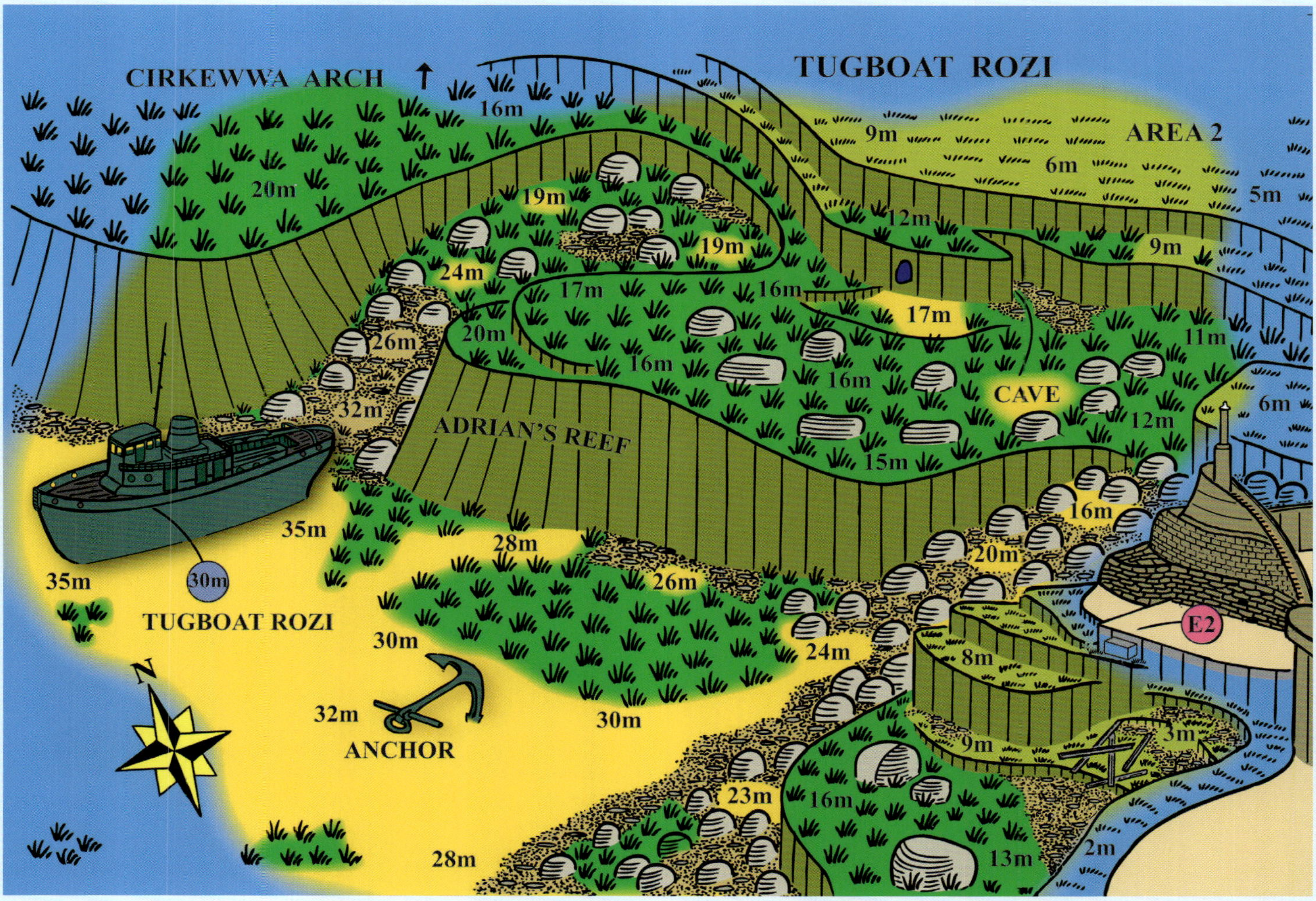

CIRKEWWA (MARFA POINT)

Sugar Loaf – Madonna Statue

Area 3

This dive area has many permutations and variations and you can navigate your way around by using the reef, generally it runs from north to south. Most divers who come to Cirkewwa (Marfa Point) normally dive this site first. A visit to the Madonna Statue, then on to Sugar Loaf, which is a huge rock detached from the main reef and rising some 8m from the seabed. Once out of the training area and over the drop off you will find the seabed reasonably flat but with many boulders littering the bottom; also the many large and small overhangs within the reef to explore, make this a good dive site.

THE DIVE
Minimum time – 40 mins

Entry for this area would normally be made at Susie's Pool E1, once under water head in a westerly direction along the stony path to the drop-off, over and down on to the bottom. Now turn right in a northerly direction and in a very short distance, in a corner you will find a small fissure at a depth of 18m. Here you will find the Madonna statue, which is also the home for many cardinal fish. Follow the reef down over the large boulders, round the corner, watch out for groupers lying on the rocks, between the main reef and Sugar Loaf, and remember they are very shy, so you have to move slowly. The large rock on your left is called Sugar Loaf.

The Madonna statue sits serenely in a small cave just below the first drop off.

Divers returning to The Ledge following a training exercise.

When it is time to return, ascend the reef to your required depth and head south, keeping the coastline reef on your left, you will come to the swim-through cave at 11m, once you have gone through or round to the other side, continue along the reef, over the Madonna cave. Within this area there are many small crevices and little over-hangs to explore. Once at the ledge at 11m, move to your right and you will find a very large over-hang, sometimes hiding right at the back on a small ledge you may see a grouper. The roof of this over hang is covered with brightly coloured small soft coral, this maybe a good opportunity for photographs. Moving from the ledge area there are depths of 6m and 3m for stops if required, through the training area and exit at the Susie's Pool E1.

A diver checks out the small boulders behind Sugarloaf for any sign of groupers resting there. PHOTO: BENT MATUSIAK

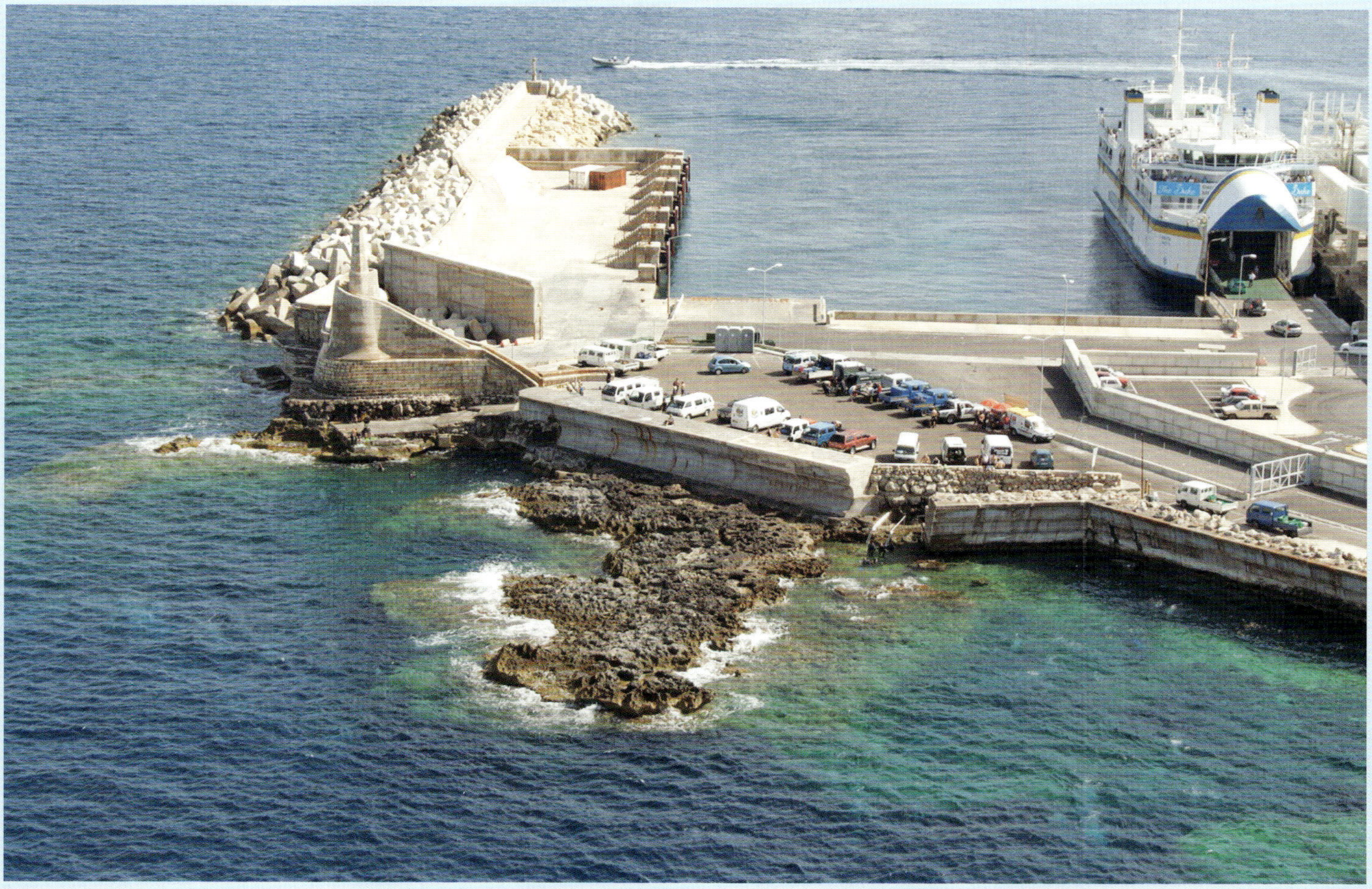

PGL AERIAL PHOTOS

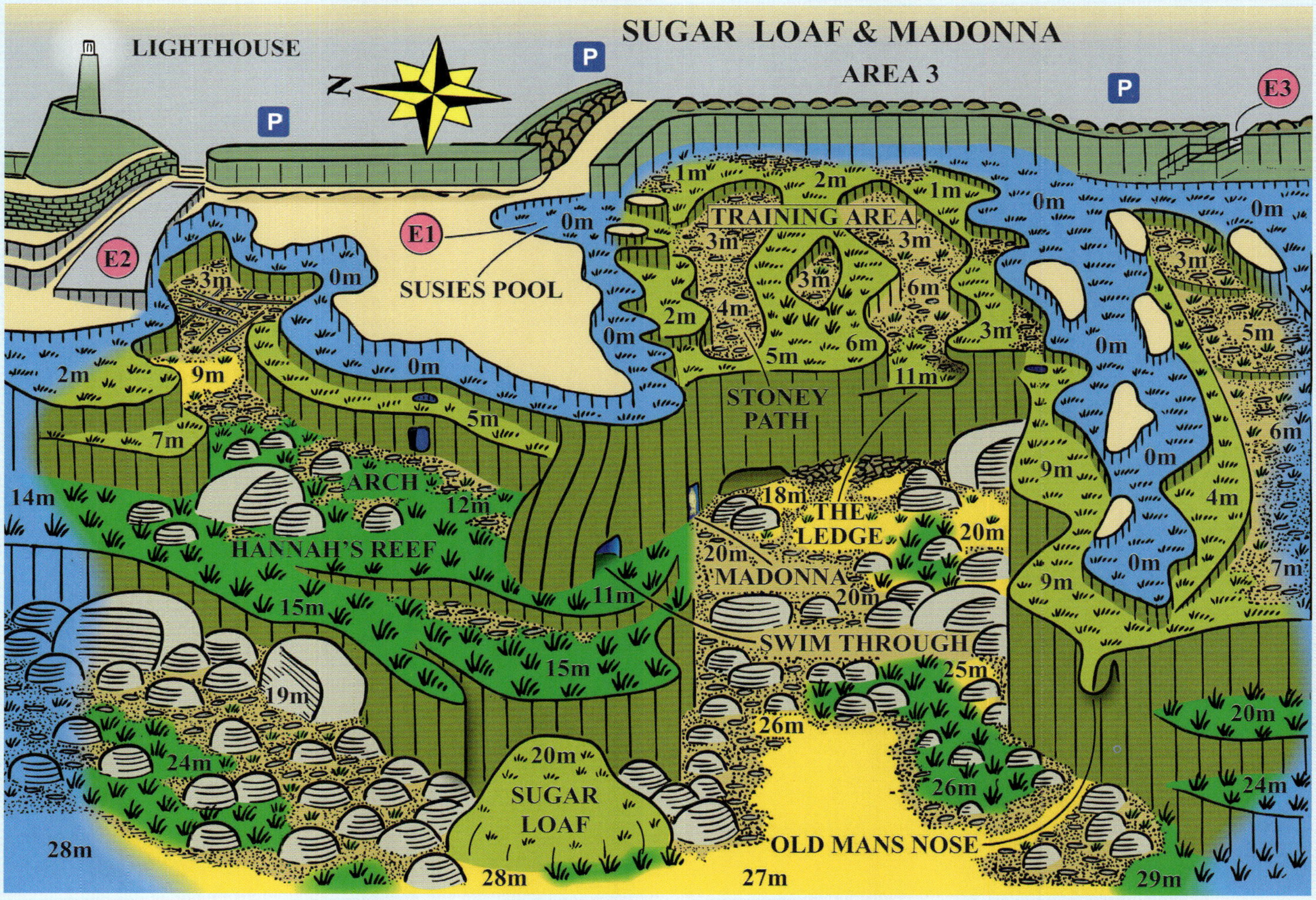
SUGAR LOAF & MADONNA
AREA 3
LIGHTHOUSE
N
P
P
P
E1
E2
E3
SUSIES POOL
TRAINING AREA
STONEY PATH
ARCH
HANNAH'S REEF
THE LEDGE
MADONNA
SWIM THROUGH
SUGAR LOAF
OLD MANS NOSE
0m
1m
2m
3m
4m
5m
6m
7m
9m
11m
12m
14m
15m
18m
19m
20m
24m
25m
26m
27m
28m
29m

A look around Cirkewwa (Marfa Point)

Entry point E3.

P29 sinking.

The Rock.

P29 anchor.

Adrian's Reef.

Towards Hannah's Reef.

Old Man's Nose.

Inside Ben's Arch.

P29 Patrol Boat

The arrival of the P29 to Malta from Germany on the 29th August 1997.

The *P29*, formerly *Boltenhagen*, started life in former East Germany. She is a Kondor-class boat designed and built on the Peenewerft, Wolgast, in East Germany in the 1960's. With a length of 52 metres and weighing 360 tons, these vessels were primarily intended as minesweepers, though several variants existed, used possibly in fisheries protection, border control or as part of the German Democratic Republic logistical fleet.

In August 1997, after a three week voyage from Germany, the Armed Forces of Malta's Maritime Squadron took delivery of their third Kondor vessel, the *P29*. When the ship arrived in Malta it was greeted by the family and friends of the crew. The Kondor vessels were the first war ships the AFM ever commissioned, and it was thanks to them that the Maritime Squadron was able to participate in naval exercises with other European fleets.

From 1997 until 2004, when she was decommissioned, the *P29* patrolled the coastal waters of the Maltese Islands, fulfilling her duties with search and rescue operations, fisheries protection duties and exercises: of course the naval exercises took her further a field into International waters of the Mediterranean. In 2000 and 2001 the Kondors supported the prestigious Royal Malta Yacht Club's Middle Sea Race off Lampedusa.

In September 2005 the *P29* was sold to the Malta Tourism Authority to be scuttled as an attraction for divers. She was cleaned and made environmentally safe and was scuttled on the 14th August, 2007, off Cirkewwa, buoyed and at a depth of 38m.

Exploring the stern of the P29 with a Torpedo DPV.

The mast and deck of the P29.

The bows of the patrol boat P29.

CIRKEWWA (MARFA POINT)

P29 Patrol Boat
Area 4

THE DIVE
Minimum time – 45 mins

Route 1
Enter the water at Susie's Pool E1, surface swim out between the two rocks, now head in a westerly direction above stony path to the drop off and descend. From here the distance is 100 metres to the stern of the *P29*. Take a compass bearing of 270° and if the visibility is good you will be able to see the reef on your right hand side until Sugar Loaf comes into view. In front of you and to the south of Sugar Loaf, on a sandy seabed will be a concrete block almost buried, at this moment in time there is a plaque on the far side. You are now half way there, if the visibility is not so good leave the drop off and drop down over the boulders, rocks and sea grass until you reach the sand; if you are taking a bearing of 270° you should find the concrete block and plaque. Continue with the same compass bearing. From the drop off to the *P29* should take you no more than 4-5 minutes.

Route 2
Entry point E3 Paradise steps. I suggest that you surface swim to the 9m ledge above the Old Mans Nose, the best way is to go around the last rock of the reef on your right to reach the ledge, which is on the north side of the rock. From here the *P29* is 100 metres with a compass bearing of 310° the same distance as Route 1 and should take no longer than 4-5 minutes.

Now descend from the ledge above the Old Mans Nose and where the reef meets the sand it forms an 'L' shape. The reef runs to the north and the sea grass runs to the west, now re-check your bearing of 310° and continue to the wreck.

Note: If the visibility is not too good and you are intending to swim mid water, beware of the currents which sometimes occur in this area, only a slight current will drift you off course and consequently you will miss the wreck.

Return route
When it is time to leave the wreck a compass bearing of 90° will take you back to the concrete block and Sugar Loaf whereas a bearing of 130° will take you back to the reef below the Old Mans Nose. Of course you can take any compass bearing between the two which will lead you back onto the main reef and your exit point.

A plaque in memory of the British diver Frank Pembridge, this is half way to the P29 *if using Route 1.*

FRANK PEMBRIDGE first started diving when he was on active service in Malaya. He saw an article in a magazine called Popular Science on how to make your own aqualung, this was completed, it worked and Frank was the first one to try it out. He began diving in Malta in 1957 with a man called Vince, in 1985 he was invited to Malta by Charles Cassar to assist in a Life Saving Course, apart from this Frank, who at the time was the National Diving Officer of the SAA, organised many other courses over the following years. Since 1990 he was a frequent visitor to the Maltese Islands, then annually with his dive club from 1994. Sadly Frank passed away on the 5th October 2006.

LEFT: *A view of the* P29 *from just below the surface.*

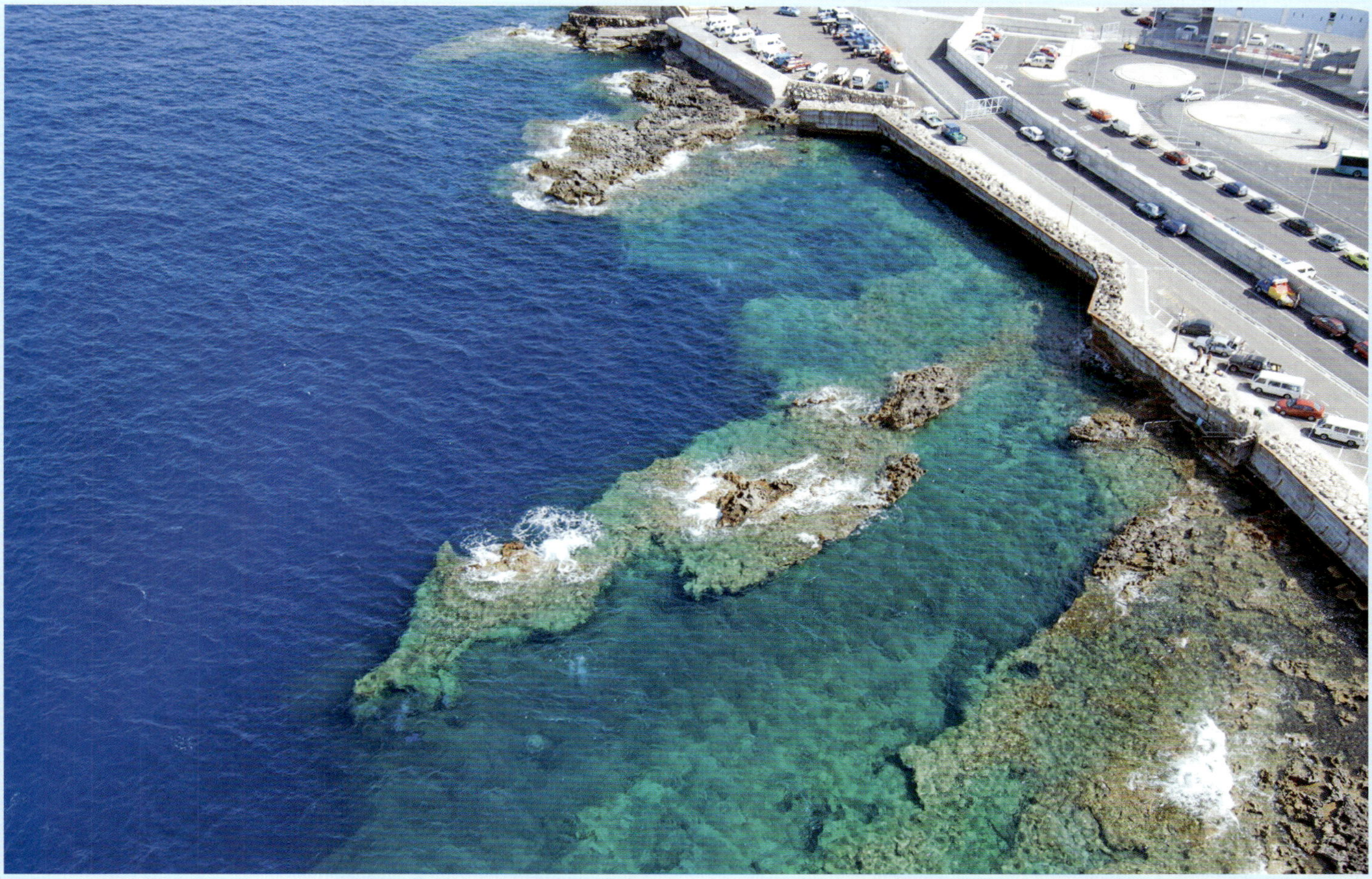

PGL AERIAL PHOTOS

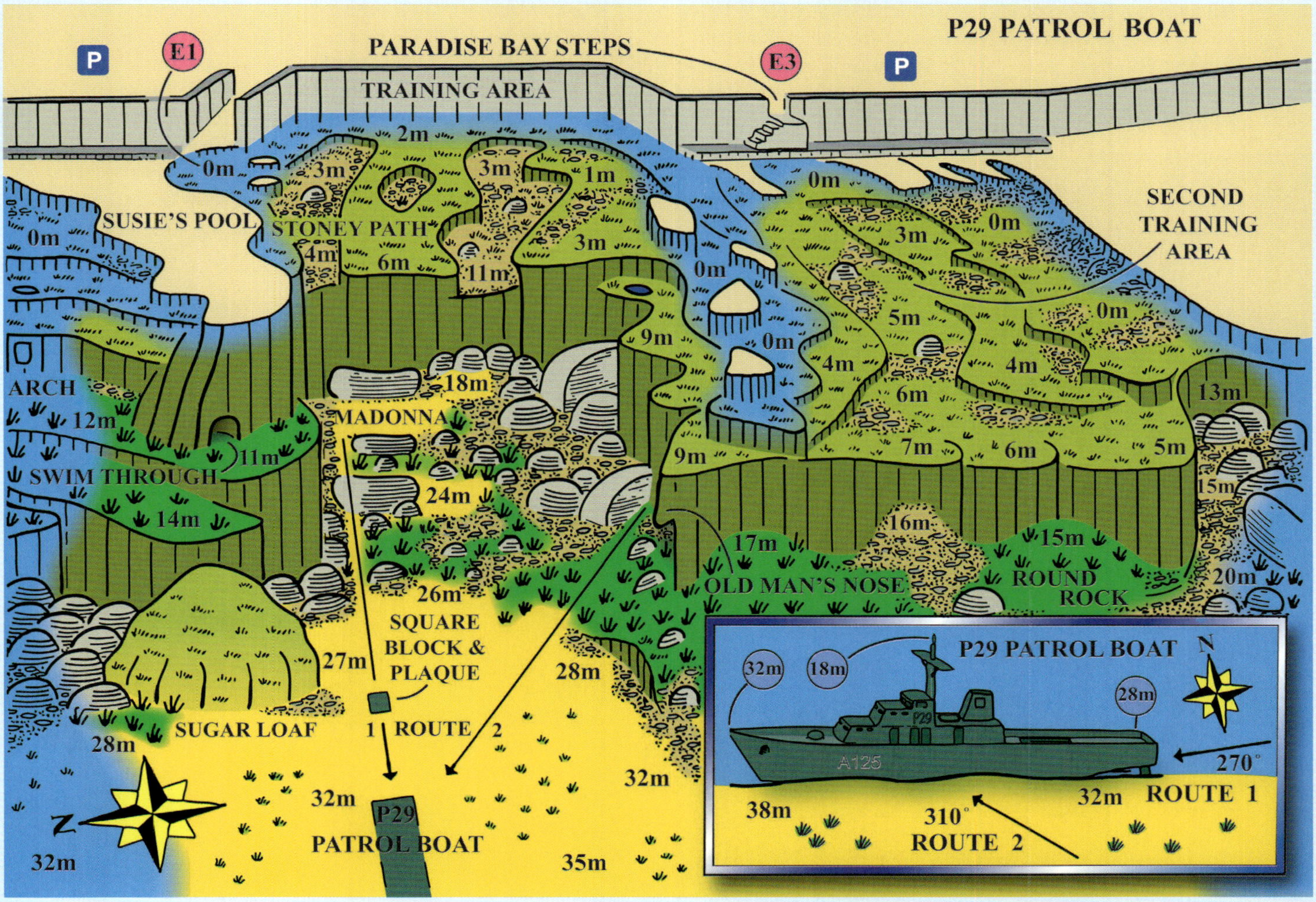

P29 PATROL BOAT
PARADISE BAY STEPS
TRAINING AREA
P
E1
E3
SUSIE'S POOL
STONEY PATH
SECOND TRAINING AREA
ARCH
SWIM THROUGH
MADONNA
OLD MAN'S NOSE
ROUND ROCK
SQUARE BLOCK & PLAQUE
SUGAR LOAF
1 ROUTE 2
P29 PATROL BOAT
0m
2m
3m
1m
4m
6m
11m
5m
9m
7m
12m
13m
14m
15m
16m
17m
18m
20m
24m
26m
27m
28m
32m
35m
N
270°
ROUTE 1
310°
ROUTE 2
38m
A125
P29

CIRKEWWA (MARFA POINT)

Paradise Bay
Area 5

Ben's Arch, which is just below the surface, I have named after my grandson.

The long swim is the nickname given to this site by myself, but in reality it can be completed, taking a leisurely swim, in less than 40 minutes. Your entry point is E4 on the western end of South Quay, there is no exit point at the quay or throughout the route. There is, however, a short distance from the quay, a little cove where you could exit in an emergency. This would involve walking over a very uneven surface. I suggest you take your vehicle to E4, unload, then park it near your exit point E3, then return to your buddies on foot.

THE DIVE — Minimum time – 50 mins

Beware, the jetty can be extremely slippery. Below your entry point E4 the depth at the side of the quay is 4m. When you are under water just follow the reef in a westerly direction keeping it on your right hand side. After a short distance you have a choice to stay on the ledge at 10m or go down to the next level at 15/18m. If you decide to stay at 10m after some 6/8 minutes you will find a curve in the reef, inside this area is an arch, good for photography. If you went to the lower reef it will take you 10/12 minutes or one minute from the arch to the large boulder right up against the main reef, it is possible to swim under it but the entrance is hidden by smaller boulders.

Once through the other side **you can take one of two routes:** the first one with a maximum depth of 32m, the second has a maximum depth of 20m. The first option is to follow a compass bearing of 270° down to an area of large boulders, with a maximum depth on the sand of 32m. Once you have run out of bottom time or you just want to move on, take an easterly compass bearing, heading back up the reef, taking your time to explore, when a depth of 20m is reached you should be between Valley Way and Round Rock.

Alternatively, continue round the reef keeping it on your right, where the seabed rises to 16m, here you will find Chris's Rock; this smallish rock resting on stones makes a great hiding place for marine life, we once found a nice cuttlefish here. From here move on along the base of the reef to a depth of 19m which is the start of Valley Way a narrow route between the main reef and boulders. In this area there are many hiding places for marine life such as Morays, Groupers, Octopuses and large Scorpion fish. When you reach 11m, bear left between two rocks, once through these looking down and slightly to your left you will see a stony seabed at 19m and the very large overhang at the base of Round Rock, explore this area and then ascend Round Rock onto the ridge at 9m and head into the second training area and E3.

ABOVE: *Can you name the divers? We were younger then!*
LEFT: *The drop off and large boulders between Bens Arch and Valley Way.*

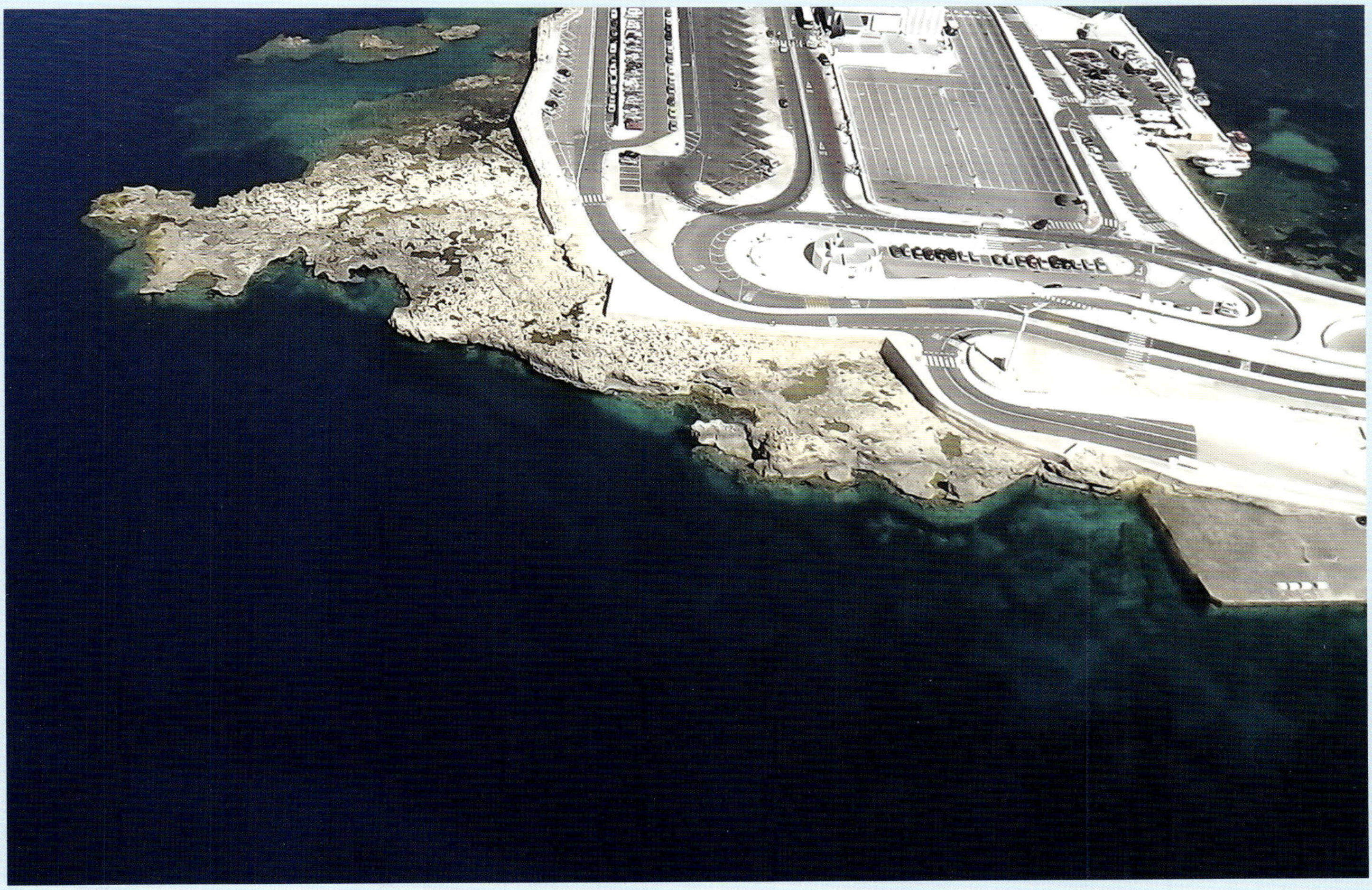

PGL AERIAL PHOTOS

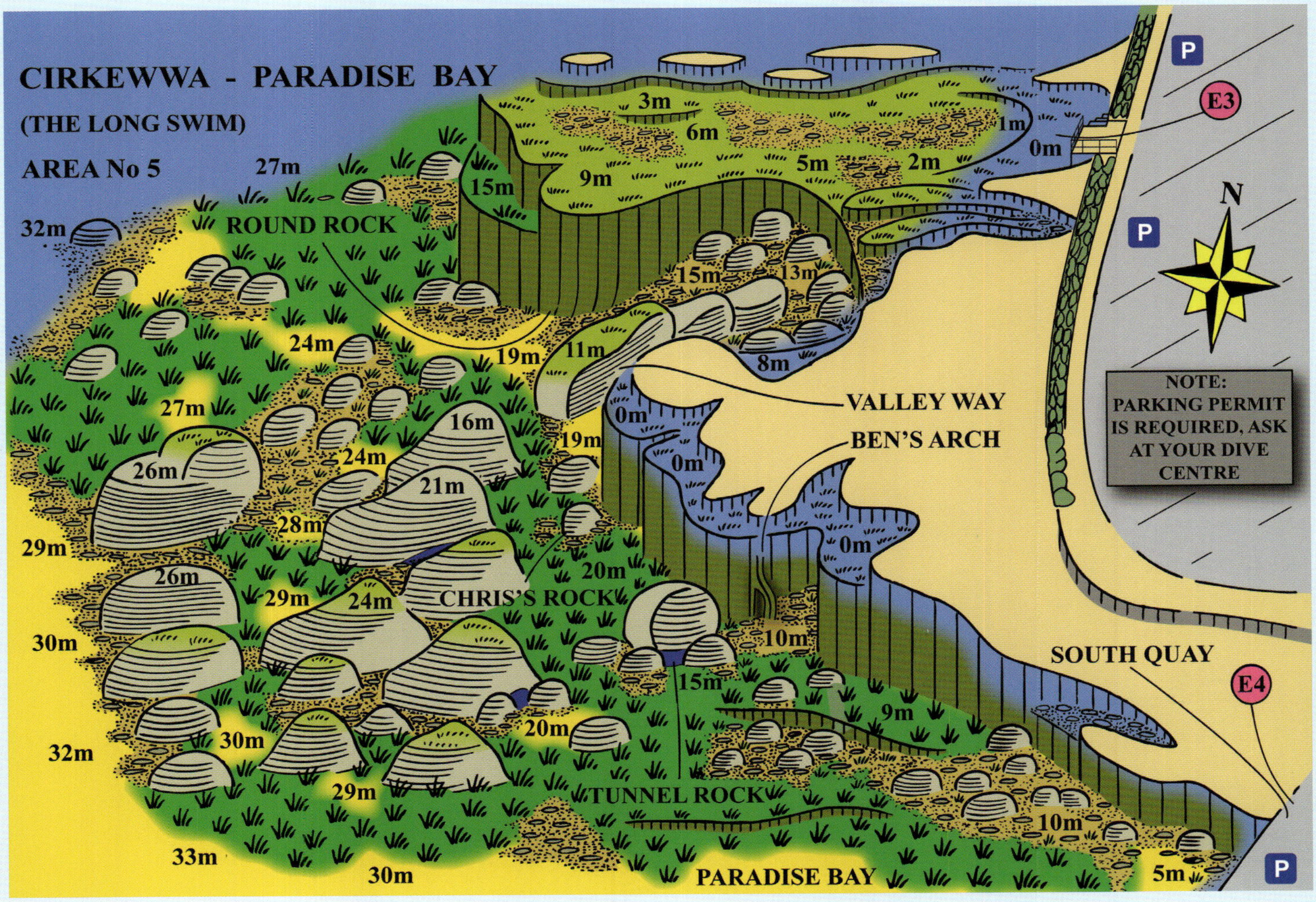
CIRKEWWA - PARADISE BAY
(THE LONG SWIM)
AREA No 5
ROUND ROCK
VALLEY WAY
BEN'S ARCH
CHRIS'S ROCK
TUNNEL ROCK
PARADISE BAY
SOUTH QUAY
NOTE: PARKING PERMIT IS REQUIRED, ASK AT YOUR DIVE CENTRE
N
E3
E4
P
P
P
3m
6m
9m
5m
2m
1m
0m
15m
27m
32m
13m
15m
11m
8m
19m
24m
27m
16m
19m
0m
0m
26m
24m
21m
28m
29m
0m
20m
26m
29m
24m
30m
10m
15m
9m
30m
20m
32m
29m
10m
33m
30m
5m

MELLIEHA – L-AHRAX POINT

PHOTO: JOE ABDILLA & PAUL GAUCI

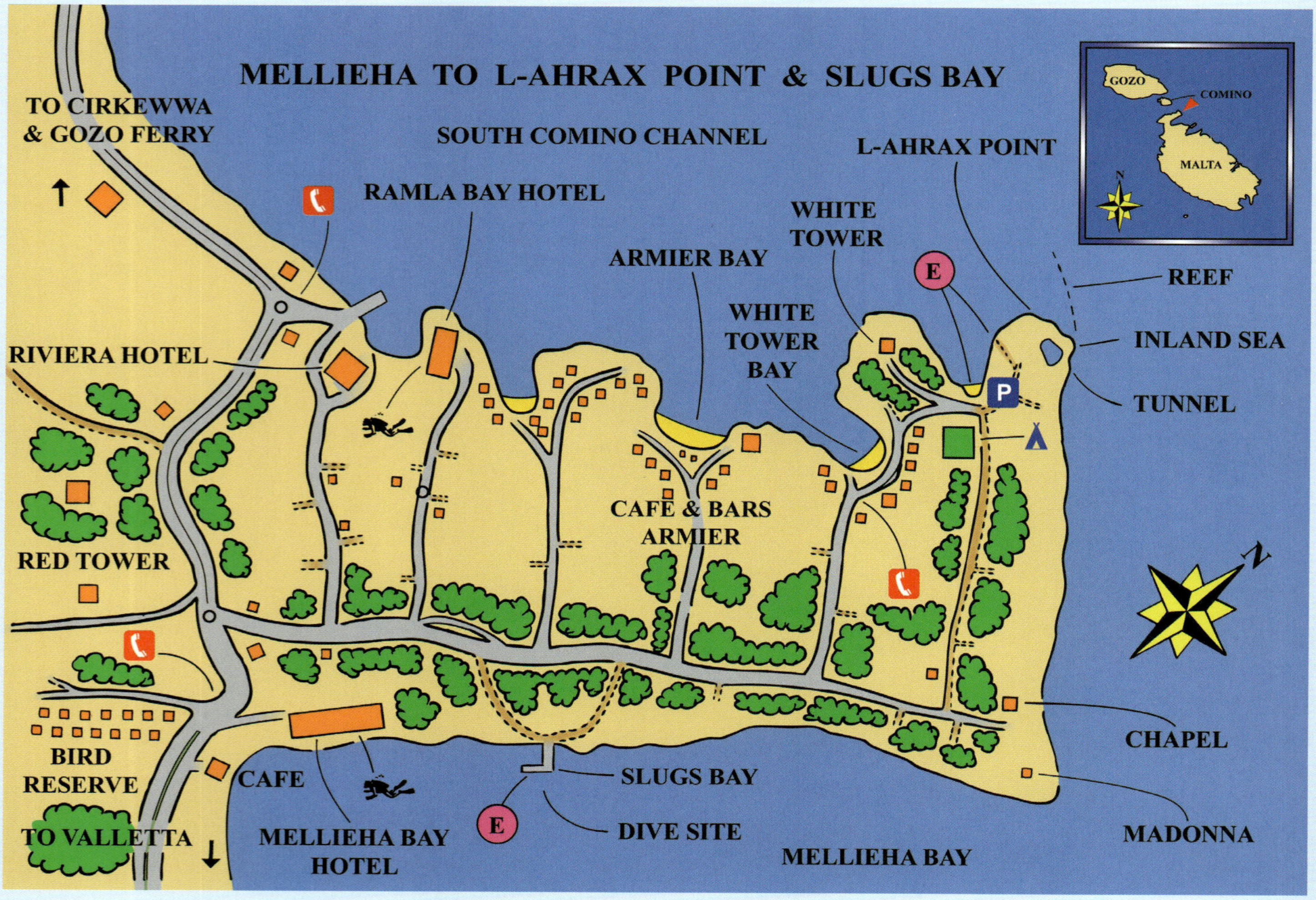

MELLIEHA TO L-AHRAX POINT & SLUGS BAY

TO CIRKEWWA & GOZO FERRY
SOUTH COMINO CHANNEL
L-AHRAX POINT
RAMLA BAY HOTEL
WHITE TOWER
ARMIER BAY
WHITE TOWER BAY
REEF
INLAND SEA
TUNNEL
RIVIERA HOTEL
CAFE & BARS ARMIER
RED TOWER
CHAPEL
BIRD RESERVE
CAFE
SLUGS BAY
MADONNA
TO VALLETTA
MELLIEHA BAY HOTEL
DIVE SITE
MELLIEHA BAY

GOZO COMINO MALTA

L-Ahrax Point

To reach L-Ahrax Point follow the road from Mellieha to Cirkewwa past Mellieha Bay and the sandy beach, continue up the hill on the other side, at the top of the hill turn right at the roundabout. Follow this road for about 2km where the road narrows you have two choices one; turn left down to White Tower Bay, in Maltese `Ramla tat-Torri`, which is a summer village for the Maltese people. Bear right and follow the bay around, and on the other side turn right again, at the next junction turn right, this will lead you to the camp site or two; continue straight on and take the first left.

The track is quite rough but it leads directly to the camp site. Entry point E1 is directly in front of you. For E2 bear to the right, and if your vehicle is able, continue along a track by the right hand side of the bay, at the end of the track is a concrete pad, E2 is a short walk from here. See plan.

This away from the madding crowd dive site is situated on the most northerly point of Malta, and is definitely worth a visit, especially if the sea conditions are westerly. If you decide to dive here remember that all amenities are some distance away. There are a number of ways to dive this site but it could be divided into two main areas, using both entry points, E1 and E2.

South reef tunnel and Inland Sea, maximum depth on the reef is 12m over the ledge depths of 22m can be reached; the tunnel is reasonably shallow at 8m.

In the right hand corner is the tunnel entrance.

A diver encounters shoal of bream.

North reef, which is reasonably level with a maximum depth of 10m, once over the edge you have a drop off down to 23m, away from the reef depths of 30m plus can be reached.

The best time to dive this site is with the sun directly on the reef, later in the day the reef will be in the shade and all the bright colours will have disappeared. The coast line around the headland is very rugged which makes it almost impossible to exit and even more difficult to walk on with diving equipment. There is one small area, which is suitable for an emergency exit if required. {see plan}. You can follow one of my two dive plans or you can plan your own to reach the reef. Many dive centers boat dive this site.

The entrance of the tunnel to the Inland Sea.

L-AHRAX POINT

South Reef Tunnel and Inland Sea

THE DIVE (1)　　Minimum time – 50 mins

Using entry/exit point E1 from here surface swim following the coastline all the way round until it meets the main reef you can of course descend at any time you wish to, this distance of approximately 250 meters will possibly take you some 20 minutes. At this point you will need to descend unless you have already done so, here the depth will be approximately 6m, keeping the coastline reef to your right and head in a southerly direction for about 6 minutes you will come to a distinct corner where the coastline reef now runs in a southwesterly direction, continue to follow its line.

The average depth in this area will be 12m. Within 2 minutes you will be able to see up on your left a rock shaped like an eagle's head, the entrance to the tunnel, which leads to the Inland Sea, is on your right. You will be unable to see straight through the tunnel, as there is a slight bend in it, the depth inside is 8m. The floor of the tunnel is covered in small rocks and they are in turn covered in red seaweed, these hard petal like flowers remind me of roses.

When you leave the tunnel return to the distinct corner, now head in a north westerly direction until you reach the drop off, you should pass a lone rock right on the edge of the drop off. Now follow the ridge along in a northerly direction until it turns and

The sea rose (Peyssononnelia squamariag) is a red seaweed, grows on rocks and poorly illuminated areas and covers the floor of this tunnel.

head west, continue to where the reef meets the coastline, it is quite easy to follow as it is shaped like the letter D. From this point your return route is the same as dive number one.

Facilities like a telephone and café are available when the camp site is open, otherwise there are no amenities within this area, the nearest telephone and café are some distance away (see plan) A reminder that you are diving a site away from it all, that means emergency services as well, so you must check the sea conditions. Although it is harder, I think it is more enjoyable to dive this site from the shore rather than a boat.

Eagle Rock with its head just below the surface, points towards the entrance to the tunnel.

Beware of small boats cutting this corner, especially during summer periods.

RIGHT: *A friendly encounter with a small ray.*

PGL AERIAL PHOTOS

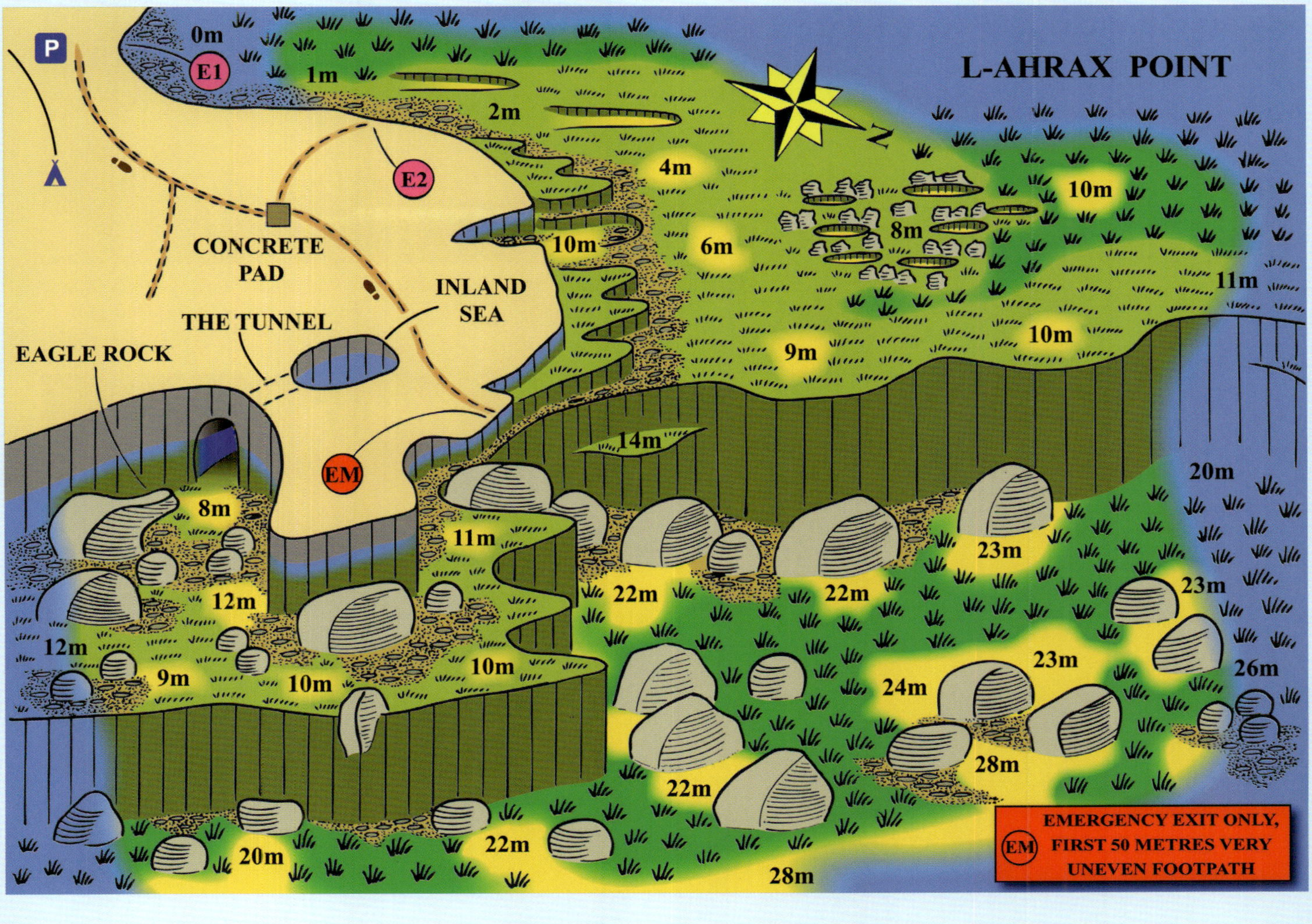
L-AHRAX POINT
P
0m
E1
1m
2m
E2
4m
6m
8m
10m
11m
CONCRETE PAD
INLAND SEA
THE TUNNEL
EAGLE ROCK
9m
14m
EM
8m
11m
12m
12m
9m
10m
10m
22m
22m
23m
20m
23m
23m
26m
24m
28m
22m
20m
22m
28m
EMERGENCY EXIT ONLY, FIRST 50 METRES VERY UNEVEN FOOTPATH

L-Ahrax Point – North Reef

THE DIVE (2) Minimum time – 50 mins

Use entry point E1 and once in the water surface swim following the coastline, keeping it on your right to the sandy gullies, depth 3/4m now descend and take a compass bearing of 350'. Most of the seabed will be covered in sea grass, after about 11 minutes you will reach an area of small jagged rocks, where the marine growth is short. The stones are in a circle and for some reason it reminds me of a mini Stonehenge. Now take a compass bearing of 30° continuing over the sea grass to an area of short marine growth just before you reach the drop off.

This distance will possibly take you a further 6 minutes. If you decide to go over and once on the bottom your depth will be around 23m or deeper if you move away from the reef, head in a southerly direction keeping the main reef on your right. Running along beside the reef are some very large boulders, the sea bed is covered with sea grass and sandy patches, don't forget to keep an eye in the blue for any dentex or barracuda passing by.

When it is time to return ascend to the top of the reef, continue to follow the edge until you meet the main coastline reef at 6m, bear right, from here it is

Once over the drop off the large boulders litter the seabed with areas of sea grass and sand.

A shoal of barracuda (Sphyraena sphyraene) have come into a shallow area off thi-s headland.

almost 250 meters to your exit point, this could take you as long as 15/20 minutes. If you have the air take your time and explore this shallow reef. On your way back you will pass a small quarry with a depth of 10m with a little cove at the rear and inside there is a small arch. Continue to follow the reef all the way round until you reach the sandy gullies from here when it becomes shallow, if you wish you could surface and swim to your exit point E1.

This pretty little nudibranch (Cratena peregrine) can be found with patience as they are so small and very difficult to spot.

PHOTO: IAN FORDER

The sea hare (Aplysia depilans) has a thin shell completely covered by its mantle, found on rocky, algae rich sea beds.

Nudibranch

Hermit crab

Squid

Red-mouthed Goby

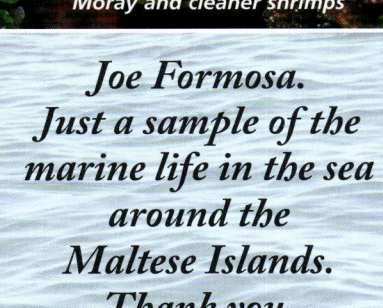
Moray and cleaner shrimps

Lobster

*Joe Formosa.
Just a sample of the marine life in the sea around the Maltese Islands.
Thank you.*

Fan worm

Joe Formosa

Seahorse

Slugs Bay

To reach Slugs Bay the directions are the same as for L-Ahrax Point, but after turning right at the top of the hill continue for just under 1 km. When you have passed the turning to Armier, continue round a slight bend and then on your right hand side you will find an entrance to a track, which will lead you down to Slugs Bay. Normally a 4x4 will be required for the 400 metre drive, but some people do take cars to the parking area above the cove, but due to the weight of diving equipment, passengers are advised to walk.

The name of this dive site does not do justice to this peaceful pretty area on the north side of Mellieha Bay, with its jetty and secluded cove and is only disturbed by walkers during the spring months admiring the many colourful wild flowers. Entry for this dive can be made from the shore or the jetty; the dive area consists of rocks, sea grass and areas of sand with a maximum depth of 12m.

To the east of the dive site in an area of small shingle/sand, fossilized sharks teeth have been found here, remember that it is illegal to remove certain items from under the water. This is not a very popular dive site, due to the conditions of the track, especially after heavy rainfall, but if you have a 4x4 that's great. It is a site used mainly when sea conditions do not permit diving elsewhere on the island, the bay is protected from the north northwesterly seas.

The ribbed helmet shell (Phalium granulatum) found mostly in posidonia meadows. PHOTO: ALAN JAMES

The Jetty at Slugs Bay. PHOTO: JOE ABDILLA & PAUL GAUCI

The giant tun shell (Tonna galea) lives on sandy seabeds feeds on sea cucumbers and often falls prey to octopus.

THE DIVE — Minimum time – 40 mins

This dive site is good for training new divers or to test your skills in navigation. The way I normally dive this area is to enter the water from the outer part of the jetty, entry point E1. Once on the bottom head out over the sea grass and sandy areas with a compass bearing of 140° for approximately 5 minutes, now turning left and a compass bearing of 50° for a further 8/10 minutes. Here you will find a small reef, where the seabed is covered in shingle: this is the area where shark teeth have been found. Now follow the reef all the way round to your left until you have a compass bearing of 270°, this will lead you towards the arch.

When it is time to return, head back to the sandy area, with a compass bearing of 180° after a short distance, bear to your right up and over the little reef on to the area of sea grass. For the next 3 minutes or so use a compass bearing of 230° then a bearing of 270° would be required in order to take you towards the jetty or into the cove and your exit point, E2. Maybe it would be a good idea to plan your own dive here and discover how good you are with the compass.

Remember that there are no facilities here at all and the nearest services are some distance away at Mellieha. When walking on the jetty extra care must be taken if it is wet or your shoes are wet, as it can be **extremely slippery**.

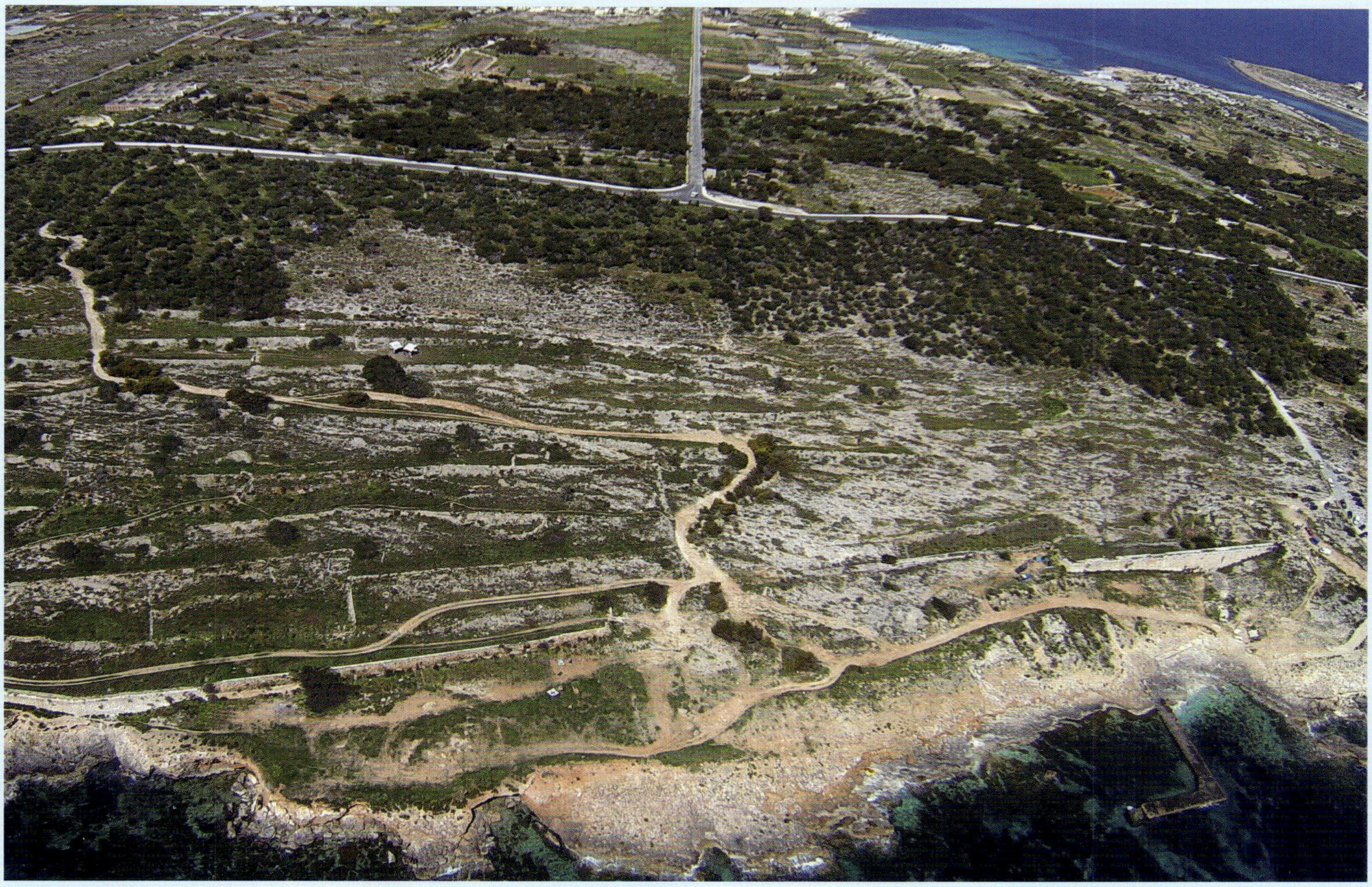

PHOTO: JOE ABDILLA & PAUL GAUCI

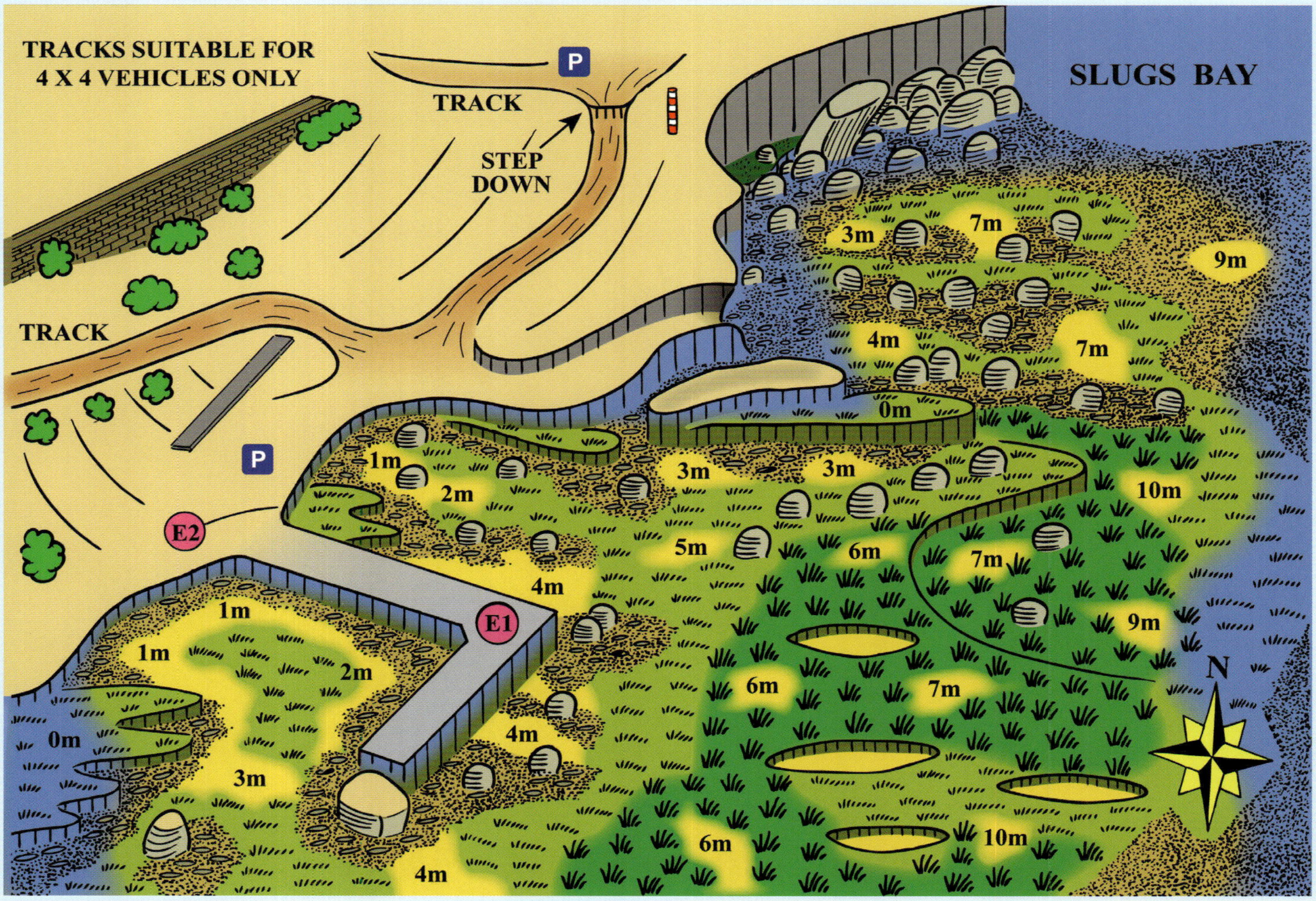
TRACKS SUITABLE FOR
4 X 4 VEHICLES ONLY
P
TRACK
STEP
DOWN
SLUGS BAY
TRACK
P
E2
E1
N
0m
1m
1m
1m
2m
2m
3m
3m
3m
3m
4m
4m
4m
4m
5m
6m
6m
6m
7m
7m
7m
7m
9m
9m
10m
10m

BUGIBBA & QAWRA POINT

PGL AERIAL PHOTOS

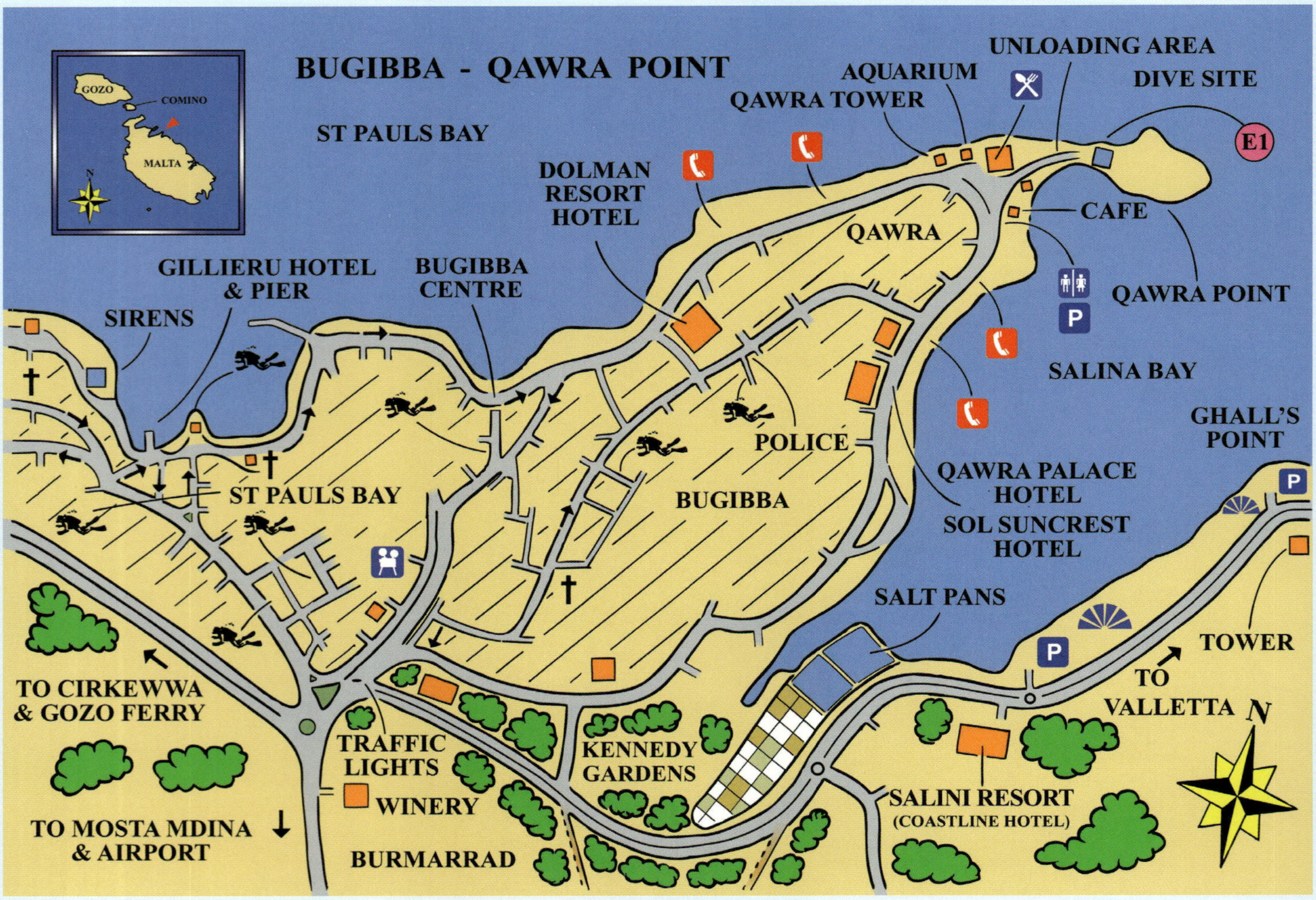

BUGIBBA - QAWRA POINT

- ST PAULS BAY
- AQUARIUM
- QAWRA TOWER
- UNLOADING AREA
- DIVE SITE
- E1
- DOLMAN RESORT HOTEL
- QAWRA
- CAFE
- GILLIERU HOTEL & PIER
- BUGIBBA CENTRE
- QAWRA POINT
- SIRENS
- SALINA BAY
- ST PAULS BAY
- POLICE
- GHALL'S POINT
- BUGIBBA
- QAWRA PALACE HOTEL
- SOL SUNCREST HOTEL
- SALT PANS
- TOWER
- TO CIRKEWWA & GOZO FERRY
- TO VALLETTA
- TRAFFIC LIGHTS
- WINERY
- KENNEDY GARDENS
- SALINI RESORT (COASTLINE HOTEL)
- TO MOSTA MDINA & AIRPORT
- BURMARRAD

Qawra Point

This dive site is situated very close to the busy resort of Bugibba / St Pauls Bay on a peninsular of land on the north coast called Qawra Point. Leave the main road at the turning into St Pauls Bay / Bugibba, almost immediately bear to the right and follow the coast road for about 2km. When you pass the large hotels on the sea front this is known as Qawra, continue on to a long sweeping bend, here turn right in front of you will be the entrance to the unloading area (see photo) Once unloaded remove your vehicle from this area and find a parking space.

There are a number of ways that you could plan your dive here and I have selected three. Just off the north shore opposite the pool and your entry point, is a large level area with average depths of 8m, further out the seabed gently slopes off to 36m. This large inshore area is an excellent place to finish your dive, a second dive, or visit the cave, here you will often find thousands of glass fish. Once through the cave you will find yourself in a small inland sea, in which you can surface and snorkel around a central rock.

The last two dives suggested are deeper, 30m plus, and are suitable for experienced divers only. Sometimes due to northerly winds it is not possible to dive this site as the entry/exit point is surrounded by jagged rocks and therefore requires calm sea conditions.

The entrance for the road leading to unloading area.

The sun shines through this large blow hole within the Fra Ben Cave.   PHOTO: ALEXANDER ARISTARKHOV

THE DIVE (1)   Minimum time – 40 mins

The first dive is suitable for all grades of divers. Once you have entered the water head in a northerly direction, this will take you over an area covered by short marine growth, sea grass and many small gullies, with an average of depth of 6m to the first point on the headland. Once you have rounded the corner head into the small bay keeping the reef on your right hand side, this will lead you to the cave and small inland sea, be careful not to miss the entrance, for if the sun is casting a shadow this will make it difficult to see.

When leaving this area, and you have enough air, turn right and head in a northerly direction, just before the end of the bay you will find an area with rough rocks and boulders they are covered in coral and marine life and if you have camera a good opportunity for macro photography. Remember you are now 15 to 20 minutes away from your entry point. When it is time to head back follow the reef in a south westerly direction not exceeding a depth of 8 to 9m. To reach the shore line / exit point take a southerly compass bearing.

A free swimming octopus (Octopus vulgaris) seems to have found a friend and attached itself to the divers arm.

QAWRA POINT

A pretty little nudibranch (Hypselodoris elegans).
PHOTO: COLIN STEAD

This jelly fish (Cotylorhiza tuberculate) sometimes known as a fried egg normally found along this coastline during summer and autumn.

THE DIVE (2)   Minimum time – 50 mins

The second dive will take you to 30m plus. From the entry point surface swim out for 8 to 10 minutes on a compass bearing of 330° you can of course go under water but you will pass over mostly sea grass and use valuable dive time. Now descend to the sea bed if your depth is 28m or less continue down and over the reef to the bottom, if your depth is 32m or more head south back to the base of the reef.

Follow the line where the reef meets the sand in an easterly direction, your depth will gradually increase to 36m, this should take you approximately 10 minutes.

Two divers outside the Fra Ben Cave doing a familiarization equipment dive.
PHOTO: ALEXANDER ARISTARKHOV

Here you will see a number of small jagged rocks dotted around in the sand.

This is possibly a good time to head south up over the reef to shallower depths, here the seabed is covered in grass with small areas of sand. Now look for the larger areas of sand at a depth of 19m and the small arch (see plan) Continue on, turning east when you reach the reef, depth 15m, this will take you on to another area of sand, cross the sand to the other side still keeping the reef on your right. In a small corner of the reef there is a plaque in memory of four Maltese divers who lost their lives in a tragic accident. Continue up over the drop off where you will find a small ledge, keeping this on your right, it will lead you towards the cave. Take your time to explore both the cave and the small inland sea.

When it is time to return, head out of the cave, keep the reef on your left, at its end head south west parallel with the shore line and towards your exit point, maybe if you have left some marker stones it will be easier for you to find.

Tube dwelling anemone (Cerianthus membranaceus) this beautiful anemone exists on sandy sea beds.

QAWRA POINT NORTH – BUGIBBA

PHOTO: JOE ABDILLA & PAUL GAUCI

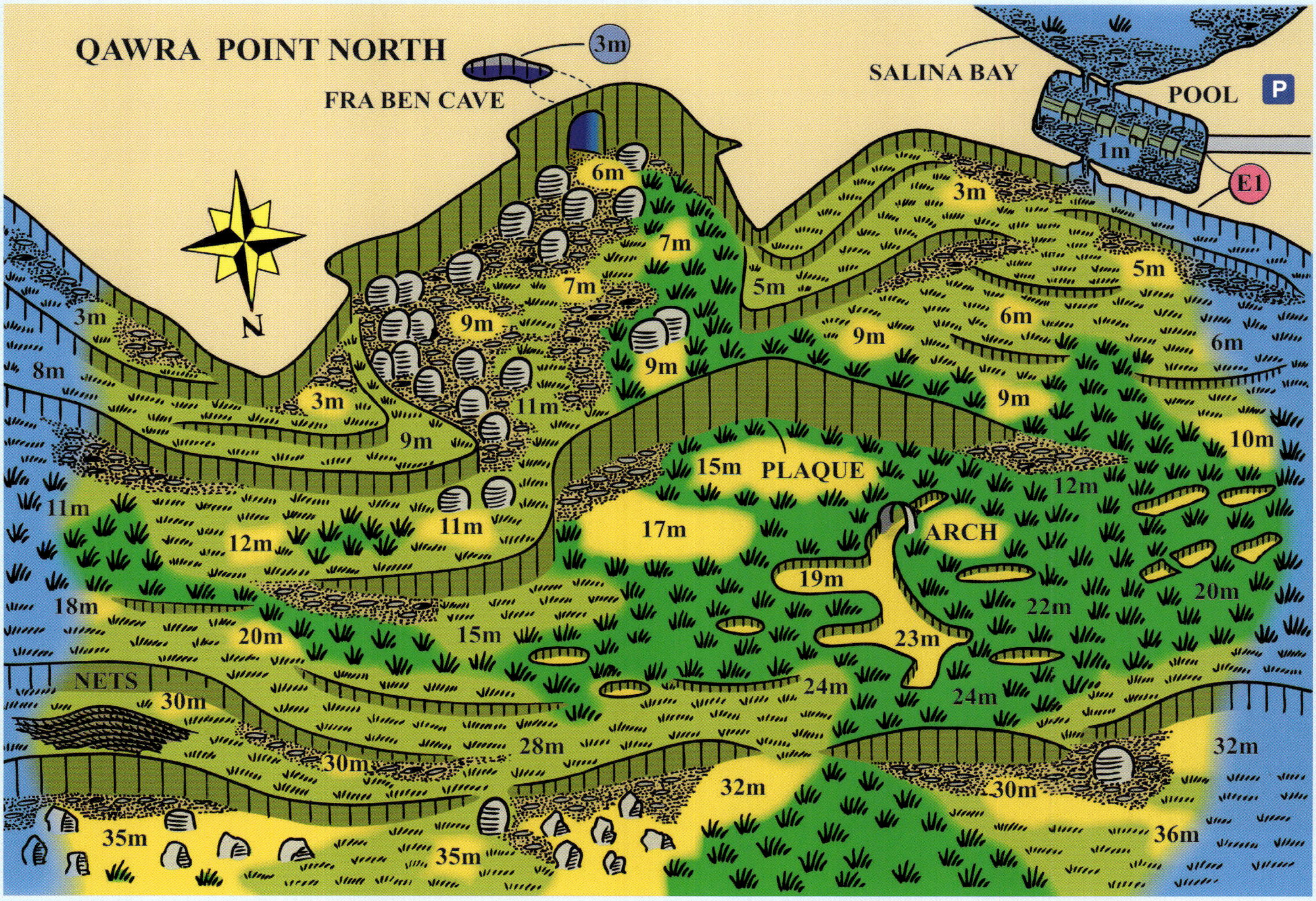

QAWRA POINT

THE DIVE (3)   Minimum time – 60 mins

In my opinion this deep and long dive should be undertaken with a 15 litre cylinder. From your entry, surface swim to the furthest point of headland, this will take 10 to 15 minutes. At this point surface swim out in a northerly direction until the shallow reef almost disappears. Descend, once on the seabed, continue down and over the reef to 30m where you will find a large old heavy fishing net, here the reef drops to sand at 35m plus.

Left – This is the commercial 'bath sponge' (Spongia officinalis) forms massive, rounded growths, with a rough spiky surface.
Middle – An encrusting red sponge (Crambe crambe) grows on rock between 5 and 30m, forming thick irregular sheets.
Right – The greek bating sponge (Spongia officinalis) has been fished for, for centuries in the Mediterranean.

Divers find a shell which was probably left over from target practice as there was a range in this area.

Tree sponges. (Asinella polypoides) this sponge's colonies look like a small tree with cylindrical branches.

If your surface swim was too far and you are unable to see the reef on your descent, head in a southerly direction. Now follow the main reef in an easterly direction, the black and yellow sponges litter this area of the dive site. Within a few minutes the reef will bear round and head in a southerly direction, continue with the reef on your right, this area of sand between two reefs approx. 30 meters wide comes to a dead end.

Now ascend the reef up to the sea grass, here your depth will be 22m bearing in mind from this point it will take you some 10 to 15 minutes to reach a depth of 9m and a further 25 minutes to your exit point. Continue on a south south-westerly direction over the sea grass slowly ascending, once you have reached a depth of 9m or less head in a westerly direction. To find the shore line and exit point take a southerly bearing.

> **Please note that Qawra Point often gets quite busy with boat traffic which are inclined to come close to the shore when rounding the headland more so in summer periods and weekends.**

On the south side of the point is a very pleasant place for those non-divers to just sit and watch the world go by, sun bathe, swim or maybe snorkel.

In this area there are a number of restaurants and café's also the Aquarium which also has a very nice restaurant. Once again this is a popular area for the local people and can become quite busy at weekends.

St. Paul's Shipwreck

St Paul's islands can clearly be seen from Qawra point and the history of the shipwreck is as follows; According to the Acts of Apostles, St Paul and St Luke were on their way to Rome to be tried as political rebels when their ship foundered on the rocks of Malta. The actual site of the shipwreck is generally thought to have been one of the islets to the north of St Paul's Bay. The islanders welcomed the Apostles and for an entire winter they sheltered in a cave at Rabat. It was from here that St Paul preached the Gospel, converting the Roman governor, Publius, who became the first Bishop of Malta.

SLIEMA – ST. JULIANS

PHOTO: JOE ABDILLA & PAUL GAUCI

SLIEMA EXILES REEF PACEVILLE MERCANTI REEF

- TO VALLETTA & SOUTH
- TO ST. PAULS BAY & CIRKEWWA
- TUNNEL
- SPINOLA BAY
- BULLUTA BAY
- ST. JULIANS
- CINEMAS BOWLING
- CORINTHIA MARINA HOTEL
- PACEVILLE
- NIGHT LIFE AREA BARS & CLUBS
- HILTON MALTA
- THE WESTIN HOTEL
- ST. GEORGES BAY
- HILTON TOWER
- PORTOMASO
- IL-QAUET
- DRAGONARA PALACE CASINO
- PROMENADE GARDENS
- CAVALIERI HOTEL
- E1
- EXILES REEF
- E2
- ST. JULIANS POINT
- MERCANTI REEF
- DRAGONARA POINT
- SLIEMA

Paceville – Mercanti Reef

This unique dive site with its entry point almost in the heart of Malta's main night life, is situated on the south side of Dragonara Point (Il-Qaliet).

To find this site head towards the Hilton Tower the parking and entry point are situated on the north side of this building. Most of the streets within this area are one way so follow the local map. Boat traffic should not be a problem as most of it will pass on the outside of the reef.

THE DIVE   Minimum time – 60 mins

From your entry point E1 you have just over a 250 metre surface swim, less if you are able to use the beach front on Dragonara Point (hotel property) as this is closer to the reef. When you reach the reef, descend, below the marker post is a small shallow valley of stones which run out in the direction of your route back to your exit point. Now head north until you reach a large area of flat rock with gullies running out in a westerly direction, after exploring this area, turn round head back in a southerly direction past the marker post. Now follow the reef in a southerly direction keeping it on your left hand side for some 6 minutes, in front of you will be a large rock/boulder, it looks a bit like a blackberry, **now you have a choice;**

One: you can continue all the way along the reef round the little horseshoe and the pointed end with a small hole in the reef, this reminds me of an animal sitting up with its front leg supporting its head, along the back of the reef it is much flatter once you have passed the 6 humps you will now be 20 minutes into your dive and 40 minutes away from your exit point, turn and retrace your steps to the small stony valley below the marker post, maximum depth so far is 10m. From here your return journey will take you approximately 20 minutes with a maximum depth of 12m on a compass bearing of 250°.

An unusual off-shore reef with many overhangs and places of interest to explore.

Nudibranch (Hypselodoris valenciennesi) gastropod mollusc with a body similar to a snail.   PHOTO: JOE FORMOSA

Two: go on the inside between the reef and Blackberry rock, now take a bearing of 200/210° to the southern end of the inshore reef exploring the rugged east side before returning to the end, then head in a northerly direction so that the inner reef is on your left and when the visibility is good you will see the main reef on your right. Follow this to the end of the valley here, if you have taken the time to explore, you could

Not easily found these cute little seahorses (Hippocampus ramulosus).   PHOTO: SHARON FORDER

be 40 minutes into your dive. Your return route is the same 250 metres; 20 minutes with a compass bearing of 250° this will test your navigational skills. There are far too many small overhangs fissures and places to explore to be indicated on this small map, this is an excellent dive and should not be rushed. The marine life here is plentiful, so take your camera.

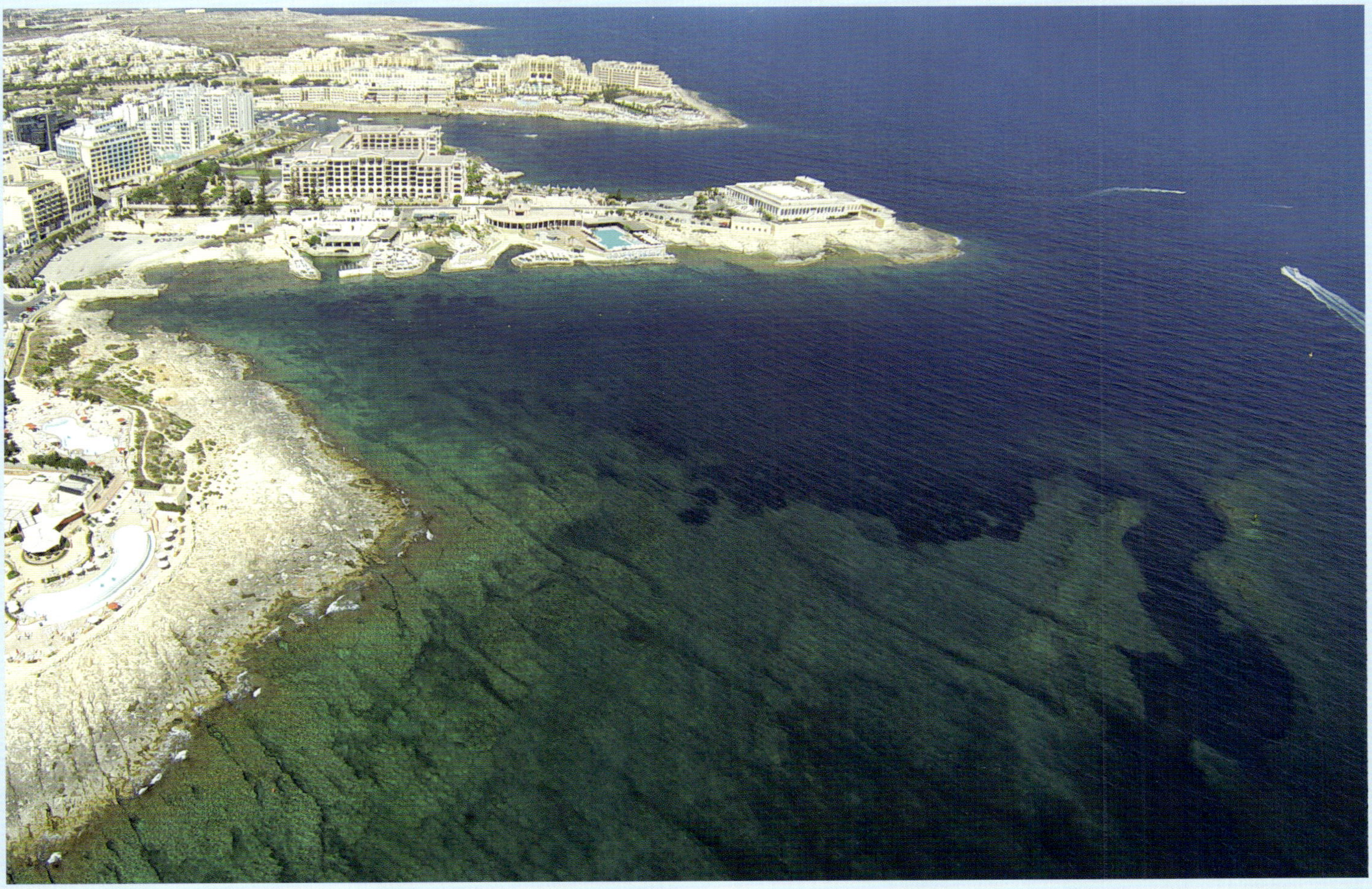

PGL AERIAL PHOTOS

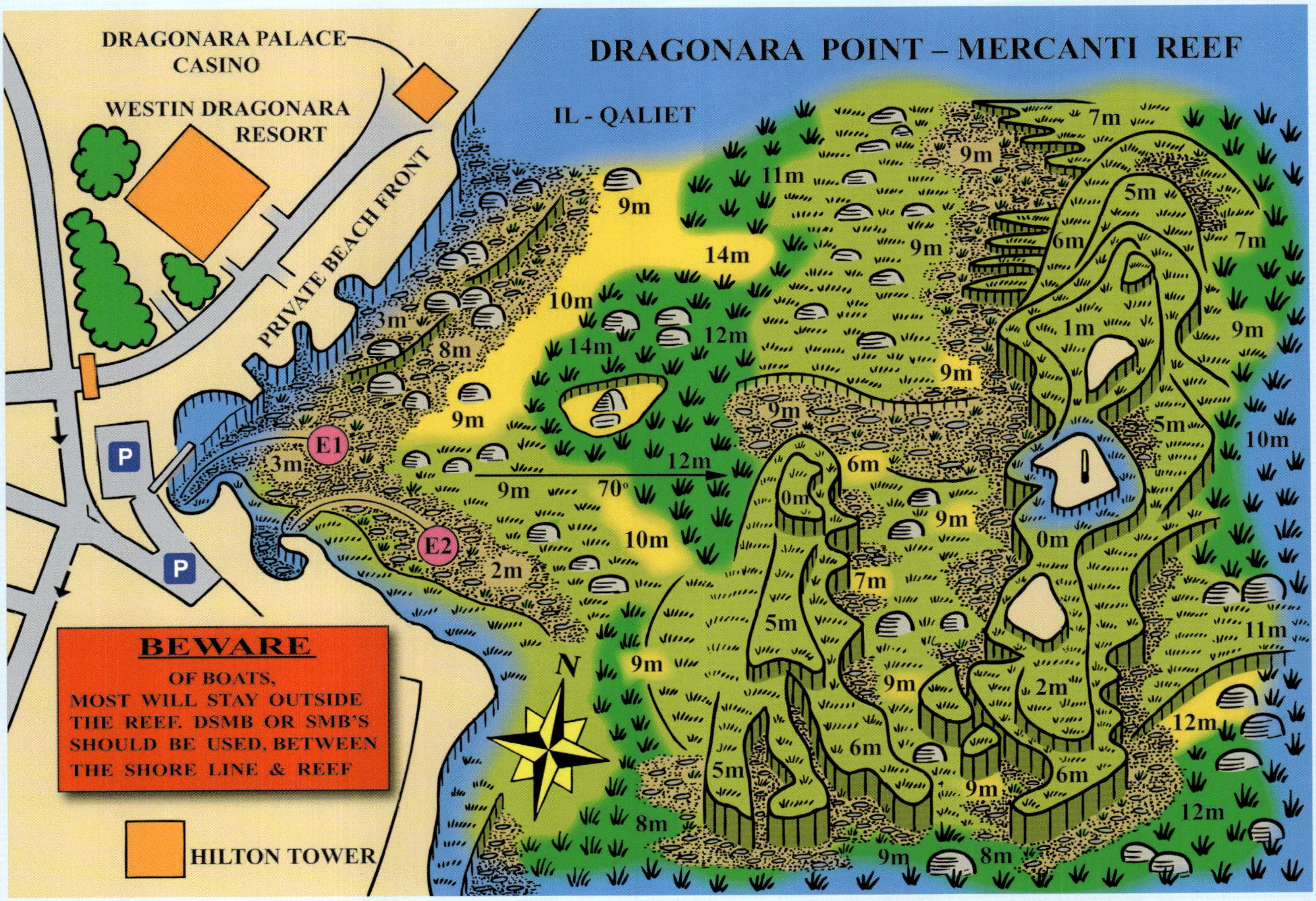
DRAGONARA POINT – MERCANTI REEF
DRAGONARA PALACE CASINO
WESTIN DRAGONARA RESORT
PRIVATE BEACH FRONT
IL - QALIET
E1
E2
70°
N
BEWARE
OF BOATS, MOST WILL STAY OUTSIDE THE REEF. DSMB OR SMB'S SHOULD BE USED, BETWEEN THE SHORE LINE & REEF
HILTON TOWER
P
P
3m
8m
9m
3m
2m
9m
14m
10m
14m
12m
12m
9m
10m
9m
11m
9m
7m
5m
6m
1m
9m
9m
9m
6m
0m
5m
7m
9m
9m
6m
5m
8m
9m
8m
9m
2m
6m
0m
5m
10m
7m
9m
11m
12m
12m

Exiles St. Julians Point – Sliema

This dive site is situated approximately half way between the main centres of St. Julians and Sliema. Leaving St. Julians follow the coast road passing the water polo pool, further on to the Barracuda restaurant, from here in approximately 500 metres turn left down a narrow road which leads to a car park and your dive site.

From Sliema front follow the coast road (Tower Road), travel for about 1 km where the St Julians Tower will be on your right. Here there is a sharp bend with a central barrier, immediately after this you will have to turn right down the narrow road to the car park and dive site. Parking is often a problem on week days.

Tugoat 2 *working in Grand Harbour.*

This dive site is situated at Exiles/St Julians Point and offers divers of all experience an interesting dive with *Tugboat 2* at 22m. There are pretty gentle sloping reefs with many small gullies, overhangs to explore surrounded by large areas of sand, there is also an abundance of marine life. The entry/exit point here is not difficult, therefore it is an excellent place for training especially in navigational skills, or you quite simply want a change.

Before scuttling.   PHOTO: LUCA PAPARELLA/ITALIAN AIR FORCE

The scuttling of Tugoat 2.   PHOTO: DIVE SYSTEMS MALTA

Tugboat Number 2 – Tuo Lun Er Hao

Tugboat Number 2 was built by Malta Drydocks, Marsa in 1975 for the Chinese Government, named *Tuo Lun Er Hao* and registered in Tientsin China. With her sister tugboat *Tuo Lun Yi Hao* worked together on the China Dock 6 project in French Creek, Grand Harbour. They soon became known as Number 1 and Number 2 tugboats. Originally owned by Kalaxlokk Co. Ltd, in 2000 she was purchased by Bezzina Marine Services Ltd and for the following 12 years she had been laid up in their shipyards. Her sister ship, now named *Anni* is still working and was present at the scuttling. *Tugboat 2* has a gross weight of 141 tons, a length of 30 metres, a beam 7.5 metres and a height of 9.5 metres.

The Professional Diving Schools Association in conjunction with the Malta Tourism Authority requested permission from the planning authority to scuttle *Tugboat 2* some 250 metres on the sand off St Julians Point. After going through the process of planning applications and being made environmentally friendly, *Tugboat 2* was scuttled as a diver attraction on the morning of the 20th June 2013. She now sits on the sand in an upright position at a depth of 22m, lying parallel and some 17 metres in distance from the closest point to the reef. Another unique dive site has been created by scuttling the ninth diver attraction/artificial reef just to add to the excellent variety of diving in the Maltese Islands.

For the more time spent on artificial reefs the less time will be spent on the natural reefs this new wreck will allow newer divers with a qualification to this depth to visit a wreck and see for themselves how the marine life gradually moves in. It could take you

The plaque in front of the bridge reads: Malta Dry Dock No. 101 Built 1975

between 12 and 20 minutes to reach this wreck depending on your dive plan.

Maybe on the way to the wreck, just concentrate on the route and navigation and leave exploring the reef and its marine life for your return journey.

Approaching the end of the reef where the boulders are and looking out over the sand towards the tugboats resting place, my first sighting was a dark shadow in the blue, then moving forward, soon the whole wreck came into view, she looked quite peaceful just sitting there on the sand. While exploring the outside of the hull, take time to stop and resting on the sand in front and below the bow, just look up, it is quite awesome.

Already the fish life are taking up residence on the wreck, a grouper and a shoal of saddle bream under the bows, a small octopus in a pipe with only two very small eyes looking up at me. It is also possible to enter the engine room; the engine is still in place. Please ensure that care is taken and penetration diving procedures are followed.

Beware of boat traffic – especially at weekends in the summer. The yellow Marker Buoys could possibly be removed from the sea in the winter months then a Surface Marker Buoy would be a must and at other times a Delayed Surface Marker Buoy would be advisable.

A shoal of saddle bream taking up residence below the stern.

Calypso plaque and stones.

THE DIVE   Minimum time – 50 mins

There are a number of ways in which to reach the wreck of *Tugboat 2*, but I am going to suggest three. All my choices for this dive use entry point E1, check your entry point for the steps probably will have been removed during the winter months

Choice 1.

From entry point E1 descend and take a compass bearing between 300° and 330° this will take you over the short marine growth, then over the sea grass down onto the sand at 12m, time about 3 minutes. If you have navigated correctly and with a little bit of luck, you should come across the Calypso plaque and stones on the sand, the letters read CSAC (Calypso Sub Aqua Club) at Christmas, I understand a Christmas tree is placed here! This plaque is a good marker point on your return journey. Now follow the reef edge where it meets the sand, for a short while your heading will be 30° in about 2 minutes the reef will be heading in a northerly direction, depth 13m. Continue for some 10 minutes until you reach a depth of 18m, here the

The bows and bridge of Tugboat 2 *in her final resting place.*

The stern of Tugboat 2.

Mini Car Rock – 17 metres from the wreck.

reef changes direction slightly to 30°; at this point there is no reef as such on your right, only sea grass. When reaching a depth of 20m your approximate total time to this point could be 17 minutes. You should find in this area, partly in the sea grass and surrounded by sand, a large smooth boulder almost a metre high and from above appears to be the shape of a heart, so I have given it the name 'Heart Rock'. Facing out over the sand use the right hand side as a directional line and a compass bearing of 20°, from here it is 30 metres to the wreck, or you can follow the edge of the sand passing three more boulders each separated by sea grass, the fourth one is shaped like a small car, 'Mini Car Rock', this is the wrecks' closest point to the reef, a distance of 17 metres with a northerly compass bearing. Total time to reach the wreck approximately 19 minutes, of course you may be a lot faster than me!

Choice 2
From entry point E1 descend and take a compass bearing of north to 330° continue down and over the reef until you reach the sand, basically this way you are cutting off a corner. Now follow the edge of the reef where it meets the sand all the way to Heart Rock, as in choice 1, this route could save you 3 to 4 minutes making a total time to the wreck of approximately 16 minutes.

Choice 3
Possibly this is the best way to complete this dive. From entry point E1, surface swim parallel with the land to the end of St Julians Point. Stay on the western side of the reef, using it for protection from boat traffic. Now descend to a depth of 5m and take a northerly compass bearing; it will take you about 12 minutes and If your navigation has been good, you should be in the area of the six boulders that line the end of the reef, bearing in mind they are only a metre in height. From here you should be able to see the wreck, if not, see details in choice 1. Total time to the wreck approximately 14 minutes.

Return Routes
You have a choice of routes over the reef to entry point E1, compass bearing 180° or E2 compass bearing 130°/140°. I would normally follow the reef where it meets the sand all the way back to the Calypso plaque and stones at approximately 11 to 12m. I found the reef to be full of life, octopus, painted comber, cardinal fish and nudibranchs to name but a few. It is always a good idea to check out on the sand for tun shells, rays, flying gurnards and dabs. Lots to see – a great dive – even better if you have a camera.

Heart Rock some 30 metres from the wreck.

The engine room. PHOTO: DIVE SYSTEMS MALTA

TUGBOAT 2 – EXILES – SLIEMA

PHOTO: JOE ABDILLA & PAUL GAUCI

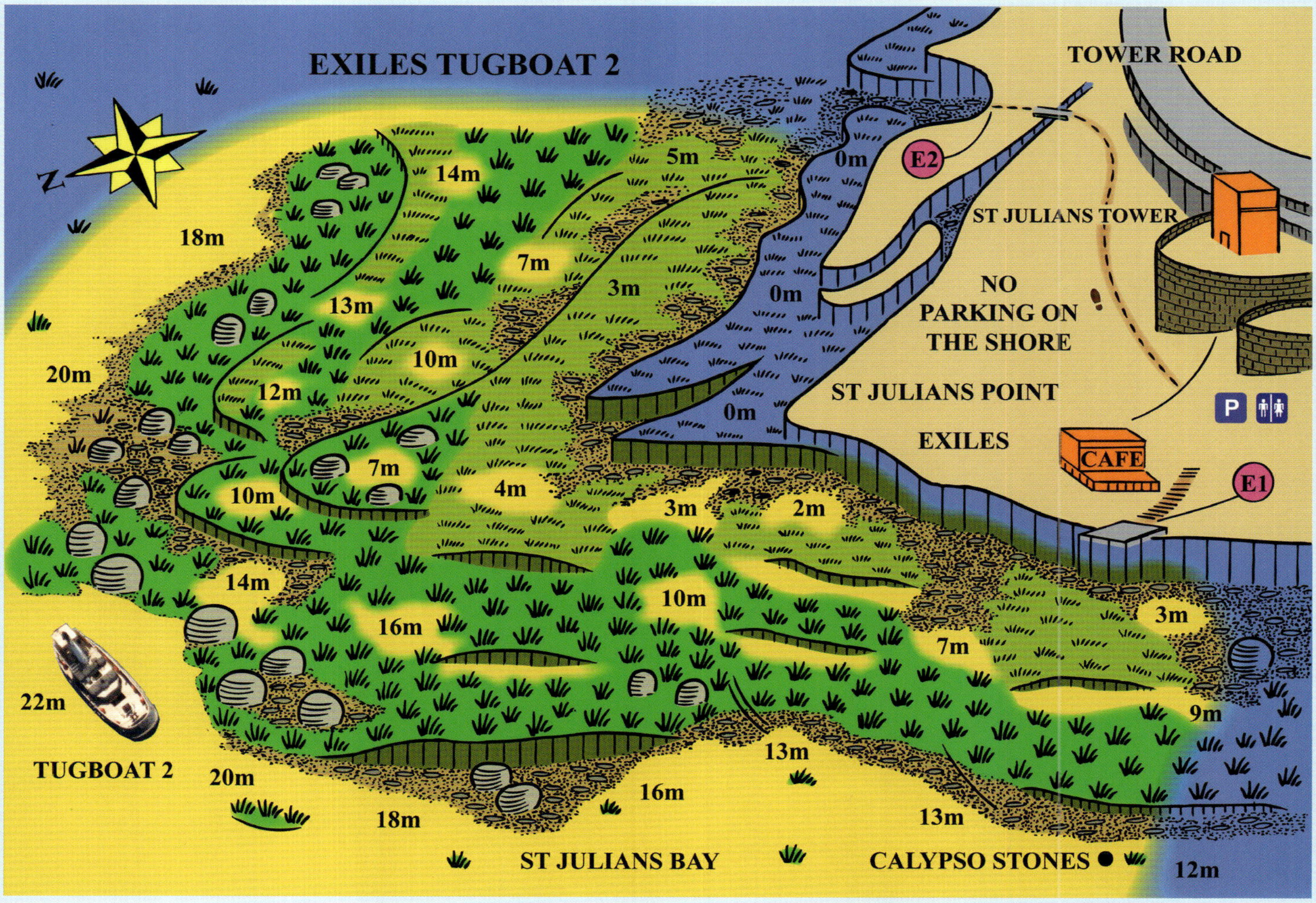

EXILES TUGBOAT 2

TOWER ROAD
E2
ST JULIANS TOWER
NO PARKING ON THE SHORE
ST JULIANS POINT
EXILES
CAFE
E1

14m
5m
0m
18m
7m
3m
0m
13m
10m
0m
20m
12m
7m
4m
3m 2m
10m
14m
3m
16m
10m
7m
9m
22m
TUGBOAT 2
20m
18m
13m
16m
13m
12m

ST JULIANS BAY   CALYPSO STONES

Founded in 1970, the Calypso Sub-Aqua Club is a BSAC affiliated non-profit club organising all year round recreational and technical diving, training for all levels and social activities for members and friends. More information from the informative club website.

www.calypsosac.org
email: info@calypsosac.org

SLIEMA - FORTIZZA REEFS – MANOEL ISLAND

PGL AERIAL PHOTOS

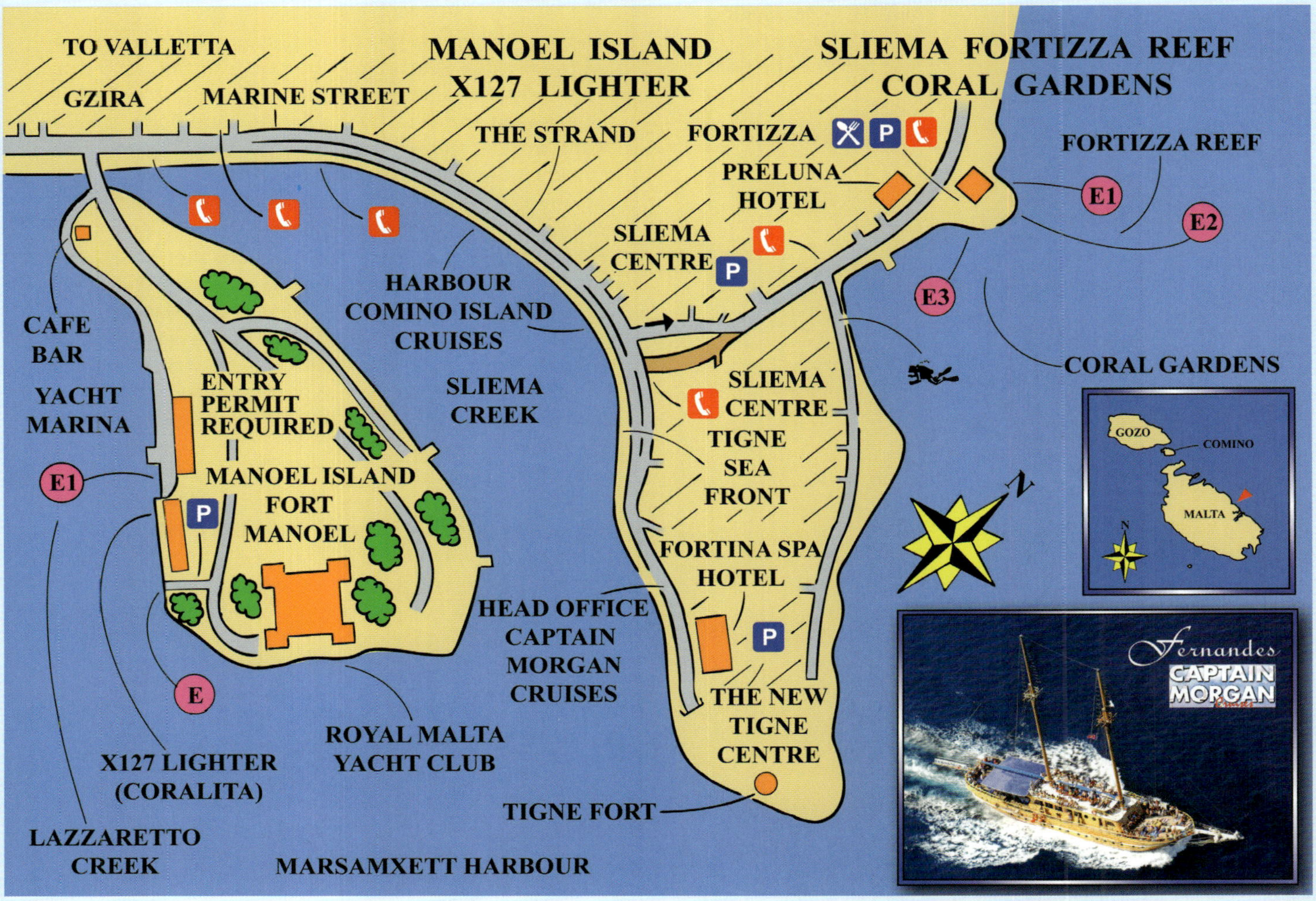

MANOEL ISLAND X127 LIGHTER
SLIEMA FORTIZZA REEF CORAL GARDENS

- TO VALLETTA
- GZIRA
- MARINE STREET
- THE STRAND
- FORTIZZA
- PRELUNA HOTEL
- FORTIZZA REEF
- E1
- E2
- SLIEMA CENTRE
- E3
- CAFE BAR
- YACHT MARINA
- HARBOUR COMINO ISLAND CRUISES
- CORAL GARDENS
- E1
- ENTRY PERMIT REQUIRED
- MANOEL ISLAND FORT MANOEL
- SLIEMA CREEK
- SLIEMA CENTRE
- TIGNE SEA FRONT
- FORTINA SPA HOTEL
- HEAD OFFICE CAPTAIN MORGAN CRUISES
- THE NEW TIGNE CENTRE
- E
- X127 LIGHTER (CORALITA)
- ROYAL MALTA YACHT CLUB
- LAZZARETTO CREEK
- TIGNE FORT
- MARSAMXETT HARBOUR

Fernandes CAPTAIN MORGAN

Fortizza Reef & Coral Gardens – Sliema

This dive site is only a few minutes away from the bustling centre of Sliema, with its shops, cafes, bars and seafront promenades. Travelling from St Julians drive along the coast road with the sea on your left, when you pass the St Julians Tower; continue on for 800 metres. The car park is next to the Fortizza restaurant, which will be on your left. From the other direction, turn right into the car park almost opposite the Preluna Hotel, just after the zebra crossing. Sometimes you may have to wait for a space, you will find much better availability in the afternoons on week days or mornings at weekends.

Fortizza

This dive site has a maximum depth of 16m, if you continue further out it gently gets deeper. There are many places of interest to explore on this reef with a surprising amount of marine life, given the locality and due to the reef being reasonably shallow makes it an excellent place for photography. It is also good for practising your navigational skills, either with a compass or by pilotage, with a tunnel, arch and a short cave to find. May I suggest you check out your route and entry/exit E2 E3 ladders first. Once you have rigged go down the narrow road to the lower level, you will be above the polo pool, cross over to the far corner and down on to the sun terrace, bear left and go to the furthest corner where you will find steps leading onto the rocks and the little horseshoe cove which is entry/exit point E1. Once upon a time we had to walk past the front of the Fortizza restaurant along the street.

The first time I did this I felt most strange walking along the street in full diving kit! Just past the restaurant there is an entrance into the Preluna Beach

These shallow limestone reefs have been shaped by the sea over many years.

Hermit crab (Dardanus arrosor) sits on a rigid sponge.

Club, sun terrace and swimming pool, if you are using this route may I suggest you ask permission first.

THE DIVE   Minimum time – 45 mins

The entry point for this dive site is E1, which is in front of the Preluna Beach Club pool. Once in the water you will find an area shaped like a bowl, swim straight out of this area and drop over a 3m wall and down to 6m keep close to the reef on your left. Stop at the end of this reef, depth around 8m, your compass bearing to Mushroom Rock is 35° and approximately 60 metres in distance; this should not take more than 3/4 minutes. First of all you will swim over sea grass then short marine growth, and then you should see what is called Mushroom Rock, which from certain angles looks just like a giant mushroom. Drop over a little reef just to the left of this rock, when on the bottom bear left and on your right will be the tunnel. Go through the tunnel, on emerging the other side keep going forward taking a compass bearing of 60° you will pass three distinct rocks on the left reef.

After the third one, bear left into an open area covered in sea grass, in front of you there will be another reef, here there is small cave which leads on to the top of the reef. Return to the third rock and continue with a compass bearing of 60° there are two more bowl areas to explore, if you reach the furthest one, your depth will be 18m you are some 15 minutes from Mushroom Rock and a further 5/6 minutes to your exit point E1. Your return route is to follow the opposite side of the valley back to Mushroom Rock and then use the same route back to E1, E2 or E3. Of course you can plan your own dive but it would be wise to include Mushroom Rock, as this is a good pilotage point.

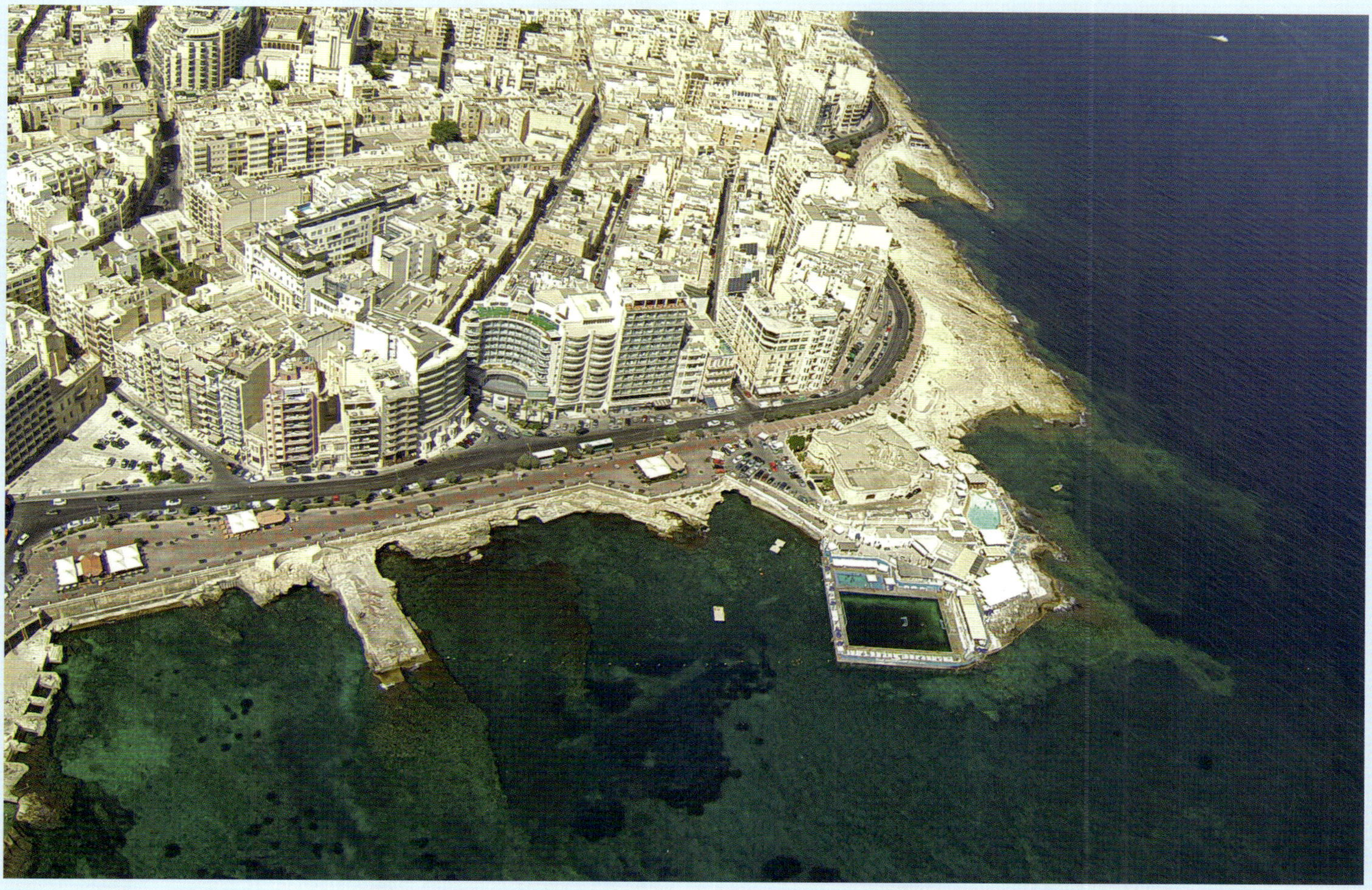

PHOTO: JOE ABDILLA & PAUL GAUCI

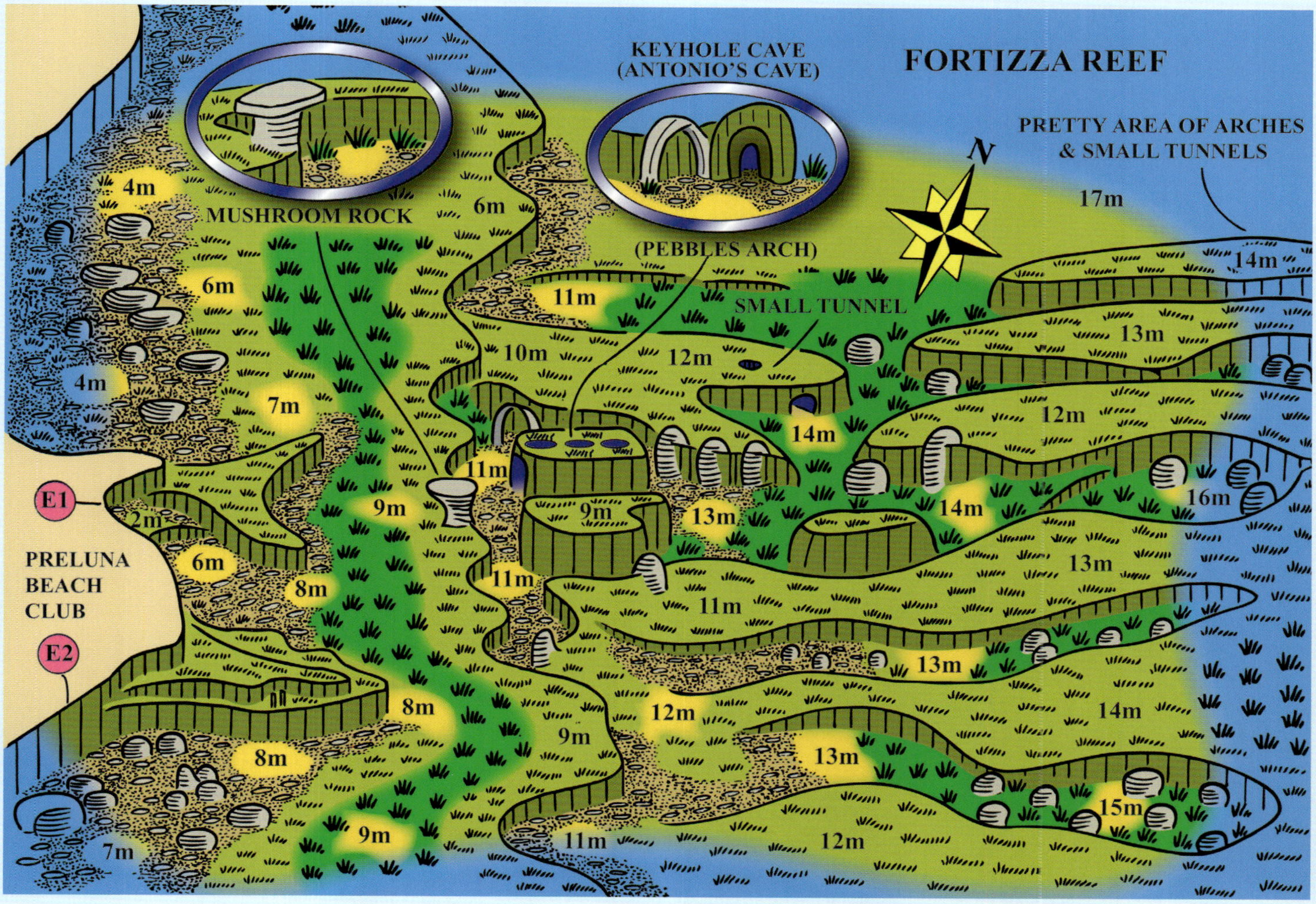
FORTIZZA REEF
KEYHOLE CAVE
(ANTONIO'S CAVE)
PRETTY AREA OF ARCHES
& SMALL TUNNELS
N
MUSHROOM ROCK
(PEBBLES ARCH)
SMALL TUNNEL
PRELUNA
BEACH
CLUB
E1
E2
4m
6m
4m
7m
6m
2m
6m
8m
9m
8m
8m
9m
7m
10m
11m
11m
9m
11m
12m
14m
13m
14m
17m
14m
13m
12m
16m
13m
11m
13m
12m
14m
9m
13m
15m
11m
12m

SLIEMA – CORAL GARDENS

The painted comber (Serranus scriba) will hide in the sea grass and always good for a photo opportunity. PHOTO: SHARON FORDER

Coral Gardens

When you have rigged go down to the lower level to reach your entry/exit points E2 & E3 are on the opposite side of the water polo pool. Navigating this dive is much easier when the visibility is good, otherwise if it is new to you maybe you should consider taking a dive guide with you, as you may miss so much of this extraordinary dive, with a maximum depth of 17m if you explore further to the East reef. In good visibility a camera here is a must.

It has taken millions of years for the canyon system to form. Fragile caves and windows have formed and in turn provided unique ecosystems within themselves. Please avoid the temptation of swimming through the windows in the reef limestone, you would surely damage them!

Gerrard De Waal – Dive Instructor & Guide

A diver moves away from Mushroom Rock.

A tiny octopus (Octopus vulgaris) has made its home in an empty tun shell. PHOTO: JOE FORMOSA

THE DIVE   Minimum time – 55 mins

From your entry point E2 follow the small reef on your left in a north westerly direction to its furthest point, depth will be 7m. From here take a compass bearing of 60° over the sea grass, within 2/3 minutes you will reach Wedge Rock and its distinct little cove. Go down into this narrow valley where you are going to turn right, note, if you had turned left it would have led you to Mushroom Rock. Keeping the reef on your right hand side continue to the three little tunnels, once you have checked them out cross over to the other side and turn down the valley with a depth of 13m, on your right are the Coral Gardens, your direction is north easterly.

There are many small mushroom shaped rocks covered in coral and surrounded by sea grass on this plateau. From the end of this valley take a compass bearing of 150° or southerly, this will lead over the reef at 11m and maybe you will find the white battery.Before you enter the Limestone Reef please explore this area with extra care and good buoyancy as you admire this unique underwater landscape, around the area of pinnacle rocks the depth is 14m, this could be the deepest part of your dive,. Now, head in a westerly direction into Boulder Canyon and from the narrow exit bear to the right across the bottom of Scorpionfish Valley. Head north keeping the reef on your left, pass the double swim through to Wedge Rock. Take a bearing of 240° which will take you over to your starting reef and your chosen exit point. Of course there are many dive permutations for this area; I have chosen probably the most popular one.

You must be aware that many small yachts and motor boats travel along this coastline, some passing directly over the reef.

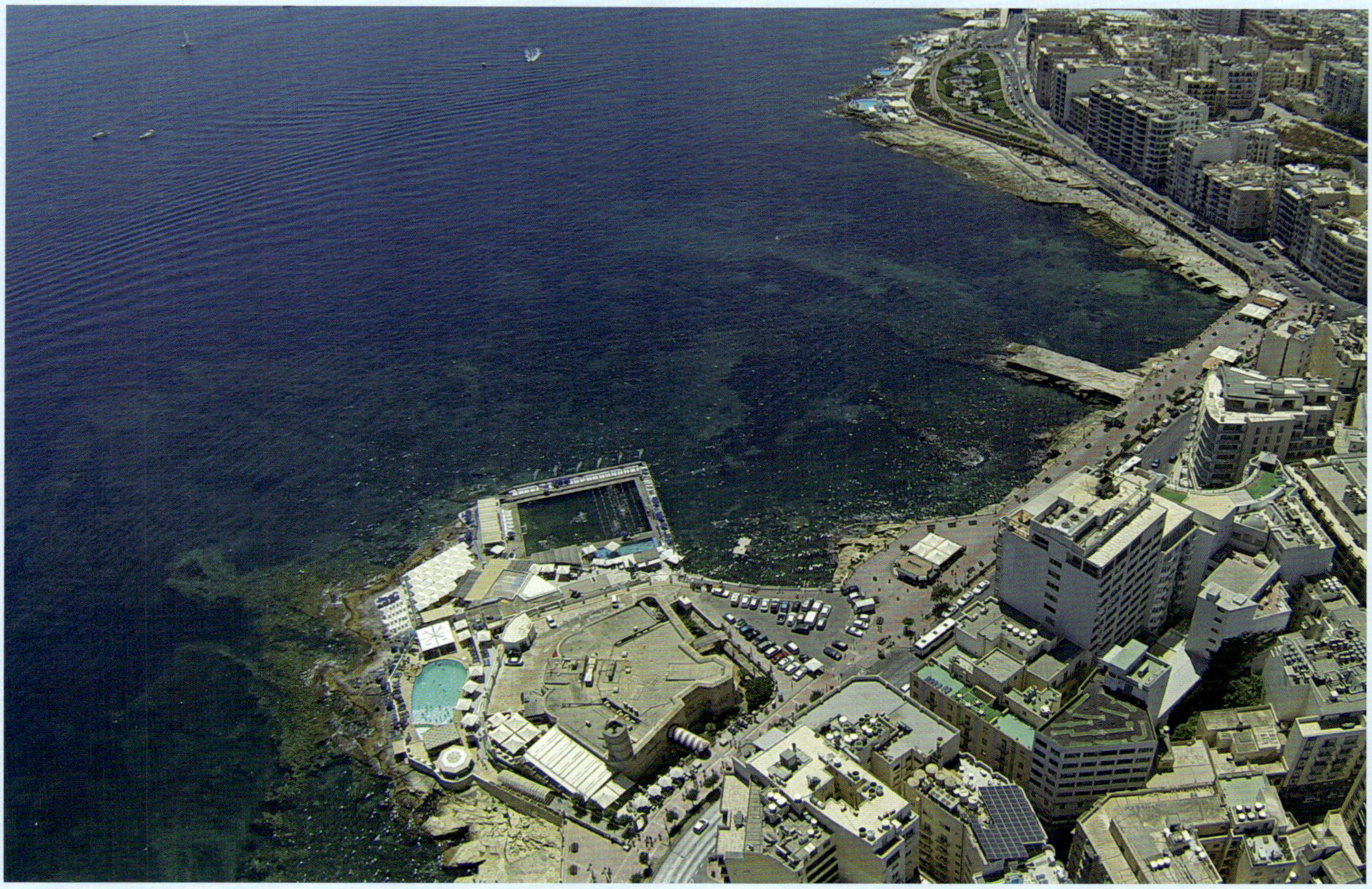

PHOTO: JOE ABDILLA & PAUL GAUCI

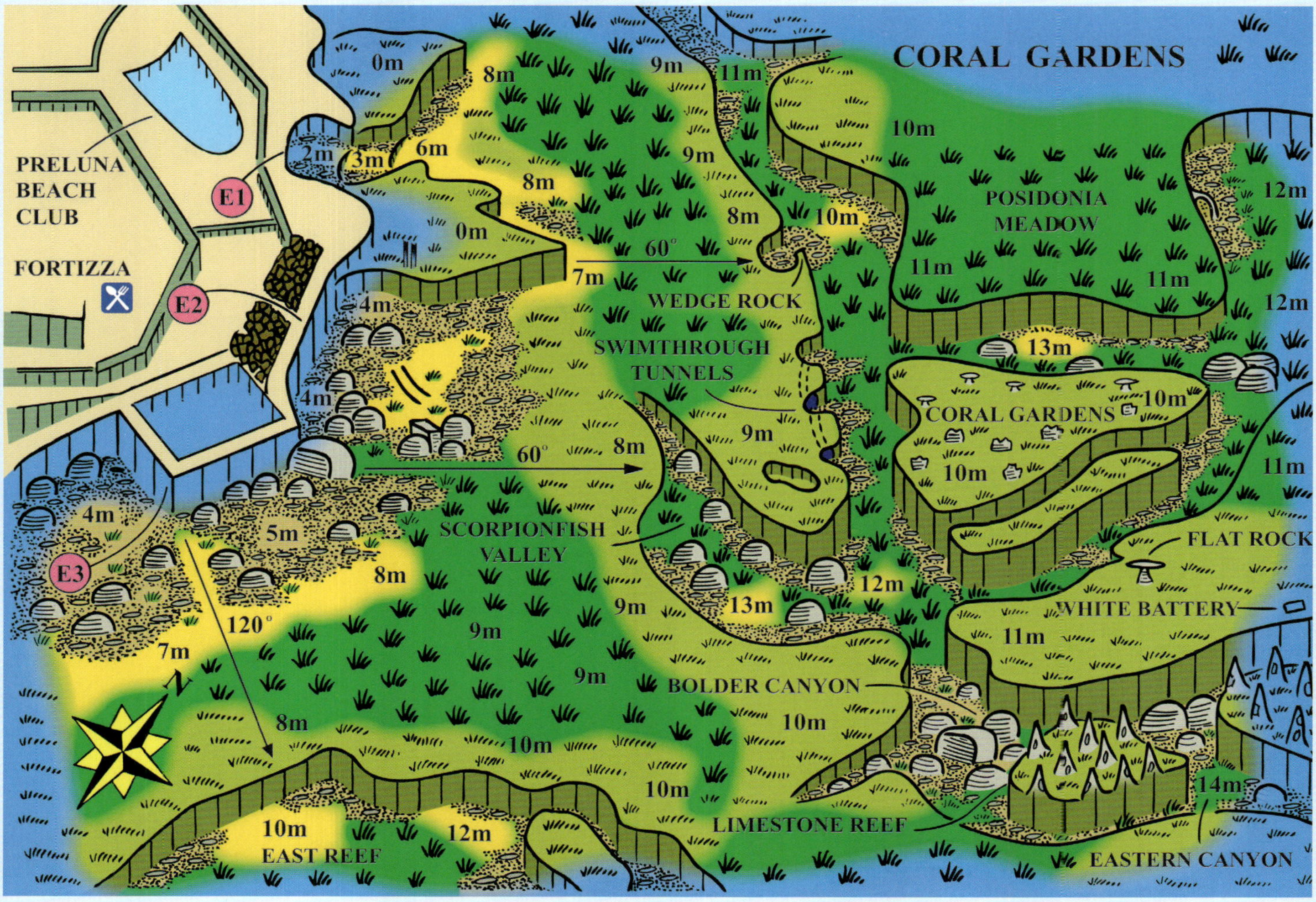
CORAL GARDENS
0m
8m
9m
11m
2m
3m
6m
PRELUNA
BEACH
CLUB
E1
8m
9m
10m
POSIDONIA
MEADOW
12m
8m
10m
0m
60°
11m
11m
FORTIZZA
E2
7m
WEDGE ROCK
12m
4m
SWIMTHROUGH
TUNNELS
13m
4m
10m
CORAL GARDENS
9m
8m
60°
10m
11m
4m
5m
SCORPIONFISH
VALLEY
FLAT ROCK
E3
8m
12m
9m
13m
WHITE BATTERY
120°
11m
7m
9m
9m
BOLDER CANYON
N
8m
10m
10m
10m
14m
LIMESTONE REEF
10m
EAST REEF
12m
EASTERN CANYON

Manoel Island –
The *X127* Water Lighter (*Coralita*)

Manoel Island is situated between Sliema and Valletta and is reached by the coastal road over a little bridge. **Before diving this site consult with your Dive Centre**. Once over the bridge, turn right, where there is a barrier before you enter the marina. The road runs alongside the water's edge, technically you are on private property, at the end of the road park courteously, whilst here please have respect for local residents.

Walter Pollock of James Pollock & Sons was asked to design and oversee the construction of 200 motor landing craft (support vessels) built for the 1915 Dardanelles landings in the Gallipoli campaign during World War 1 and they would be designated as X Lighters.

The hull construction would be based on the river Thames barges with a 60% parallel bottom and a spoon shaped bow with a drop down ramp. Each would weigh 135 tons, 35 meters in length with a beam of 6.5 metres to carry a crew of 12 men.

These X Lighters would be built in 30 ship yards in England and Scotland. *X127* was built by Goole Shipbuilding and Repairs Co. Beverly, Yorkshire, fitted with a Campbell 80 BHP engine with twin props. The *X127* was converted to carry water and fitted with a Tangye water pump engine to pump the water out of the hull to the reservoirs on shore.

These vessels were towed the 3,000 miles from Immingham on the river Humber via Plymouth to the large natural harbour of Mudros on the Agean island of Lemnos, this took 25 days. At Cape Hellas on the Gallipoli peninsular two reservoirs were built, the Water Lighters would have transferred water from the ships to the beach then pumping it to the reservoirs.

The *X127* was involved with the successful withdrawal of troops and horses after what some would say was one of the bloodiest battles in WW1. From 1920 many of the 200 Lighters were sold to private companies, shipping agents and the governments of Greece Egypt, France and Spain, then

ABOVE: *New Entry Point for the X127.*

The route from the little bridge to entry point. PHOTO: JOE ABDILLA & PAUL GAUCI

MANOEL ISLAND – *X127* WATER LIGHTER (*CORALITA*)

A Water Lighter, probably the X127, taking part in the successful evacuation of the troops from Gallipoli, Turkey in 1916.
PHOTO: DAVE MALLARD, ISLE OF WIGHT

British diver Dave Mallard, (centre front) completed four years research on the X Water Lighter, with the help of four colleagues from Malta. Front left: Antonio Anastasi, Front right: Patrick Milton. Back row, left to right: Rupert Mifsud, Darrel Borg Carsdona, Martin Vella – 4th December 2004.
PHOTO: BY KIND PERMISSION OF DAVE MALLARD, ISLE OF WIGHT

16 Lighters went to Malta, *X127* was one of these.

The *X127* was converted to carry fuel oil for the tenth Submarine Flotilla, HMS *Talbot*, Manoel Island, Malta. On Friday 6th March 1942 the submarine base was attacked by dive bombers and during a second attack the *P36* and *P39* were damaged by near misses and the Fuel Lighter *X127* caught fire, listed and shortly afterwards sunk. She remains in the same position today laying upright the bow at 5m and the stern at 22m. Listed by Lloyds as Wreck No. 37379.

The research for this wreck has been undertaken by David Mallard of the Isle of Wight. For over thirty years this wreck has been known as the *Coralita*. In March 2003 David decided to start his research into this wreck and a year later it seemed possible that it was the Lighter *X131*, he discovered a photograph of the fishing trawler *Coral* together with the *X131* in dry dock No.3, Grand Harbour; both vessels had been damaged by an air raid on 21st April 1942. The name *Coralita* may have originated from this trawler but found no evidence to support this. Further research ruled out the *X131*, and in 2006 David found the vital information proving what everyone has always known as the *Coralita*, is actually the Lighter *X127*.

The wreck of the WW1 Lighter X127 now lies below the surface of what was the submarine base HMS Talbot.
PHOTO: DAVE MALLARD, ISLE OF WIGHT

THE DIVE   Minimum time – 35 mins

Once in the water, surface swim along in front of the buildings, now descend and head in an easterly direction at a depth of 10/12m staying at this depth until you reach the wreck. Starting at the spoon shaped bow, on the forward deck are footholds for the horses, a fitting for the mast and on each side fairleads and towing bollards. Moving down the starboard side passing over the chain locker, on your right on the small upper structure are two hatches, inside is one of the two Tangye water pumps, just

Two divers above the main water tanks and in the foreground towing bollards.

Divers on the bow of the X127 Lighter.

look, in the deck there is a hole where something has been removed.

The next four hatches on your right, are for the water tanks, above the tanks is the gun platform, although a gun was never fitted. Further down is the steering pedestal and the compass plate, around the

The stern quadrant rudder gear, the steering chains would have run along the deck on each side of the engine room.

front of this is what remains of the bullet-proof screen.

Next are the living quarters, the scuttle entrance with a ladder and the large skylight. Moving down to the stern you will pass the engine room, from here you will be able to see the quadrant rudder, unfortunately the rudder and props are covered with silt. The steering chains run along the deck on both sides of the engine room. The flag pole fitting, rear fairleads and towing bollards can be seen and looking in the engine room doorway you can see the twin cylinders of the Campbell engine with the flywheel in front, the weight of the engine is 5.5 tons. Fitted to the engine room walls are four sixty gallon water tanks, also the remains of the engine silencer.

On the port side of the engine room are the brackets for the spare anchor. Moving up and along the portside deck, is the much visible bomb damage, showing the damaged hull plating with bent and twisted metal. Continue along the wreck where you will find further damage possibly caused by the submarine *P39* being pushed up against the Lighter, when the three bombs were dropped alongside.

This original entry point could be used as an emergency exit.

Return Route
Moving away from the bow in a westerly direction staying reasonably close to the wall, as you do not want to miss your exit steps and continue into an area where large boats are moored. **Remember this is a busy harbour**.

Explore this man made reef looking out for cuttlefish and octopus which frequent this area, whilst making your way to your exit.

MANOEL ISLAND – *X127* WATER LIGHTER (*CORALITA*)

Key to insert on dive plan for the *X127* Lighter/*Coralita*

- A Crew quarters
- B Engine room
- C Rudder
- D Rudder gear
- E Engine room
- F Skylight
- G Engine exhaust
- H Accommodation
- I Skylight
- J Steering gear
- K Gun platform
- L Water tanks
- M Main tanks
- N Water hatches
- O Tangye engine
- P Air intake
- Q Footholds
- R Ramp

PGL AERIAL PHOTO

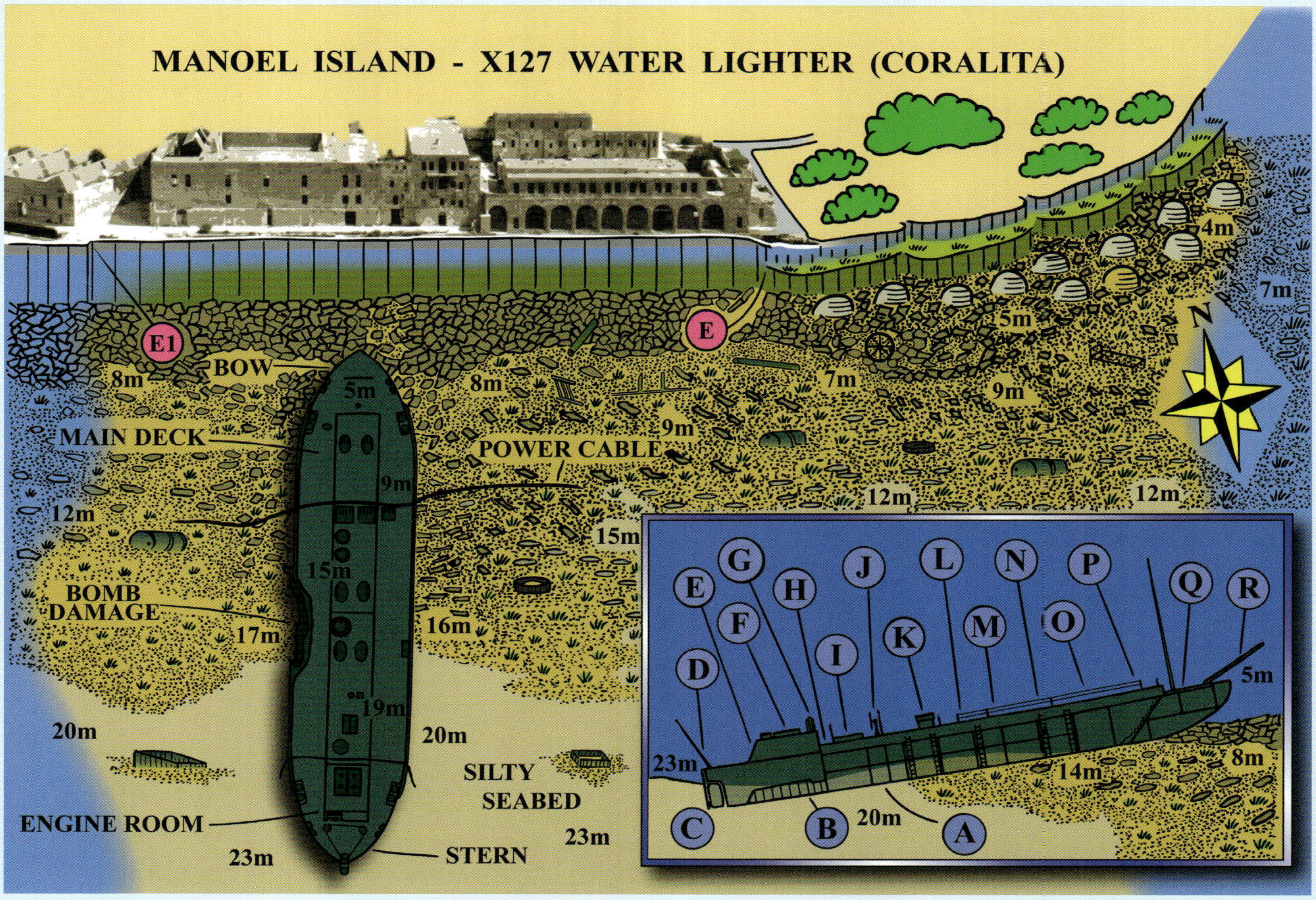

MANOEL ISLAND - X127 WATER LIGHTER (CORALITA)

4m
7m
E1
BOW
5m
8m
8m
E
5m
MAIN DECK
7m
9m
9m
12m
9m
POWER CABLE
12m
12m
BOMB DAMAGE
15m
15m
17m
16m
5m
20m
19m
20m
14m
8m
ENGINE ROOM
SILTY SEABED
23m
23m
STERN
23m
20m

GHANJSIELEM TO XATT L-AHMAR (RED BAY)

PGL AERIAL PHOTOS

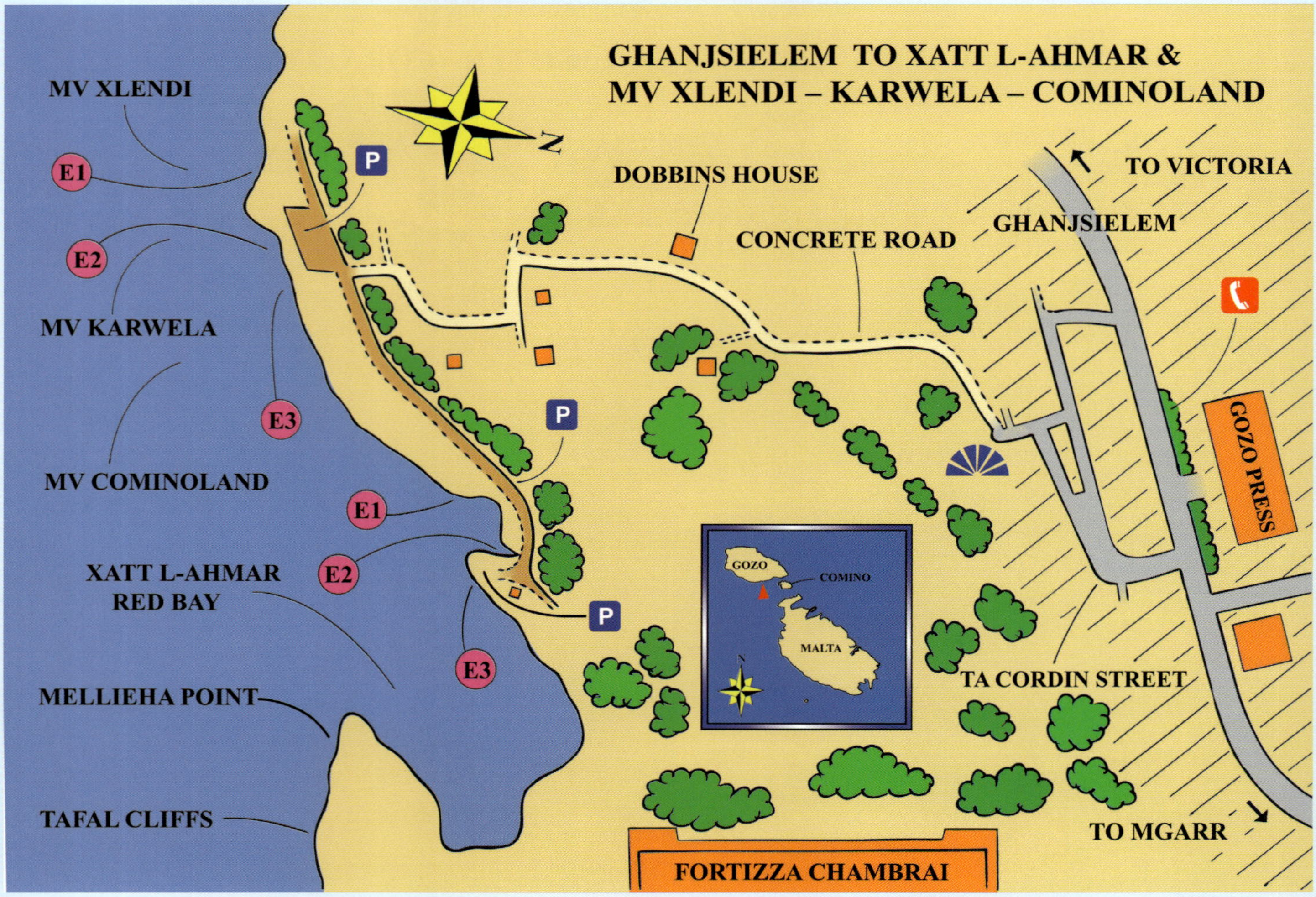

GHANJSIELEM TO XATT L-AHMAR & MV XLENDI – KARWELA – COMINOLAND

- MV XLENDI
  - E1
  - E2
- MV KARWELA
  - E3
- MV COMINOLAND
  - E1
  - E2
- XATT L-AHMAR RED BAY
  - E3
- MELLIEHA POINT
- TAFAL CLIFFS
- DOBBINS HOUSE
- CONCRETE ROAD
- GHANJSIELEM
- TO VICTORIA
- GOZO PRESS
- TA CORDIN STREET
- TO MGARR
- FORTIZZA CHAMBRAI

GOZO — COMINO — MALTA

Xatt L-Ahmar – MV *Xlendi, Karwela* and *Cominoland*

Once in the village of Ghanjsielem, which is situated on the main road between Victoria and Mgarr, turn opposite the Gozo Press, from this point the dive site is approximately 800 metres. Follow the route plan to the viewpoint, stop to look at the view of Comino and Malta with the boats going to and fro, a good point for photographs. From here the single concrete track winds down the hillside to the sea, for a short distance near Dobbins stable the track is unmade and can be difficult after heavy rain. When you reach the coastal track turn left for Xatt L-Ahmar (Red Bay) and right to park for the wrecks, see aerial photo.

MV *Xlendi*

MV Xlendi *leaving Grand Harbour.*   PHOTO: CHARLIE SCICLUNA

It was on the 12th November 1999 at 2.15pm, after about 3 hours getting her into position, the Gozo ferry boat *Xlendi* was scuttled off the south coast of Gozo as an artificial reef and for the use of divers. This double ended Ro-Ro car passenger ferry was built in Denmark by Helsingar Ship Builders with a gross weight of 1123 tons and a length of 77 metres.

ABOVE: *This wreck is unsafe for penetration.*
BELOW: *A diver visits the car that missed the boat, but only just!*

Two tugboats manoeuvre MV Xlendi *into place.*

Unfortunately on the way down she struck part of the reef and landed upside down on a sandy bottom at 42m at a slight angle, resting partly on the funnel and the upper structure, with the hull upturned at 24m. After a few days the funnel and part of the upper structure collapsed and she went totally in an upside-down position, she still lies on a sandy bottom at 42m, but her hull is now 36m in depth. This is still an excellent dive, with the reef so close you can dive the Xlendi and then explore the reef to complete your dive.

XATT L'AHMAR (RED BAY)

A diver has made a friend, spot the small cuttlefish, this reef below the entry point is where they normally hang out.

THE DIVE   Minimum time – 45 mins

Check your entry and exit points, for if you decide to use the westerly entry point E1, to exit from here is not possible, you will have to exit from the easterly entry/exit points, E2 or E3. The route to your entry/exit points starts at the westerly end of the car park, from here walk towards the little headland almost directly in front of you.

Which ever entry point you use surface swim round to the west side of the little headland and here the compass bearing to the *Xlendi* is 200° and approximately 60 metres in distance. Enter the water at this point E1, but remember your exit is on the other side of the little headland, E2. I normally surface swim for a short time following the compass bearing towards

Diver hovers above one of the huge rudders and propellers.

the *Xlendi*, just before losing sight of the reef below me I descend.

Staying above the reef, but just keeping it in sight, will guide you down to the upturned hull; this should take you no more than 4 minutes. Follow your dive plan whilst on the wreck but I suggest you leave the hull at the western end as the sandy slope leading to the reef above is much closer. Follow it up to your required depth, when this is reached, turn right, and follow it in an easterly direction when the reef drops away close to the headland, continue on into a large area of shallower waters now you are not far from your exit points, E2 or E3. Of course you can spend as much time as your air will allow on this reef.

The marine life in this area is very good with a good chance of finding octopus also cuttlefish, I once saw three cuttlefish all grouped together.

A diver above the upturned hull of this large car ferry.

XATT L-AHMAR

PHOTO: JOE ABDILLA & PAUL GAUCI

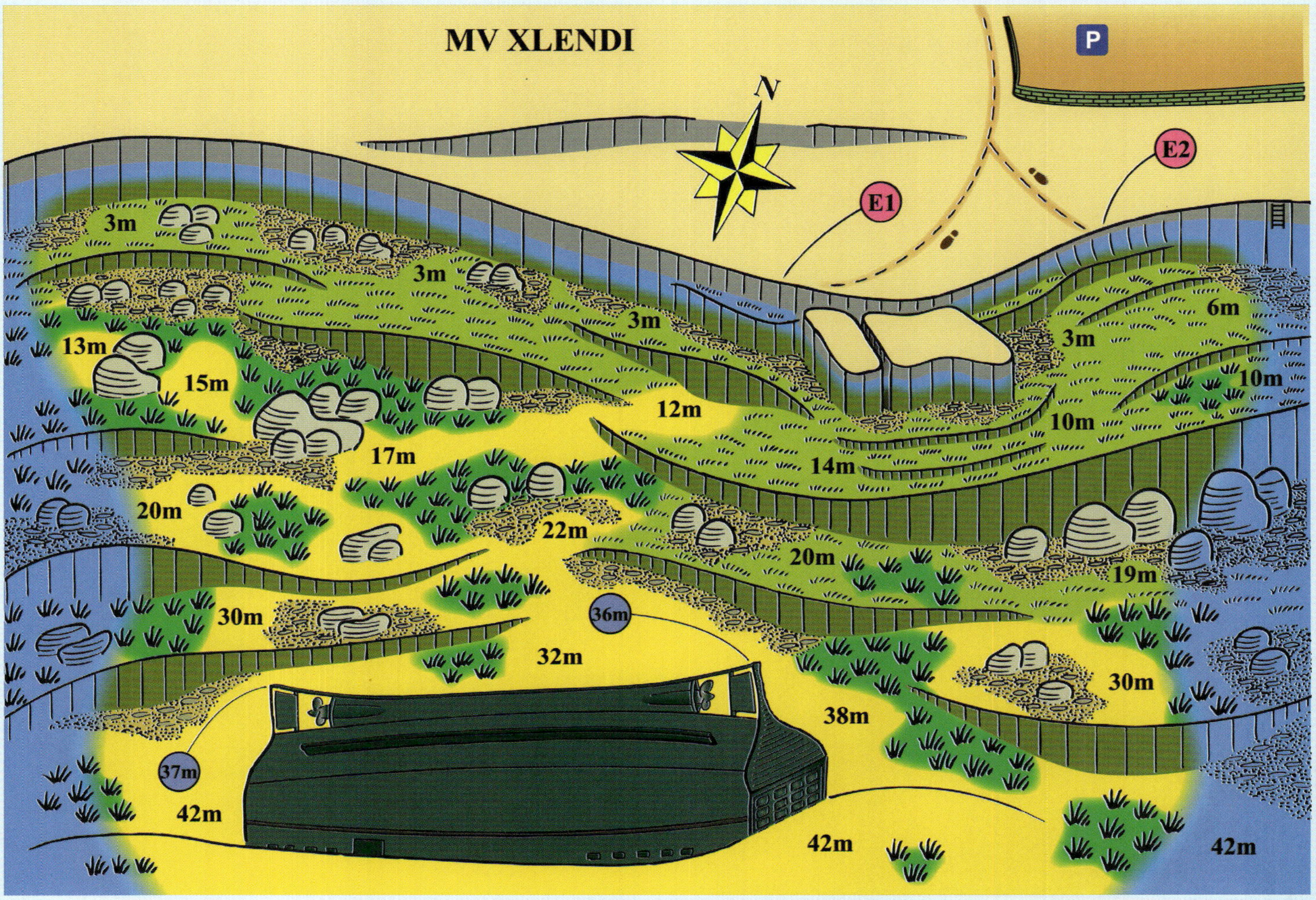

MV XLENDI

XATT L'AHMAR (RED BAY)

The Scuttling of the MV *Karwela* and MV *Cominoland*

On the 12th August 2006 at 0100 hrs the MV *Karwela* and MV *Cominoland* were towed out of Marsa and through Grand Harbour, Valletta to Gozo. It took over seven hours to scuttle these two wrecks; the *Karwela* was finally sunk at 16-00 hrs followed by the *Cominoland* 25 minutes later. So with their air filled blue buoyancy tanks they sank below the waves and now they both sit upright on the sandy seabed at 42m, some 60 metres apart and in my opinion due to their depths they are separate dives. Both wrecks had been made environmentally safe by Cassar Ship Repairers of Marsa, Malta.

ABOVE: *Entry point for the MV* Karwela *and the MV* Cominoland.
BELOW: *On the side of the bow the ships name* Karwela.

MV Karwela *(Jylland Cruises) in Marsamxett harbour, in the background St Luke's hospital in the early 1990's.*

PHOTO: GEORGE ZAMMIT BRIFFA. CAPTAIN MORGAN CRUISES

MV Cominoland *in Marsamxett Harbour during her last working days.*

PHOTO: GEORGE ZAMMIT BRIFFA. CAPTAIN MORGAN CRUISES

MV Karwela *sinks slowly beneath the surface watched by many spectators on 12th August 2006.*

PHOTO: BRIAN AZZOPARDI, ATLANTIS DIVE CENTRE

MV Cominoland *just west of Xatt L-Ahmar (Red Bay) before the scuttling on the 12th August 2006.*

MV *Karwela*

The MV *Karwela* was built in West Germany in 1957 by Jos. L. Meyer of Pepenburg. This passenger ferry with a steel hull weighing 497 tons and 48 metres in length and a beam of 8 metres was first registered in West Germany as the Nordpaloma. She came to Malta in December 1986 and in May 1992 she was purchased and registered by Captain Morgan Cruises. Sliema, Malta.

A diver above the bridge and funnel of the MV Karwela.

THE DIVE   Minimum time – 40 mins

Your entry point will be E2 or E3 now surface swim to the east side of the little headland, from here follow the underwater reef out with a compass bearing of 160° to the drop off, when you can see this drop off, descend to 9m. Now follow the ridge in an easterly direction until your reach the Finger, on the far side there is a crack running all the way down the reef. From this point take a compass bearing of 150° slowly descending to her depth, the distance from the Finger to the *Karwela* is 40 metres, you will approach her side on.

Now you can explore the wreck, when it is time to leave, head in a northerly direction, once on top of the reef take your time to explore the areas of boulders and gullies whilst doing your safety stops. Now follow the reef in a north westerly direction to your exit point either E2 or E3.

The crack which runs down the reef.

Under the stern of the MV Karwela.

Above the bows of the MV Karwela.

MV *Cominoland*

Built in England in 1942 by Philip & Son Ltd of Dartmouth and named *Minor Eagle*. This 295 ton passenger ship 34 metres in length and with an 8 metre beam, she was first registered in Malta in May 1992, when it had been purchased by Captain Morgan Cruises. Sliema, Malta and she was re-named *Cominoland*.

ABOVE: *The bows of the MV* Cominoland, *in the background, the bridge.*
BELOW: *Diver below the stern of MV* Cominoland.

Hovering above this huge rock sitting on two boulders. I have named this The Altar, as in the dive plan.

THE DIVE   Minimum time – 45 mins

Using entry points E2 or E3 and once in the water surface swim out heading in a south-easterly direction. While you are still able to see the seabed descend and continue on your course until you come to the edge of the drop off. Follow it along in an easterly direction past the Altar stone to the area of boulders where you will find the old fishing net, here you need to descend and moving forward with a compass bearing of 150°, the wreck will be side on to your course.

Taking this route you should be on the wreck within 8 minutes. After you have explored this wreck and it is time to return to the reef and higher ground; **you have two choices. One**: from the wreck head north towards the reef, once there stay on your course until you reach your safety stop depth, now turn and head in a westerly direction. At a depth of 6m or less will lead you to your exit points E2 and E3.

Second choice: If you wish to return to your exit point via a different route and you have the air then try this, only if the visibility is good and there are no currents. Leave the bows of the Cominoland head in a westerly direction 270° slowly ascending whilst moving forward, after you have passed over the *Karwelas*' bows, take a bearing of 330° to the top of the Finger, 9m. The distance you have travelled will be 100 metres and will possibly take you 10 minutes to reach a depth of 9m. Now head north into a large shallow area of small gullies and short marine growth, where you can explore and complete your safety stops close to the exit points, E2 and E3.

XATT L-AHMAR – MV *KARWELA* & MV *COMINOLAND*

PGL AERIAL PHOTOS

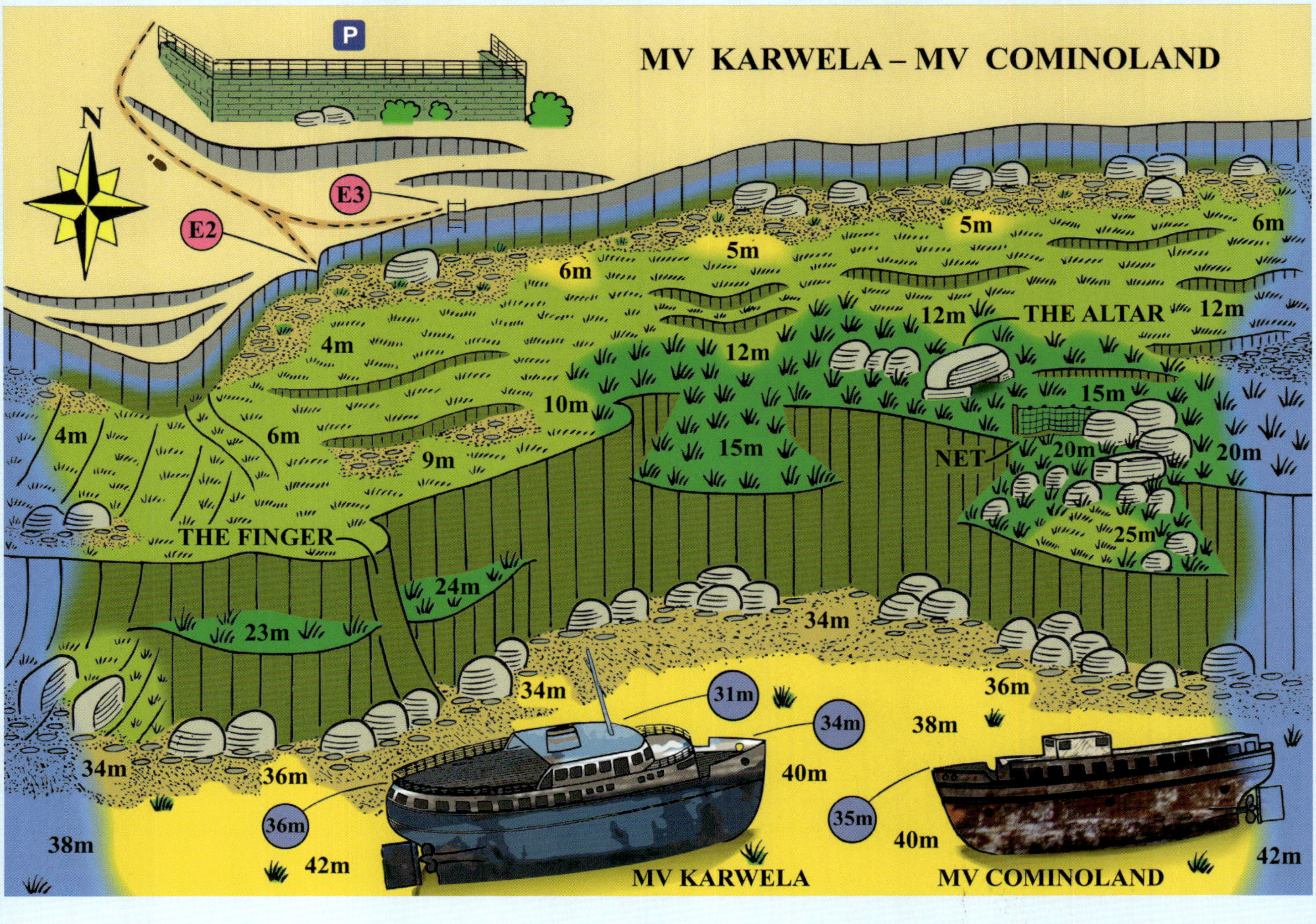

MV KARWELA – MV COMINOLAND

Xatt L-Ahmar (Red Bay)

There are three entry /exit points at this dive site and also there are a number of ways to dive this area, I have selected just two choices.

THE DIVE (1) Minimum time – 45 mins

Using entry point E2, surface swim taking a compass bearing of 200° before you lose sight of the seabed, descend to 6/9m and continue on the same course. You should reach a depth of 20m within 6 minutes, which is at the top of the slope which is covered in sea grass and boulders and drops down to 30m plus. Descend down the eastern side of the slope to the bottom depth 34m.

Now follow the base of the reef in an easterly direction, the reef now becomes a cliff face. Along this route, visit the cave, the lone rock at 40m and the overhang, continue for a further 3/4 minutes your dive time now should be 20 minutes.

Now ascend the cliff face to its ridge at 24m and head north over the sea grass on to the short marine growth, at 6m you should see the headland and a large rock which rises to the surface, if not turn left and follow the coastline to it. From the large rock take a north westerly bearing to exit point E3, at a leisurely swim this will take about 15 minutes.

The edge of the reef where it slopes away to the seabed at 30m plus.

Can you spot the eyes of this well camouflaged turbot (Psetta maxima). PHOTO: JOE FORMOSA

THE DIVE (2) Minimum time – 50 mins

From entry/exit point E3 on a south westerly bearing surface swim across the bay to the headland on the other side, this will only take a few minutes. Pass over the large rock at the end of the headland and descend on to the short marine growth at 9m then head south to the edge of the drop off, 24m, turn right and continue along the edge in a westerly direction until at 20m the drop off becomes a slope covered in sea grass and boulders, your dive time should now be around 10 minutes.

An unusual sighting of an octopus (Octopus vulgaris) out of his hiding place. PHOTO: SHARON FORDER

Descend the slope on the eastern side down to 30/34m now at the foot of the slope turn left and head in an easterly direction. If you follow the line at the bottom of the drop off then not missing the cave, then out to the lone rock at 40m and back to the overhang. Continue on for another 3/4 minutes your dive time at this point will possibly be 25 minutes. Ascend the cliff face to 24m now head in a northerly direction to the large rock at 6m at the end of the headland. Return across the bay taking a north westerly bearing to exit point E3. At any time you wish change your dive plan and head for shallow water, take a northerly bearing, this will lead you directly into the bay.

Just another small reminder that the emergency services are some distance away. Also there are no facilities or refreshments so it maybe a good idea to bring some along with you.

XATT L-AHMAR (RED BAY) – GHANJSIELEM

PGL AERIAL PHOTOS

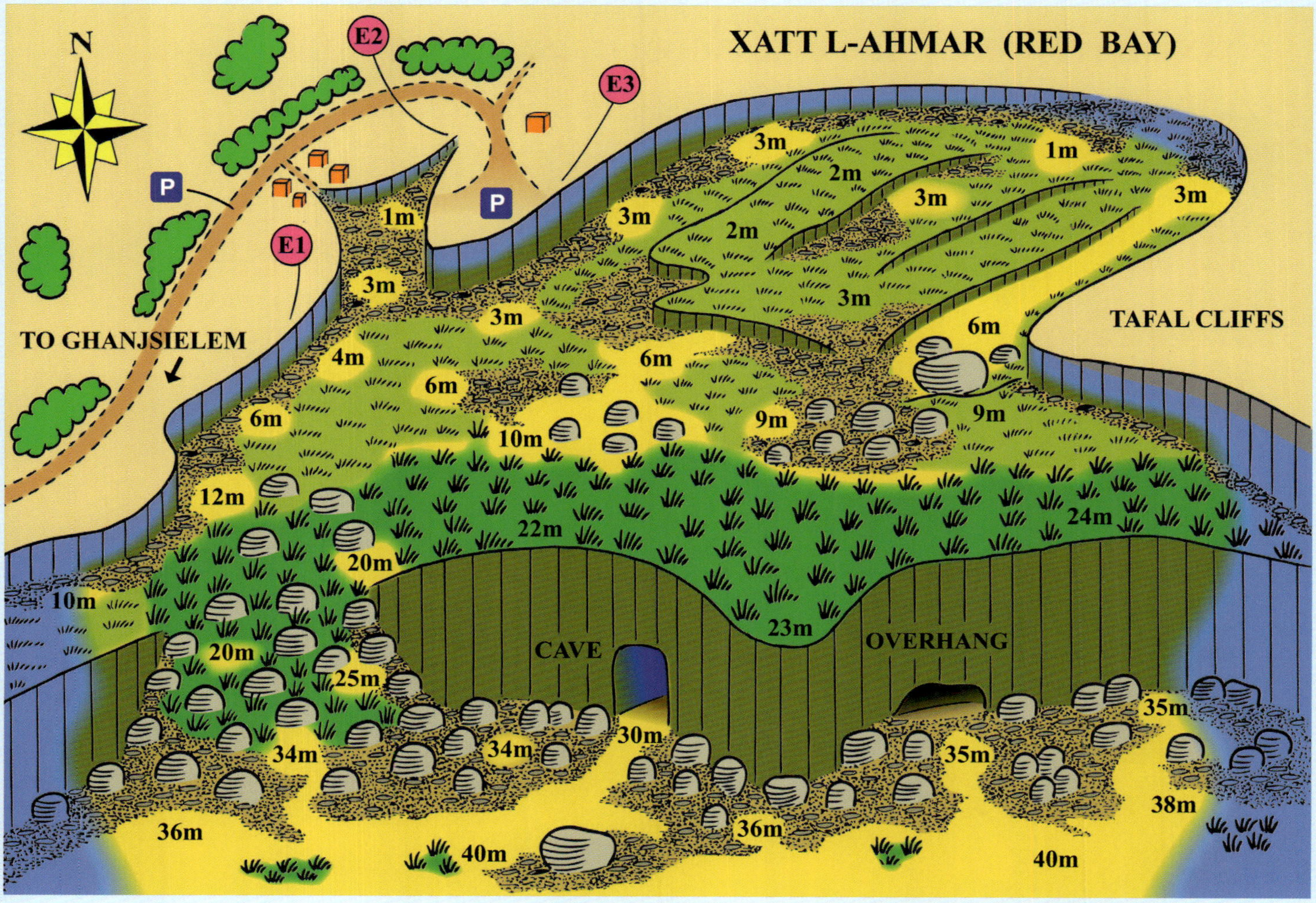

XATT L-AHMAR (RED BAY)

TO GHANJSIELEM

TAFAL CLIFFS

CAVE

OVERHANG

RAS IL-HOBZ – MIDDLE FINGER – GHANJSIELEM

PGL AERIAL PHOTO

GHANJSIELEM TO RAS IL-HOBZ - MIDDLE FINGER

← TO VICTORIA

TO MGARR

GOZO PRESS

ROUGH TRACK

GHANJSIELEM

RECYCLING HARDCORE WORKS

TO XATT L-AHMAR

TO XEWKIJA ←

E1 RAS IL-HOBZ

MIDDLE FINGER

FESSEJ ROCK

E2

PHOTOS: JOE ABDILLA & PAUL GAUCI

Ras il-Hobz – Middle Finger

Once in the village of Ghanjsielem, coming from Mgarr turn left opposite the Gozo Press building or from Victoria take the first turning right, at the bend head right or the T junction turn right. Turn left down the first track, Triq Ta' Brieghen, at the next bend follow the road to the right; continue through the rubble recycling area and graveyard for heavy machinery. At the next junction fork left down the hill on the concrete road, a high wall will be on your right, follow this road with the help of the local map. Just above the area at sea level is a small car park, from here there is a short hill down to sea level, may I suggest you check the bottom of this hill for road conditions before taking your vehicle down, unless you have a 4 x 4. The whole distance is approximately 1.5km.

Another unique diving site has been opened up for us, adding to the variety of diving in these Maltese waters. If you gather your fingers together pointing upwards, it would give you some idea of the shape of the top of the pinnacle rising from the depths below, just 20 metres from the coastline, with the highest point of only 9m below the surface, this is called Middle Finger.

Between the coastline and the pinnacle is a valley only 2 metres wide at its narrowest point at a depth of 30m and at the other end 4 to 5 metres wide and a depth of 34m. On the south western side of the pinnacle there is a large anchor at 63m. This is an ideal site for technical divers, whether under training or not, to reach these depths close to the shore line. Around the pinnacle below depths of 22m there are a variety of sponges and corals, also with plenty of marine life including shoals of bream, salema fish, damsel fish to name just a few, this attracts the deep water fish such as tuna, amberjacks and barracuda. This is an excellent dive which I am sure you will enjoy.

This is where the dive is usually completed.

Parking and entry points E1 and E2.

Divers leaving the water at exit point E1.

RAS IL-HOBZ – MIDDLE FINGER

Technical divers heading out from entry point E2.

THE DIVE — Minimum time – 40 mins

The choice of entry point will probably depend on which side of the sea level area you have parked. Entry point E1 on the eastern side is usually the most

I guess this diver has a macro lens?

One of the many shoals of salema fish (Sarpa sarpa).

popular, maybe due to the larger parking area. In the immediate area of your entry point the reef is only 1 to 2m deep and you will have to go out and around the very shallow areas before heading to the pinnacle. Entry from E2, if you have parked on the western side, here the depth increases reasonably quickly to 5m, but there is not that much difference in distance to the pinnacle, but E1 is slightly shorter.

From E1 take a compass bearing of 140° ensuring that you go around the very shallow reef, once around the shallow reef take a bearing of 230° keeping the main coastline on your right until reaching the drop off.

Continue on with the reef on your right at a depth of around 8m, when your compass starts to move towards a westerly direction, move away from the reef and shortly the pinnacle should come into view. It is approximately 15 metres in distance from the underwater shore reef and due south of the headland, only 9m below the surface.

Between the pinnacle and the underwater shore reef there is a valley with an average width of 3 metres and 32m in depth.

From E2 follow a compass bearing of 130° keeping the coastline reef on your left, down over a large number of small rocks and boulders until you come to the drop off at 16m, here bear round to the left. If you have decided to swim out at a shallower depth, just keep the main shore line in sight and on your left hand side. Once your compass bearing starts to give you an easterly direction you should be below the headland, move south away from the underwater shore reef, the pinnacle is approximately 15 metres from here.

Your actual dive around the pinnacle will depend on your dive plan and chosen depth, normally ending at the top of Middle Finger: this is an excellent opportunity for a photograph of your buddies at the top of the pinnacles.

RAS IL-HOBZ – MIDDLE FINGER

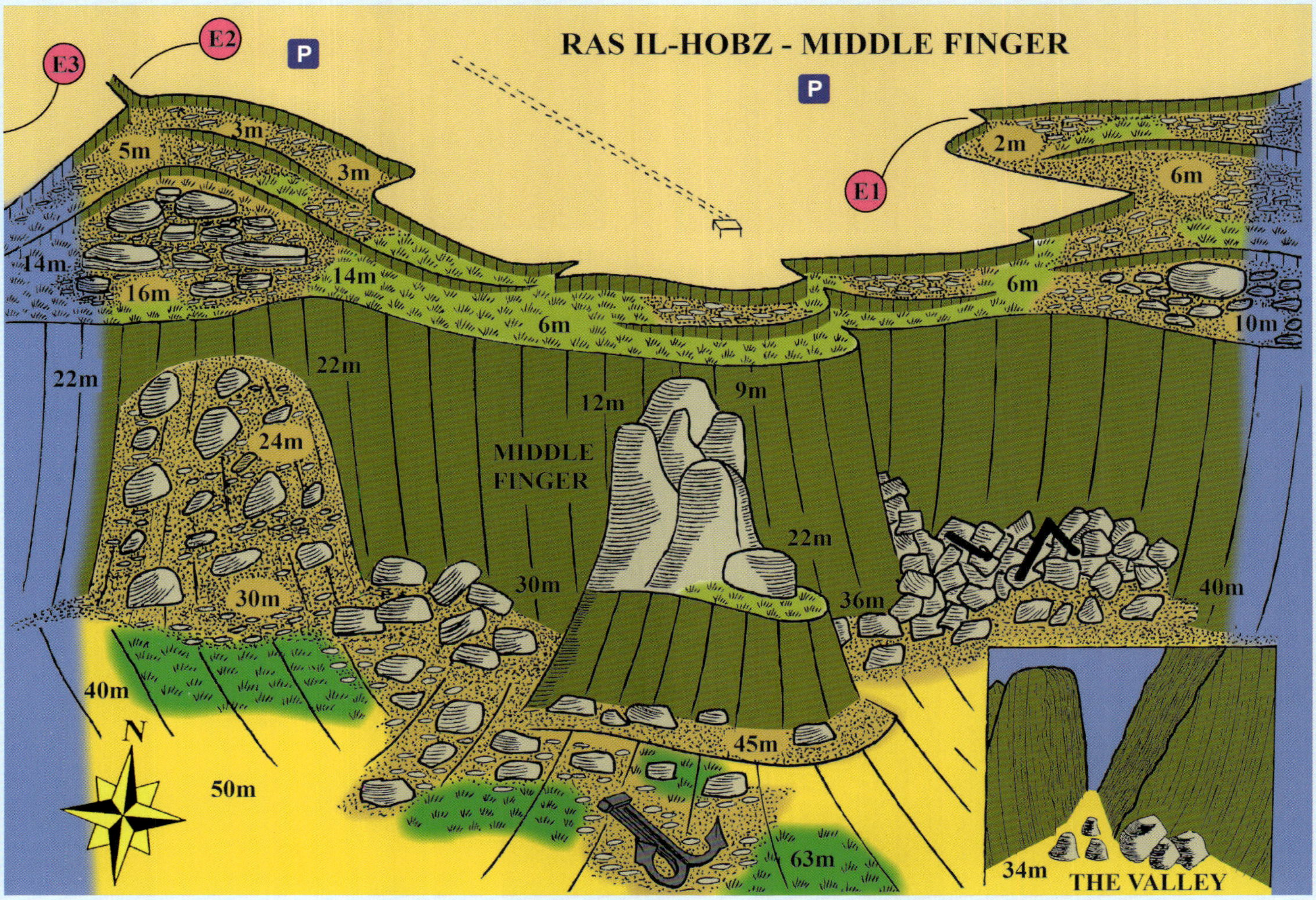

RAS IL-HOBZ – MIDDLE FINGER

Return route: From the pinnacle a north compass bearing will take you back to the main coastline. Your route will depend on which entry point you used, to E1 keep the main reef on your left hand side. Make sure you give the shallow reef a wide berth for you may run aground! A good idea is to stay at a depth of 3m when you reach the shallow area. For E2 keep the reef on your right hand side, it will lead you into the bay and your exit point.

The valley between the headland and the pinnacle.

A shoal of bogue (Boops boops) looking for cover around the rocks.

Using a torch lights up the spectacular colours of the reef.

There are experienced divers who use entry point E3 to surface swim and dive Fessej Rock, this is usually a boat dive and therefore can be found in the boat diving section of this book. May I suggest that if you are going to do this dive from the shore, that you use an instructor/guide from one of the local dive centres.

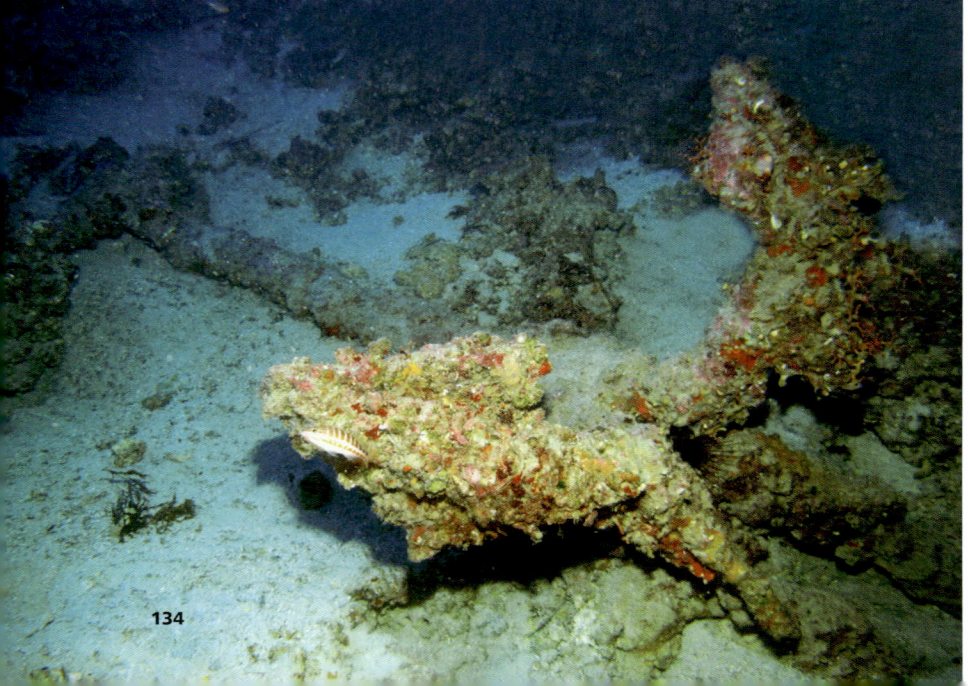

The huge (3 metre long) anchor at 63m.
PHOTO: BRIAN AZZOPARDI – ATLANTIS DIVING CENTRE

MGARR IX-XINI – TA' CENC

PGL AERIAL PHOTOS

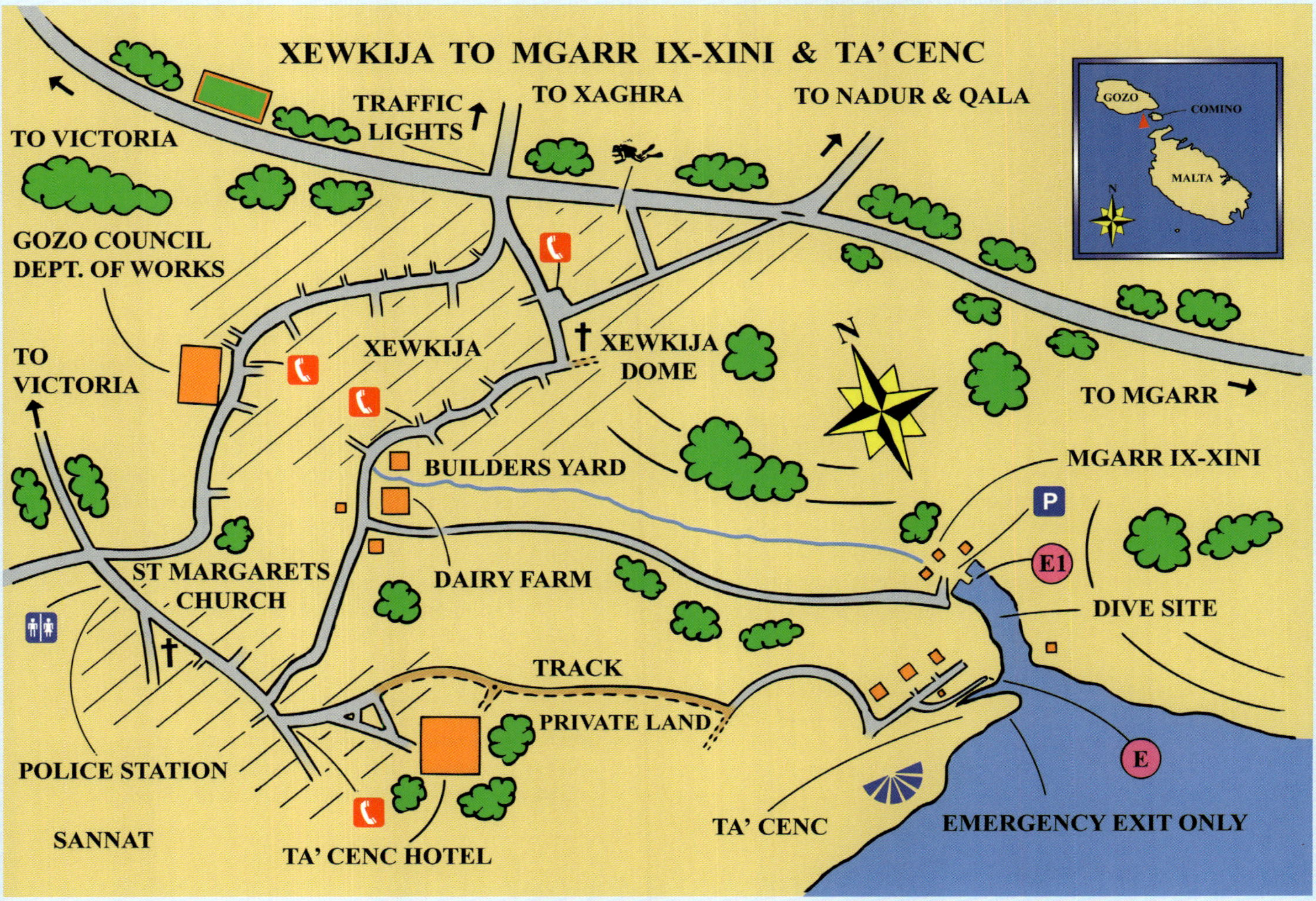

XEWKIJA TO MGARR IX-XINI & TA' CENC

- TO VICTORIA
- TRAFFIC LIGHTS
- TO XAGHRA
- TO NADUR & QALA
- GOZO COUNCIL DEPT. OF WORKS
- TO VICTORIA
- XEWKIJA
- XEWKIJA DOME
- TO MGARR
- BUILDERS YARD
- MGARR IX-XINI
- ST MARGARETS CHURCH
- DAIRY FARM
- DIVE SITE
- TRACK
- PRIVATE LAND
- E1
- E
- POLICE STATION
- SANNAT
- TA' CENC HOTEL
- TA' CENC
- EMERGENCY EXIT ONLY

GOZO COMINO MALTA

Mgarr ix-Xini

There are two main routes to this dive site; either will take you through Xewkija, a third route is from Victoria. From the traffic lights at Xewkija to your dive site the distance is approximately 6 km. At Sannat centre, bear left at the church and at the top of the hill just before a fork in the road and the telephone box, turn sharp left. Be careful you can easily miss this turning; there is a signpost to Mgarr ix-Xini. Follow this road down to the farm buildings at the bottom of the hill; turn right, this is a single-track road with passing places.

Alternatively drive directly to the Xewkija dome church, either from the traffic lights or the small roundabout, on the road that leads to Mgarr. The distance for this route is approximately 4km. The only problem is that the road from here to the farm buildings is through the residential area and is not easy to follow, but is sign posted to Mgarr ix Xini and Ta Cenc. Once at the farm buildings you have to turn left along the single-track road, which will lead you right down through the valley to the little hamlet of Mgarr ix Xini and your dive site.

Striped seabream ((Lithognathus mormyrus) this fish feeds on small invertebrates which it drives out by digging in the sediments.

Not easily visible the cute little seahorse (Hippocampus ramulosus) likes to attach itself to the Posidonia leaves swaying in the currents.   PHOTO: SHARON FORDER

This out of the way pretty little inlet is the perfect place for a night dive, but also used for a second dive or when sea conditions elsewhere are not so good. With a gentle sloping bottom and an easy channel to navigate, for all intents and purposes the inlet runs from north to south. The bottom is mostly sand with some sea grass but this changes to mostly sea grass the deeper and further you go. Remember that there are no places to exit the water other than the exit points shown on the plan.

THE DIVE   Minimum time – 50 mins

Once rigged walk to the right hand side of the bay along the little jetty to the steps at the end, this is where I would enter the water. My dive plan would be to surface swim along the west wall of the channel until the depth below me is about 5m. This is the area where the small boulders end and the sandy area begins. Once on the bottom I would head in a southerly direction following the line where the rock face/coastline meets the sand. The depth gently descends to 10m; here there is a cave with a 3m entrance, which narrows at the rear, your time to this point will be approximately 15/20 minutes. To reach the second cave from here will take you a further 10 minutes and down to a depth of 16m.

This is quite a large cave, which can be safely entered for it does not go back too far. At this point you are within three to four minutes of the exit point at Ta'Cenc which you could use only in an emergency. Now take a compass bearing of 60° to cross over the inlet, this will take you about 3 minutes, your return journey from here to E1 is approximately 25 minutes. During the summer this site is a good place to find and maybe photograph seahorses. If you cover the full route it could take you up to 60 minutes but of course you can make your turning point to suit your own dive plan. Refreshments are available here during the summer and some weekends for the rest of the year.

At this dive site when making your dive plans please remember that the emergency facilities are some distance away should they be required.

MGARR IX-XINI

PHOTO: JOE ABDILLA & PAUL GAUCI

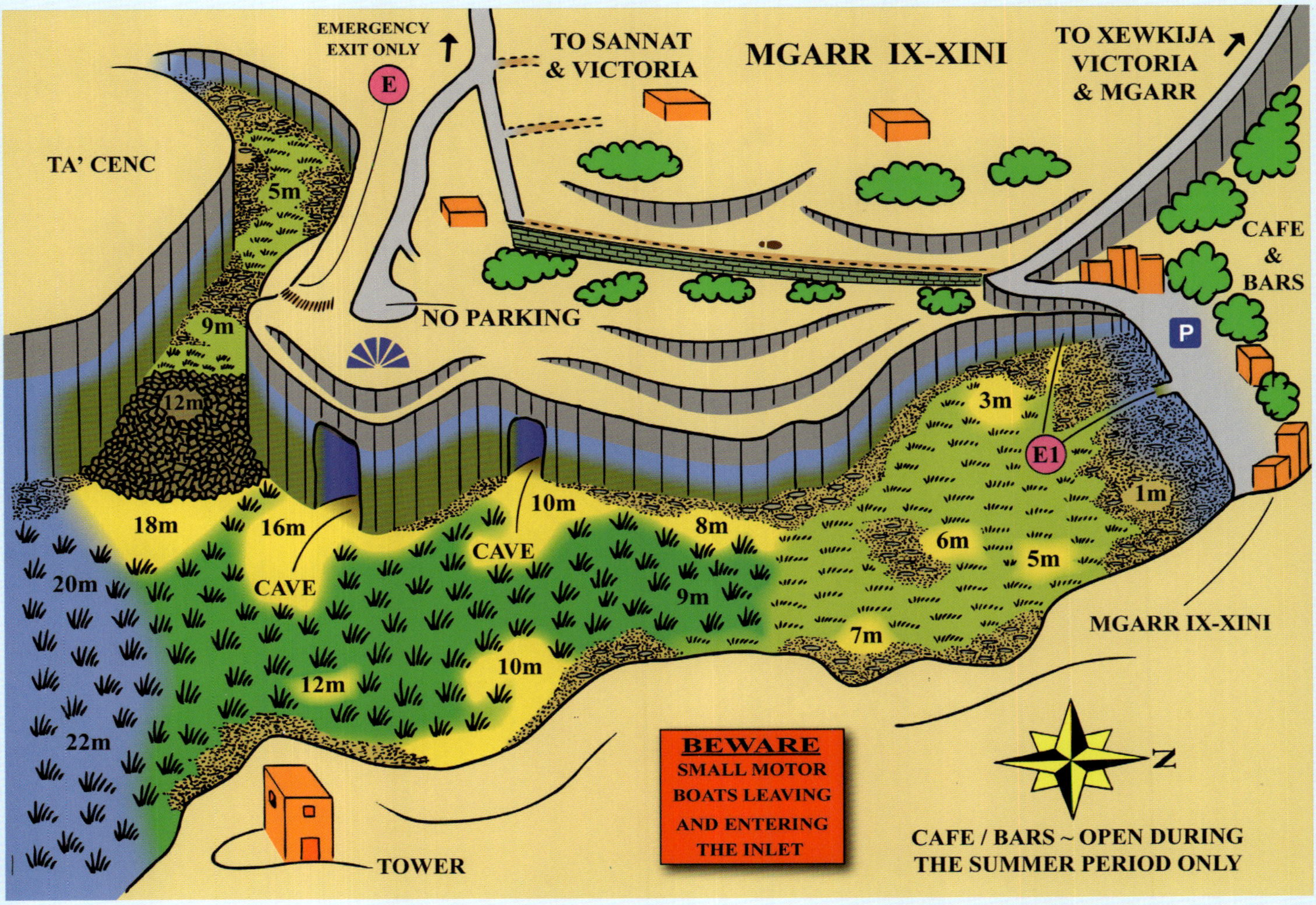

EMERGENCY EXIT ONLY E

TO SANNAT & VICTORIA

MGARR IX-XINI

TO XEWKIJA VICTORIA & MGARR

TA' CENC

5m
9m
12m
18m
16m
CAVE
20m
CAVE
10m
8m
9m
12m
10m
22m
7m

NO PARKING

CAFE & BARS

P

3m
E1
1m
6m
5m

MGARR IX-XINI

BEWARE
SMALL MOTOR BOATS LEAVING AND ENTERING THE INLET

TOWER

N

CAFE / BARS ~ OPEN DURING THE SUMMER PERIOD ONLY

XLENDI – TUNNEL

PHOTO: JOE ABDILLA & PAUL GAUCI

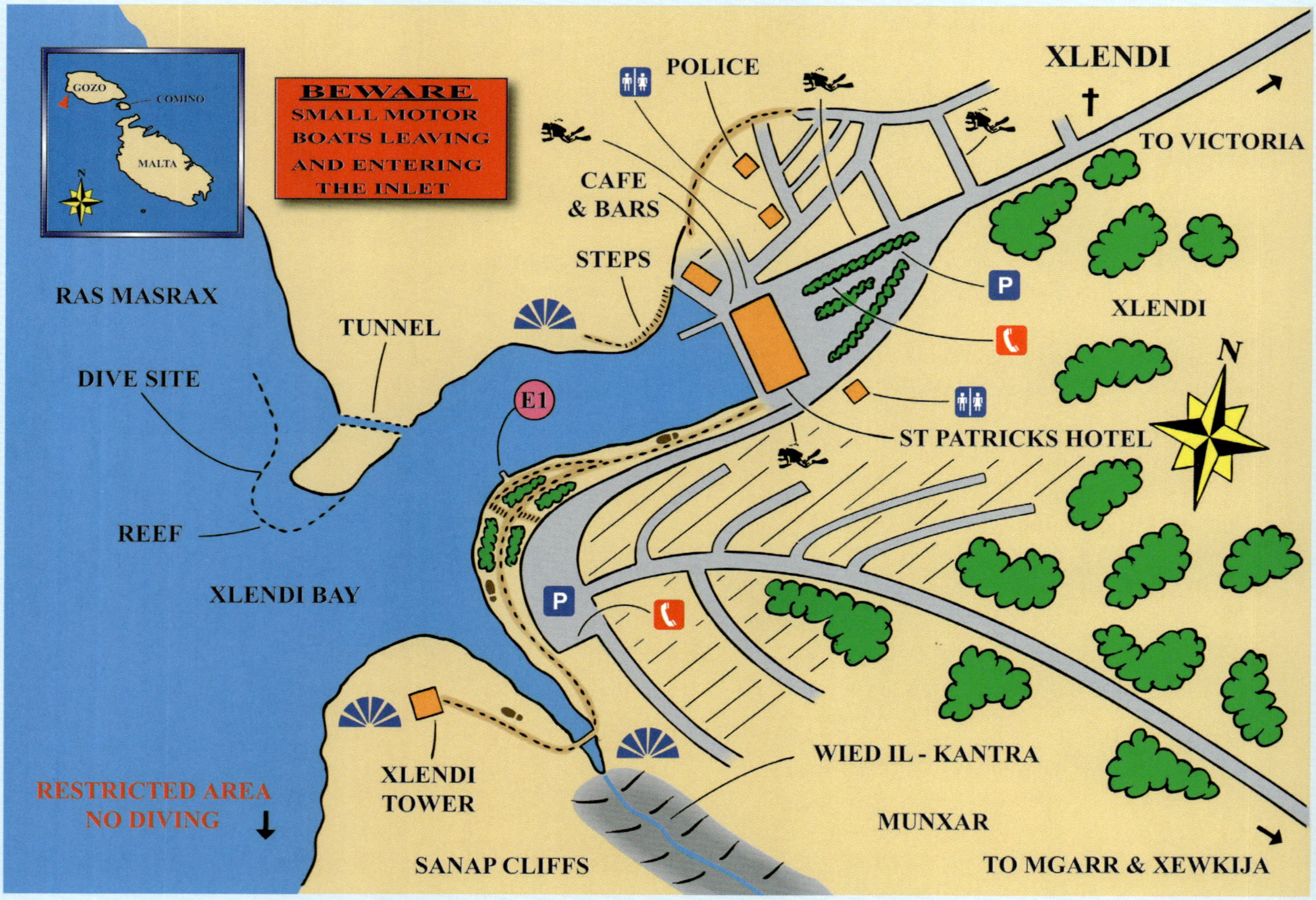

Xlendi

This quaint little village of Xlendi is situated on the southwest coast of Gozo with its large sandy inlet and excellent facilities. There is really only one route to Xlendi and that is from Victoria, a distance of approximately 3 km. When driving through the residential area of Victoria be careful not to miss the sign posts for Xlendi, as the streets are narrow with many turnings. Once you head out of the built up area of Victoria the road winds down through a small fertile valley. As you enter Xlendi fork left, past the car park continue up the hill, at the top, the road widens out and here on the right hand side is where you park, you will find the entrance to the path and steps which lead down to your entry/exit point E1. From this vantage point you will have a full view of Xlendi Bay, its reef, the entry point and the sea front promenade.

The actual dive site is around the headland on the opposite side of the bay, with a 70-metre long tunnel which runs through the headland with a maximum depth of 8m, for which you will require a torch. The main reef just off the headland forms part of the dive plan.

THE DIVE   Minimum time – 50 mins

It is best to rig where you have parked the car and then walk down to the entry point E1, which is next to a concrete diving platform with some metal steps for your entry/exit. Please do remember that these steps are normally removed during the winter months. It is not quite deep enough close to the shore for a stride entry, so do be careful for entry is not easy.

Divers take to the water and in the background some of the water side cafes which line the promenade of this bay.

To locate the entrance of the tunnel which is below the surface, look for the steep cliffs on the other side of the bay, running down is a formation of rock which looks like a spine, directly below this is the entrance or take a compass bearing of 330° from your entry point; the swim across the narrow bay will take 3/4 minutes. The depth at the entrance to the tunnel is 5m, with a ledge rising to 3m just inside, within a few metres there is a large rock in the centre which you will pass on the left, at this point it is quite dark and you will need a torch. Once you have passed this point the depth increases to 8m and from here normally you can see the exit.

From this point in the roof of the tunnel are cracks

The exit of the Xlendi tunnel on the far side of the cliff, this is at a depth of 8m.   PHOTO: CHRIS GRAY

which allows the light to shine through, with this light and the light from the exit this makes a unique opportunity for some unusual photographs. Once through the tunnel and on the other side you will find that this is a good area for looking for morays and octopus.

If you wish to dive with a pony cylinder they are available at most dive centres, best to book in advance.

Octopus (Octopus vulgaris) out for a nights hunting.

This young damsel fish (Chromis chromis) still shows its fluorescent shade of blue the adults are a brownish colour.

When it is time to move on, head in a southerly direction, keeping the reef on your left, when the inner reef direction turns to the east and there is an area of sea grass in front of you, providing the visibility is good; from here you will see the outer reef. If this is not possible take a compass bearing of 180° and continue over the sea grass until you come to the outer reef follow the reef all the way round, keeping it on your left, this route will lead you back into the bay. You can of course follow the inner reef round which is a much shorter route and has a maximum depth of 12m, unlike the outer reef which has a maximum depth of 25m. Once you are heading in a northerly direction and you reach depths of 8/9m you are in the area where you started the dive and the exit point.

Xlendi village is quite a busy little place with some small shops to visit which sell locally made crafts. It is also a very pleasant pastime to sit at one of the restaurants or bars on the waters edge with a lovely view of the bay and soak up the atmosphere of the place.

A diver explores the outer reef for some good photos.

Red mullet (Mullus surmuletus) normally found in groups on the sandy shingle seabed.

You will find that the restaurants give good value many serving the fresh local dishes also the delicious Gozo wines. If you fancy a climb, on one side of the bay there is a footpath to a viewpoint and if you are feeling really fit you can climb to the top, an excellent position to take some souvenir photographs. On the other hand you could take a stroll along the promenade by the water and sit and soak up the sun on one of the many seats provided. This is a very peaceful and picturesque bay to spend some time and just relax.

The grey triggerfish (Balistes carolinensis) lives among rocks and seaweed near shore feeding on small organisms as its mouth does not open very wide. PHOTO: KEVIN DEBATTISTA

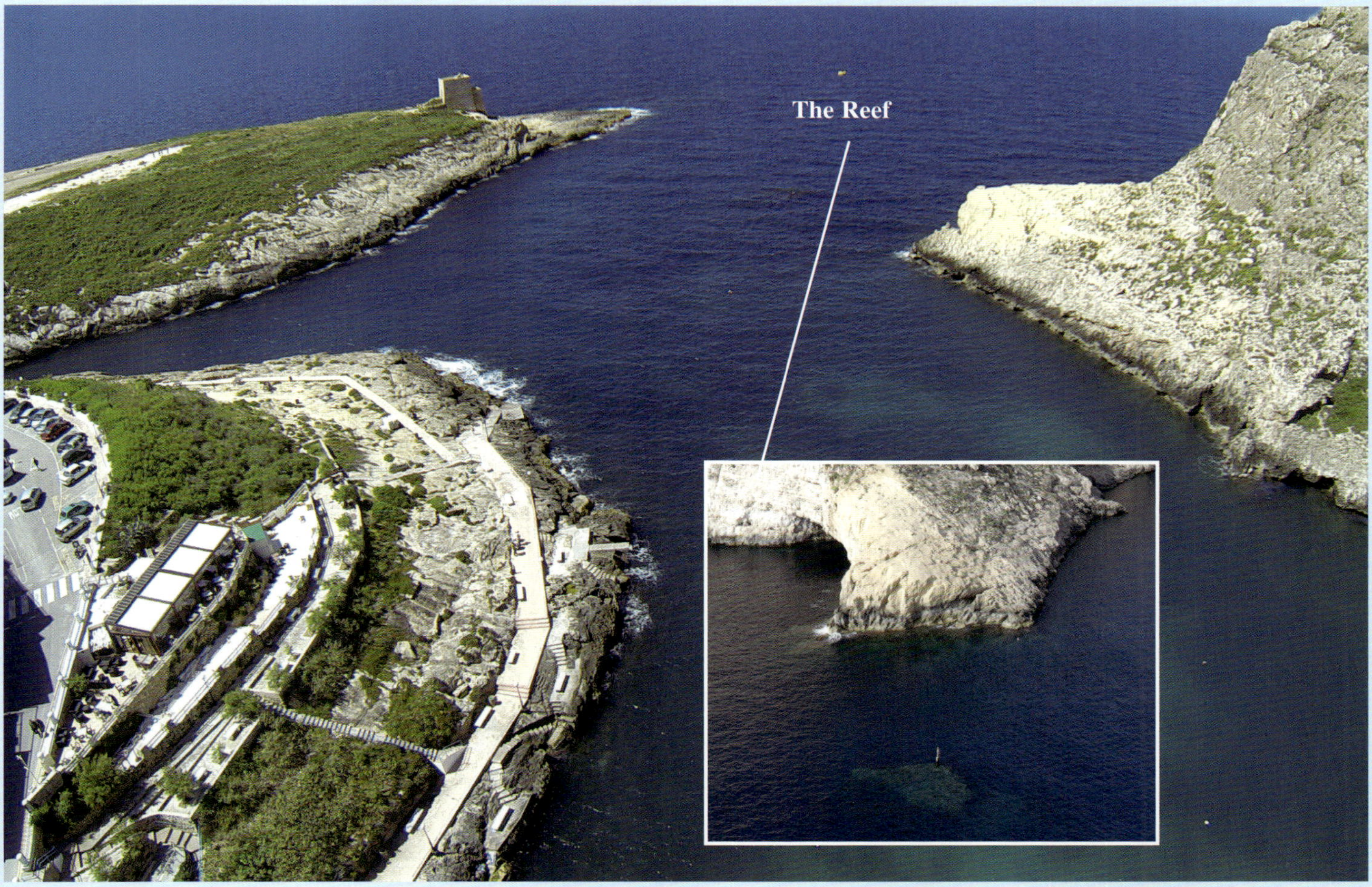
The Reef

PHOTO: JOE ABDILLA & PAUL GAUCI

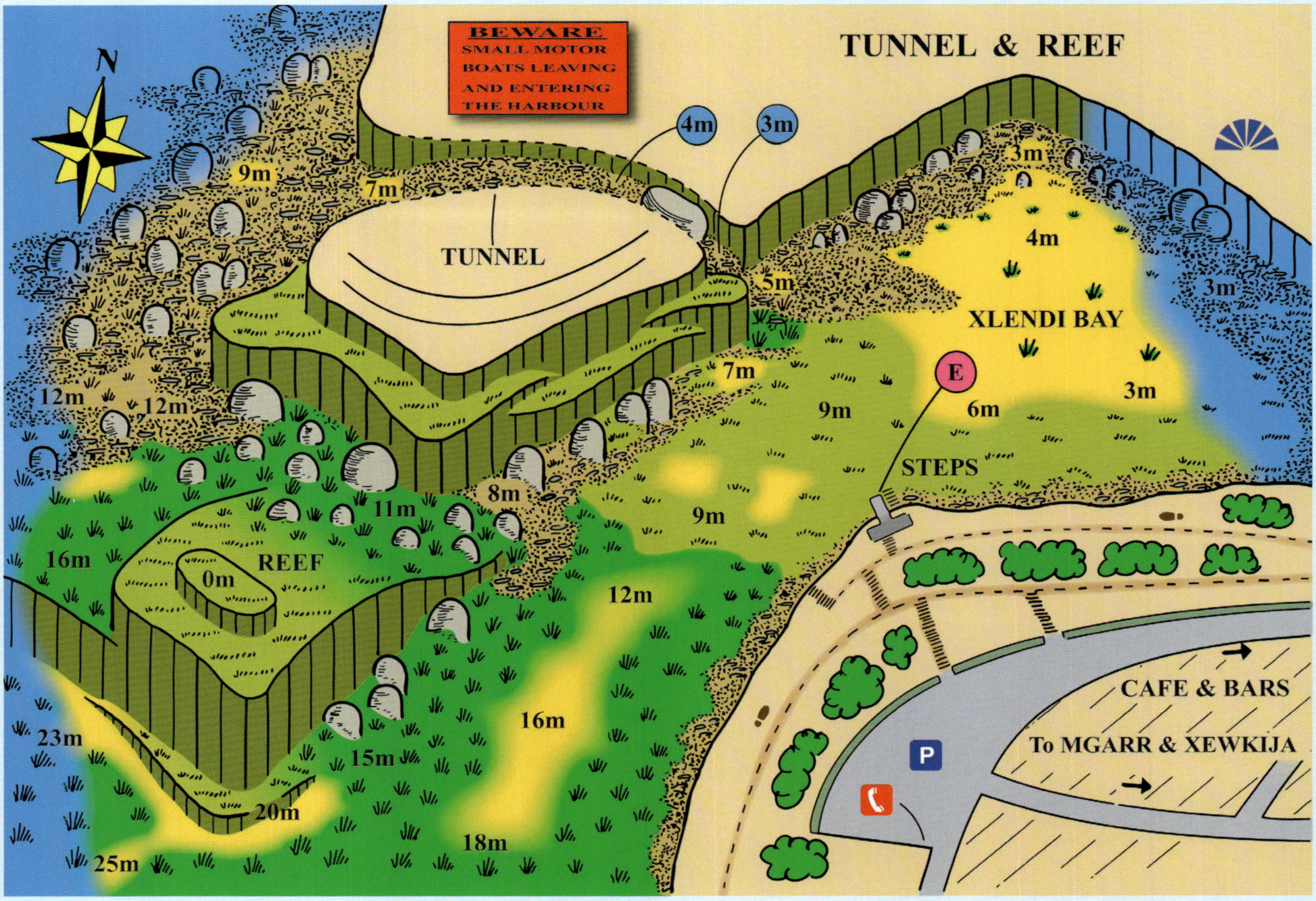
TUNNEL & REEF
BEWARE
SMALL MOTOR BOATS LEAVING AND ENTERING THE HARBOUR
N
4m
3m
9m
7m
TUNNEL
3m
4m
5m
XLENDI BAY
3m
E
7m
9m
6m
3m
12m
12m
STEPS
8m
11m
9m
16m
REEF
0m
12m
CAFE & BARS
To MGARR & XEWKIJA
23m
16m
P
15m
20m
18m
25m

DWEJRA & INLAND SEA

NSET: PGL AERIAL PHOTOS

PHOTO: JOE ABDILLA & PAUL GAUCI

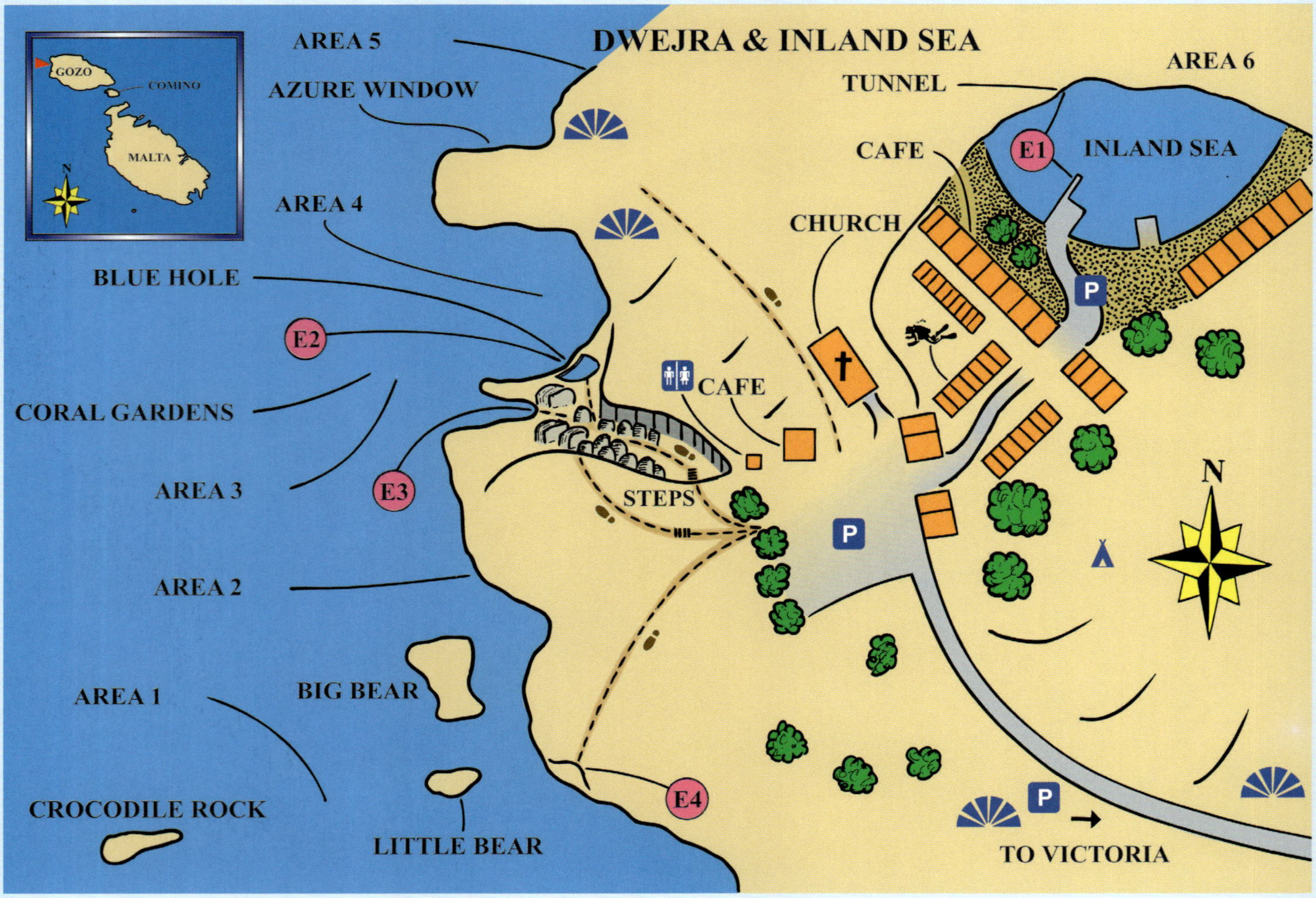

DWEJRA & INLAND SEA

- AREA 5 — AZURE WINDOW
- AREA 4 — BLUE HOLE
- CORAL GARDENS
- AREA 3
- AREA 2
- AREA 1
- BIG BEAR
- CROCODILE ROCK
- LITTLE BEAR
- AREA 6 — TUNNEL
- CAFE
- E1 — INLAND SEA
- CHURCH
- CAFE
- STEPS
- E2
- E3
- E4
- TO VICTORIA

Dwejra

This proposed World Heritage site at Dwejra normally referred to by divers as the Blue Hole and Inland Sea, is just 5km from Victoria on the west coast of Gozo. Its unique coastline has been the backdrop on many film sets, with outstanding landmarks above the surface and its beauty below, has given pleasure and enjoyment to thousands of tourists and divers alike. From Victoria follow the signs to Gharb after 2.5km turn left to St Lawrenz and follow the signs to Dwejra.

The Dwejra Village Inland Sea with diver parking.
PHOTO: JOE ABDILLA & PAUL GAUCI

A number of small boats use this route from the Inland Sea to reach the open sea.

The Inland Sea is a small expanse of shallow water with a maximum depth of 2m linked to the sea outside by the tunnel 80 metres in length and inside the seabed drops from 3m at the entrance to 26m at the exit. Both the Inland Sea and the tunnel are routes for small tourist pleasure boats.

The Azure Window is a column of rock 80 metres in circumference and rising 20 metres out of the sea which supports a bridge of rock from the headland forming an arch/window. This is very picturesque on a beautiful day, but look for the post card which shows the full force of the sea.

The Blue Hole is round and 16m to the seabed where there is a large window which allows you to venture out into the spectacular underwater world of Dwejra Point. On the opposite side to the window there is a cave.

All these wonders have been created by waves and rough seas over thousands of years, only time and the sea will change these massive structures.

Dwejra Point attracts more divers than any other dive site on Gozo and most of the divers that travel from Malta visit here first. With its normally excellent visibility and a number of unique dive sites, it is no wonder it is so popular.

For the dives, I have listed six areas or dive sites for your consideration, but of course you can mix and match your dive plan.

There are many species of fish, types of marine plants and coral to be seen in these areas. Watch out for groupers lying on rocks and under the over-hangs. Don't forget to keep an eye out in the blue, for this is where you are likely to see the larger fish such as dentex and shoals of barracuda.

> **I strongly suggest that you check out all entry/exit points before you kit up. Please take care when walking these routes especially when it has been raining.**

The Blue Hole and the Window behind the photographer, the cave.

Little Bear to Crocodile Rock
Area 1

To find the entry/exit point, E4, for this dive is not easy, you first have to navigate your way to a small ledge opposite the rock called Little Bear, which has a compass bearing of 220° from the café' in the car park. This is not a straight path but a twisty route over the rocks and holes. E4 is not visible until you are immediately above it and this is the only place along this part of the coastline that you can enter/exit the water (see aerial photograph).

This is an excellent dive with a reef which runs from Little Bear to Crocodile Rock and continues to the north point of Dwejra Bay. The average depth on the reef is around 8m, with drop-offs from 25m to 36m, depending on your location. Swim away from the rock face and the depth will quickly increase to 50m plus. During a dive along this ridge I had a visit from a lone Barracuda who came right up along side me, we made eye contact and within a minute he was gone, I felt I had had a visit from an alien.

THE DIVE — Minimum time – 50 mins

Enter the water, E4, when on the bottom move over to the right hand side of Little Bear, then drop over the edge of the reef, bottom depth about 25m. Face the reef and on your left will be the entrance to Rogers Cave, when you have had a look follow the reef in a south westerly direction, allow around 30 minutes to reach Crocodile Rock. This of course depends on how long you spend at Rogers Cave and exploring areas below the drop off.

Normally, when you are below Crocodile Rock you will be able to see the reef rising to the surface, another indication that you are below Crocodile Rock is that the line of the reef changes to a southerly direction. When it is time for you to return ascend to the top of the reef to retrace your steps at a shallower depth along the ridge to Little Bear, an excellent area for photographs, then on to your exit point, E4. Don't forget to look out into the blue for that elusive alien (Barracuda) and other large fish that may pass by.

Face to face! Two banded sea bream (Diplodus vulgaris).
PHOTO: IAN FORDER

Fan worm (Spirographis spallanzani) brightly coloured against the blue, any movement causes retraction of fan into tube.
PHOTO: JOE FORMOSA

Jellyfish (Peleegia noctiluca) artistic photography underwater.
PHOTO: SHARON FORDER

Cardinal fish (Apogon imberbis) in one of their favourite places, a small crevice and hanging like a curtain are squid eggs which hatch in June/July.

LITTLE BEAR TO CROCODILE ROCK – DWEJRA

Crocodile Rock. PHOTO: JOE FORMOSA

PGL AERIAL PHOTOS

Big Bear & Coral Gardens

Area 2

For this dive site I would use entry/exit point, E3. From the main car park to E3, head in a westerly direction towards the sea, down a few steps and bear to the right; continue down some timber steps into the gully. Follow the gully all the way down to the bottom, take your time as in places it is not an easy route. Once you reach sea level pass through a narrow gap between the cliff face and a large boulder, bear round to your left and E3 will be in front of you. Here you have a nice reef with a drop-off to 30m away from the reef and like many areas here it slopes away quite quickly to 50m plus. Big Bear rock is the largest of the three rocks in this area, once under the water it can be explored all the way round. To the south of this reef are a number of large boulders surrounded by areas of sand and small rocks; on the north side is Rogers Cave. On the east side is a valley of rocks and boulders that cover the seabed.

THE DIVE — Minimum time – 45 mins

Be careful at this entry point for the water is very shallow at first, so you have to paddle. Once in the water surface swim out to the middle of the reef where the depth will be around 3m, now swim towards the open sea in a southerly direction and out of the 'U' shaped opening, now descend to the sea bed you will

During their dive these divers have found a tun shell (Tonna galea) nobody at home, good for a photo shoot.

Big Bear and Little Bear the best place to see this likeness is from halfway down the hill to Dwejra.

have a drop of approximately 25m. Turn left and follow the reef you will pass in front of Coral Cave, this is not normally a problem but if the visibility is poor it would be possible that you could mistakenly enter the cave, as the entrance is very wide. Once past the cave take a south westerly bearing over the large rocks down to the lower reef at 30m. When you have explored this area and it is time to head for higher ground continue up the slope in an easterly direction this will take you to the cliff face of Big Bear and Rogers Cave, your dive time will be approximately 35 minutes.

Ascend to the ledge at 8m above Rogers Cave and cross over to the coastline reef, now turn left and head in a northerly direction down the inside of Big Bear. As you now possibly will be staying above 9m once you have passed over the top of Coral Cave, ascend to 6m here you will see a distinct 'U' shape in the top of the reef, this is your route back into Coral Gardens. The depth of this entrance is 6m, once further in the depth will decrease to 5m and to your exit, E3.

> **Coral Cave has a very large opening and goes back into a secondary cave. I am going to give a warning and make a request! Sadly in 1999 two divers tragically lost their lives within this cave for it is difficult to navigate when the silt has been stirred up. If you are in the entrance of the cave please take care as damage is being caused to the coral, not only by divers' equipment, but also bubbles.**

Just below the ledge on Big Bear a diver has spotted something of interest.

BIG BEAR & CORAL GARDENS – DWEJRA

PGL AERIAL PHOTOS

BIG BEAR & CORAL GARDENS

- AREA 2
- CORAL GARDENS
- LITTLE BEAR
- E3
- E4
- THE "U"
- BIG BEAR
- CORAL CAVE 30m
- ROGERS CAVE

Depths marked on map: 2m, 5m, 6m, 8m, 10m, 0m, 5m, 6m, 6m, 15m, 14m, 19m, 25m, 28m, 21m, 28m, 28m, 33m, 30m, 30m, 32m, 34m, 34m, 33m, 36m, 37m, 45+, 45+

DWEJRA

The Blue Hole & Coral Gardens

Area 3

For this dive site I would use entry/exit point, E3. From the main car park to E3, head in a westerly direction towards the sea, down a few steps and bear to the right; continue down some timber steps into the gully. Follow the gully all the way down to the bottom take care, as it is quite un-even and with steps cut into the rock, which are difficult to negotiate. Once you reach sea level entry point E2, to the Blue Hole will be on your right and on your left will be two large boulders, go round these and you will find your shallow entry point, E3. This dive allows you to explore the outer underwater reef, which takes you further away from the shore than any other dive here.

A view from above the Blue Hole with divers and swimmers on the surface.

THE DIVE Minimum time – 50 mins

Once in the water swim away from the shallows and descend towards the open sea, your depth here will be 2m and 6m when you come to the 'U' shaped opening. From this opening the drop off to the seabed is approximately 25m. At this point your minimum time to the Blue Hole is around 15/20 minutes. Once on the seabed, or your chosen depth, turn and head in a northerly direction keeping the reef on your right, when you reach the end of the reef follow it round, once you have turned the corner you will be heading in an easterly direction, from here it will only take you a very short time to reach the 'crack' as local divers refer to it. At the bottom of this 'crack' the depth is 27m, now enter this large fissure making sure your depth is below 14m, ascend slowly up into Coral Gardens where your depth will be 7m, now bear to your right and follow the gully to the 'V' opening. Your dive time at this point could be 25 minutes depending on your depth and time taken exploring around the headland.

Turn right and with the reef on your right hand side follow it all the way round to the Window and the Blue Hole, this will take some 20 minutes. I suggest that you now keep a maximum depth of 8/9m. Once inside the Blue Hole, whilst completing safety stops if required, admire your surroundings or just diver watch before you exit E2.

From the depths a view of the Blue Hole and its window.
PHOTO: SHARON FORDER

The dive starts in Coral Gardens and ends at the Blue Hole, if you check out the aerial photograph you will clearly see your entry and exit points, Blue Hole E2 and Coral Gardens E3, both the 'U' and 'V' openings and the top of the 'crack', but of course you can plan your own dive. There is from the 'U' opening, a 25m drop-off onto the seabed, with the average depth around the reef face of 30m, but if you move away the seabed quickly drops to depths of 50m plus.

Just below the surface your exit point from the Blue Hole, someone is paddling!

BLUE HOLE & CORAL GARDENS – DWEJRA

BLUE HOLE & CORAL GARDENS

- AZURE WINDOW
- STEPS
- AREA 3
- E2
- BLUE HOLE & WINDOW
- E3
- CORAL GARDENS
- THE "U"
- THE "V"
- THE CRACK

Depths shown: 10m, 12m, 15m, 18m, 20m, 22m, 23m, 26m, 22m, 33m, 34m, 40m, 45m, 0m, 4m, 6m, 11m, 8m, 0m, 11m, 30m, 34m, 45m+

PGL AERIAL PHOTOS

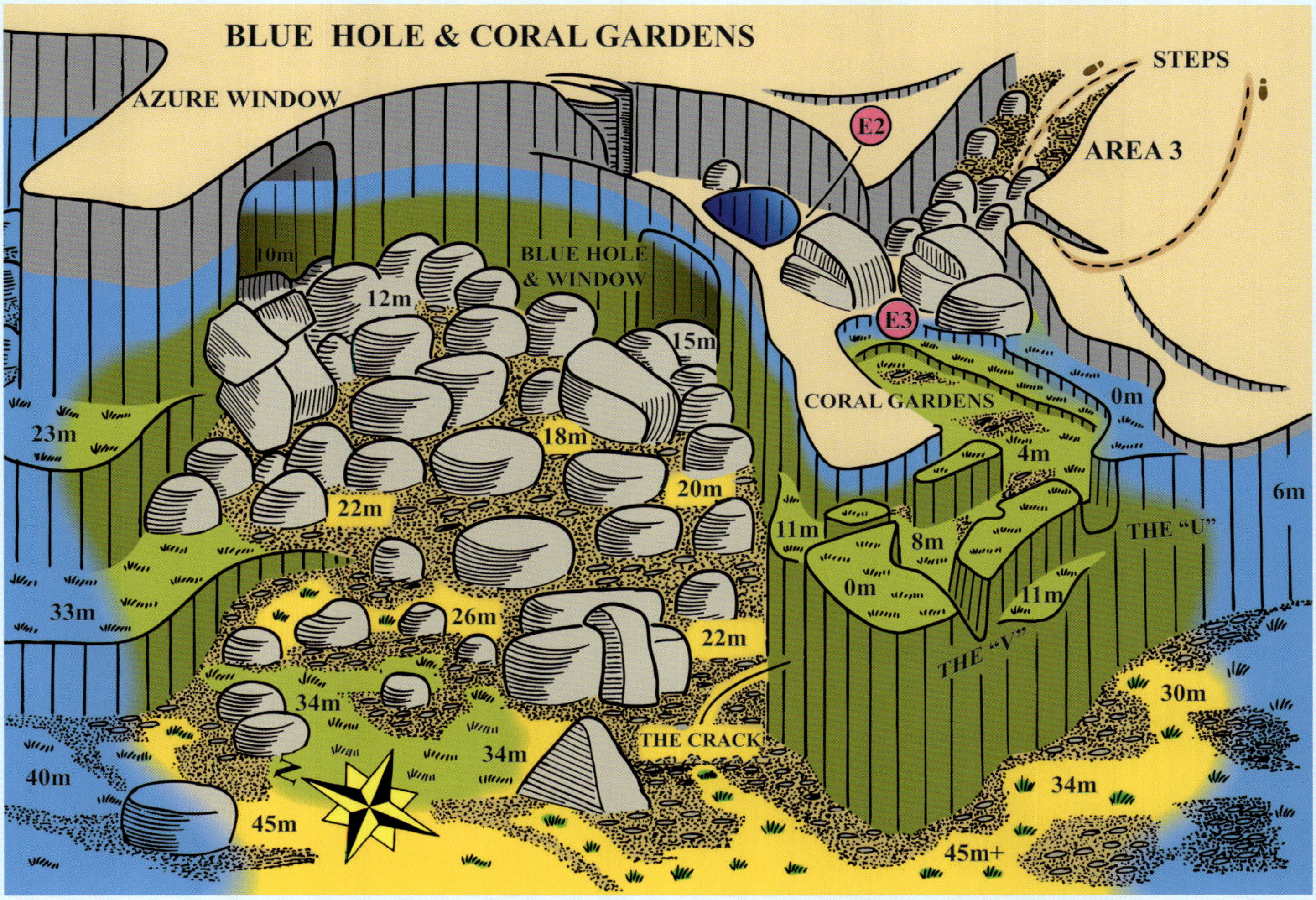

The Blue Hole & Azure Window

Area 4

For this dive site I would use entry/exit point, E2. From the main car park to E2, head in a westerly direction towards the sea, down a few steps and bear to the right; continue down some timber steps into the gully. Follow the gully all the way down to the bottom, take your time as in places it is not an easy route. Once you reach sea level pass through a narrow gap between the cliff face and a large boulder, bear round to your right and E2. The Blue Hole is possibly the most popular dive site of the six areas I have covered, quite unique, but in my opinion, not the best. On this dive you will enter the Blue Hole, circumnavigate the column of the Azure Window and a visit to the cave is worth while, a torch will be required.

THE DIVE — Minimum time – 40 mins

Once in the water descend you will pass the top of the window at 7m on your way down to the sea bed at 16m. Looking out of the window the cave will be directly behind you. When going out through the window you can go **one of two ways** to the Azure Window, take a compass bearing of 300° and swim over the many boulders and rocks until you reach the southwest corner of the column. **Alternatively**, you can turn left, follow the reef around until you reach the 'crack', from here take a northerly course, keeping your depth around 25m with the boulders on your right and the open sea on your left until you reach the southwest corner of the column.

The column will help with your navigation, for the outer and inner walls run almost north to south and the side walls, east to west. The total distance round this

During a severe winter storm a huge piece of rock has fallen from the Azure Window adding to the underwater landscape.

Two divers swimming around the column of the Azure Window.

column under water is approximately 250 metres. On the far side of the pillar there are two main ledges, below these it drops away to depths of 50m plus. On this side of the Azure Window is the best place to catch a glimpse of those giant groupers, remember that they are very shy so approach gently. When you reach the area below the arch, rocks cover the bottom and boulders, keeping the reef now on your left will lead you back to the Window and Blue Hole.

Once inside and if you have sufficient bottom time and air left, take time to explore the cave. The deepest part of the cave is at the entrance, which is 16m, once inside it slightly curves to the left, rising to a depth of 13m at the back. When it is time to go to your exit point, E2, slowly ascend within the Blue Hole.

Brown grouper (Epinephelus guazza) lives on rocky bottoms with plenty of crevices, can often be found resting on a rock.

PHOTO: VICTOR FABRI

BLUE HOLE & AZURE WINDOW – DWEJRA

PGL AERIAL PHOTOS

BLUE HOLE & AZURE WINDOW
AREA 4

E2

BLUE HOLE WINDOW & CAVE DEPTH 15m

CORAL GARDENS

THE CRACK

12m
15m
18m
20m
27m
32m
38m
45m
25m
30m
50m
45m

BLUE HOLE & WINDOW

E2

CAVE

13m 15m 16m

AZURE WINDOW

12m
15m
17m
24m
33m
34m
38m
45m

N

50m+

DWEJRA

Inland Sea to The Blue Hole

Area 5

> Beware of the small motor boats carrying tourists so during your dive through the tunnel it is most important to keep to the sides, especially if you have to surface or near the entrance.

One of my favourite places to relax and have a drink after a dive is the small bar/café next to the Inland Sea.

This dive plan will guide you from the Inland Sea E1 to the Blue Hole E2, via the tunnel and the Azure Window. A route of approximately 400 metres with a time of 50 minutes, there are no exit points along this route. Your only help is the pleasure boats, if they are running, which travel with tourists through the tunnel to the Azure Window. Once out of the tunnel stay at your required depth and keep to the coastline reef, the sides of which drop away to 50m plus in places. This dive should only be attempted in calm sea conditions and is only recommended for experienced divers.

The sheer cliffs between the Inland Sea and the Blue Hole continue under the water.

Brown meagre (Sciaena umbra) live in pairs or small groups among rocks, at cave entrances, under ledges and on drop offs. PHOTO: COLIN STEAD

THE DIVE Minimum time – 50 mins

Your entry point E1 is by the slipway at the Inland Sea, you then surface swim to the left of the entrance of the tunnel. For this dive a torch is recommended. Once under water your depth will be 3-4m, this will quickly increase to 9m and then to 16m; a further drop to 25m and the last part of the tunnel is reasonably flat with a maximum depth at the exit of 26m. Your compass bearing through the tunnel is approximately 330° and a distance of roughly 80 metres. When you are through the tunnel turn left and keep the reef on your left-hand side at all times. The first part of the reef will take you in a westerly direction, but after a few minutes it will change to a southerly direction.

The following times and depths are where the described pilotage points can be found; after 12 minutes 24m a rock wedged in-between a fissure of two rocks. 14 minutes 21m, a rock shaped like a pointing finger. 16 minutes 18m, a triple ledge close together. 20 minutes 18m and halfway with an 18m ledge and two boulders below. After around 22 minutes you will find a little cove where the seabed is covered with boulders and you might think that this is the Azure Window, but cross over to the other side (see aerial photograph) and continue to follow the outside of the reef round, 26 minutes, 19m and a whitish rock on a ledge. In approximately 30 minutes, you should be under the arch; from here it is no more than 3 minutes to the window of the Blue Hole and your exit point E2. This is only a guide; you can of course vary your depth and time to suit you and your dive plan.

Moray eel (Muraena Helena) has found a home amongst the brightly coloured corals. JOE FORMOSA

INLAND SEA TO BLUE HOLE – DWEJRA

Amberjack.

White sponges.

PGL AERIAL PHOTOS

INLAND SEA TO THE BLUE HOLE

AREA 5

BLUE HOLE — E2

CHURCH BAR / CAFE

P

CAFE

INLAND SEA 2m 1m E1

TUNNEL

BEWARE SMALL MOTOR BOATS USING THE TUNNEL

N

AZURE WINDOW

16m, 18m, 12m, 17m, 22m, 24m, 26m
18m, 16m, 26m, 17m, 18m, 45m
25m, 34m, 35m, 32m, 40m, 45m
50m+, 40m, 50m, 50m, 50m+

Inland Sea & Tunnel

Area 6

This unique dive with its 80-metre tunnel with depths from 3m to 26m and large enough to accommodate a double decker bus with space to spare, makes an exciting dive. Remember the tunnel is the only route to your exit point E1, the next nearest exit point south is 400 metres and to the north half way round the island. You will need a torch. Once out of the tunnel your selected dive plan will determine which way you want to go. Both reefs, apart from some ledges, fall away quite quickly to depths of 50m plus. Just because it is calm at the entrance of the tunnel the outer sea conditions must be checked before diving.
See note on previous dive referring to small boats using the tunnel.

The tunnel from the Inland Sea leading out to the open sea where also the pleasure boats take tourists to the Azure Window.

THE DIVE   Minimum time – 40 mins

Your entry and exit point, E1, is by the slipway near the Inland Sea car park. Surface swim to the left-hand side of the entrance to the tunnel and descend; here the depth is only 3m, so keep to the side until you are safely in deeper water. If you have to surface within the tunnel keep to the sides. The tunnel slopes down to 26m to its exit over a distance of approximately 80 metres. Once outside the tunnel, continue over the boulders to your required depth, bearing in mind, the sandy area below you is 50m once you have reached your chosen depth. The compass bearings from the exit of this tunnel are; if you turn left they start westerly and then southerly, if you turn right they are north to northeast. Your dive plan will dictate which way you turn, if you decide to turn right and head toward the northern side of the tunnel entrance, please note on your return to the tunnel there is an entrance to a cave which can be confused with the tunnel, but it is much smaller, so just double check. Hopefully you have brought your torch so you can take your time exploring the tunnel on your return. Please remember when you reach the Inland Sea entrance and you are over the boulders, your depth can be 3m or less, therefore you **must** keep to the sides.

The red scorpion fish (Scorpanea scrofa) is the largest of the Mediterranean scorpionfish easily recognised by the large number of appendices around the head.   PHOTO: IAN FORDER

All the normal facilities are here; there is a café at the top car park and another overlooking the Inland Sea. They are reasonably priced and after your dive it is nice to sit take refreshments and fill in your logbook. This area is very popular with the tourists as well as divers, but there is a lot to see and do, so it does not seem to get too crowded. When parking your vehicle by the Inland Sea keep to the area of large pebbles for it has been known that vehicles get stuck where the smaller stones are. There is a telephone box at Dwejra but if needed the next nearest one is at Gharb in the square, which is situated in front of the church.

Various sponges, soft and hard corals line the walls of the Inland Sea tunnel – of course you will need a torch to see their true colours.

INLAND SEA & TUNNEL – DWEJRA

PGL AERIAL PHOTOS

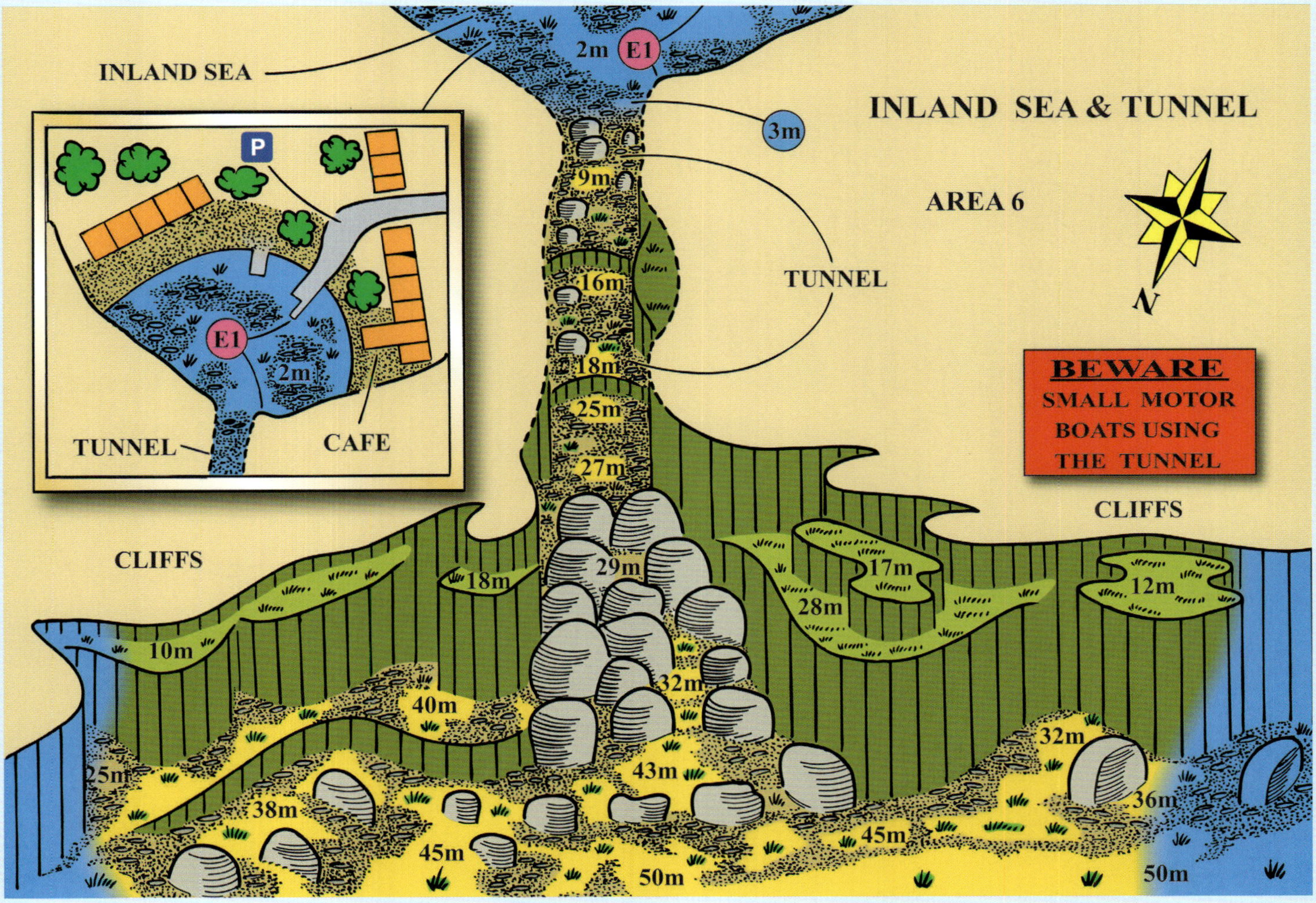

INLAND SEA

INLAND SEA & TUNNEL

AREA 6

TUNNEL

BEWARE SMALL MOTOR BOATS USING THE TUNNEL

CLIFFS

CLIFFS

TUNNEL CAFE

E1 2m
3m
9m
16m
18m
25m
27m
18m 29m 17m 12m
10m 28m
40m 32m
25m 43m 32m
38m 45m 45m 50m 36m 50m

MARSALFORN – REQQA POINT – GHASRI VALLEY

PGL AERIAL PHOTOS

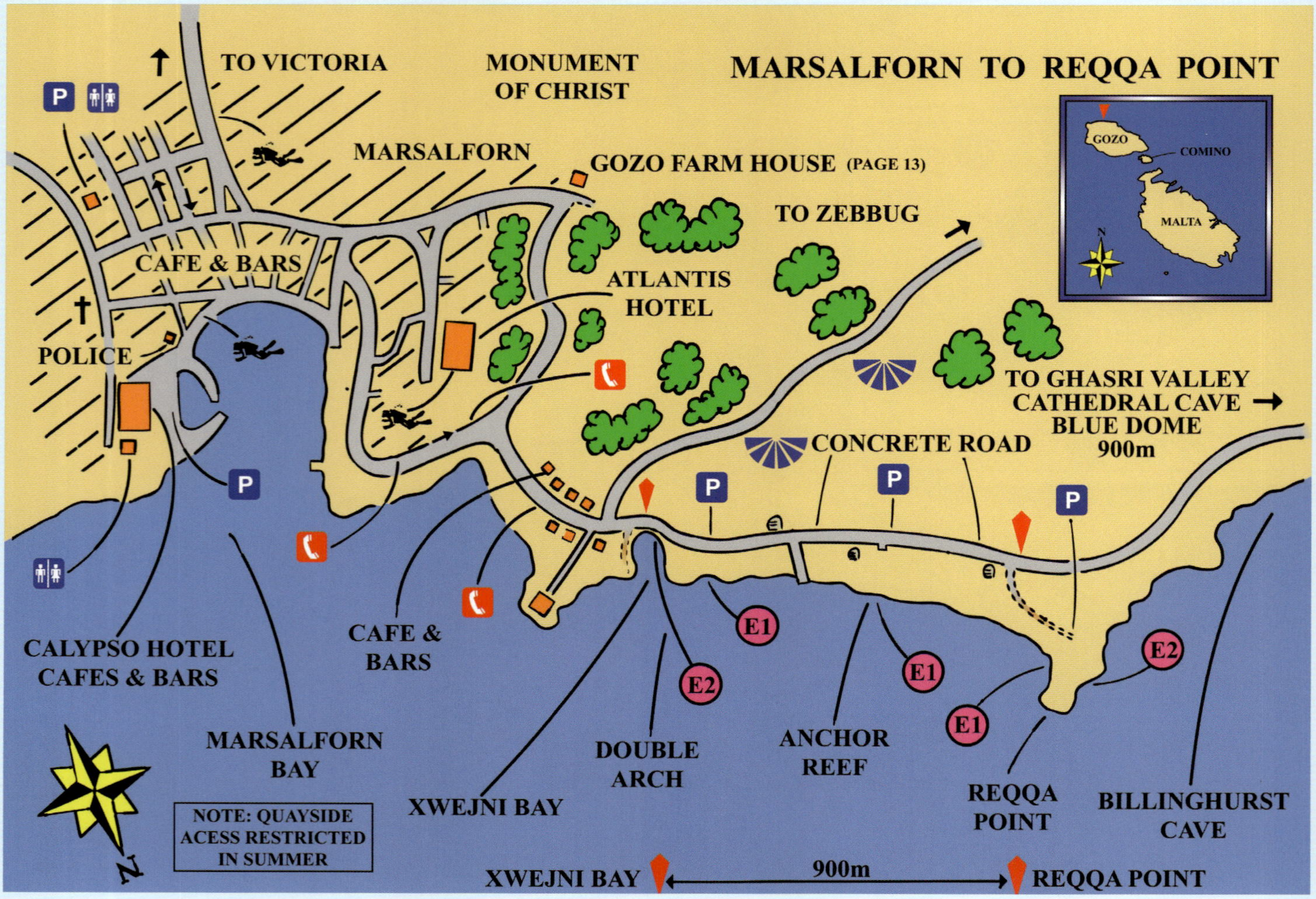

MARSALFORN TO REQQA POINT

- TO VICTORIA
- MONUMENT OF CHRIST
- MARSALFORN
- GOZO FARM HOUSE (PAGE 13)
- CAFE & BARS
- ATLANTIS HOTEL
- TO ZEBBUG
- POLICE
- CONCRETE ROAD
- TO GHASRI VALLEY CATHEDRAL CAVE BLUE DOME 900m
- CALYPSO HOTEL CAFES & BARS
- CAFE & BARS
- MARSALFORN BAY
- XWEJNI BAY
- DOUBLE ARCH — E1, E2
- ANCHOR REEF — E1
- REQQA POINT — E1
- BILLINGHURST CAVE — E2
- NOTE: QUAYSIDE ACCESS RESTRICTED IN SUMMER
- XWEJNI BAY ↔ 900m ↔ REQQA POINT
- GOZO — COMINO — MALTA

Marsalforn

These dive sites Double Arch, Anchor Reef, Reqqa Point and the Blue Dome (Ghasri Valley) are on the north coast of Gozo, not far from the seaside resort of Marsalforn.

Drive out of Marsalforn in a westerly direction, where the road narrows turn right opposite the Gozo farmhouse shown on page13. Follow this road down to the sea front then bear to your left, drive through the buildings to Xwejni Bay with its slipway, this is where the concrete road starts. The distance from Marsalforn centre to Xwejni Bay slipway is approximately 1.8 km Xwejni Bay has a distinct landmark on the east side, in the form of a large sand stone rock, which has been moulded into an unusual shape by the sea and wind.

Double Arch

There are a number of dive sites around the world with single arches, but this site with its double arch is quite unique. It is some 200 metres off shore and can take up to 20 minutes to reach and you must allow 25 minutes for your return. Do check your entry point, E1, this is known by local divers as the washing machine. If you are here when the sea is rough or there is a large swell, you will understand why it has been given this name. An excellent dive when the visibility and weather conditions are good and well recommended. This dive is only suitable for experienced divers who are skilled in navigation and should only be attempted when there are no currents and calm sea conditions.

The average depth below the arch is 36m, to the west side is a reef and the arch forms a bridge between

> To reach entry points at the Washing Machine and Anchor Reef it will be necessary for you to negotiate the salt pans, great care should be taken when doing this as they are still being worked today and if the little shop in the sandstone cliff is open you will be able to promote the cottage industry by purchasing a small bag of sea salt.

The traditional colourful boats in Marsalforn harbour.

it and the main reef. The reef has a maximum depth of 17m but is surrounded by depths of 30m plus, often haunted by shoals of barracuda coming up from the deep and swimming over the reef descending on the other side.

The little salt shop in the sandstone cliff.

A shoal of Salema fish (Sarpa sarpa) seen here at Anchor Reef. PHOTO: JOE FORMOSA

MARSALFORN

Grouper (Epinephelus guaza) Don't forget to look out into the blue! PHOTO: JOE FORMOSA

THE DIVE   Minimum time – 55 mins

For this dive may I suggest that you follow my dive plan, normally I would enter and exit at the washing machine, E1, but of course you can exit at Xwejni Bay, E2, but I do not use this as an entry point for the Double Arch. At entry point E1 just below the surface where you enter the water, are two large vertical round holes, which have been created by the sea. Once you have entered the water surface swim out just past the two points of land, about 8/10 minutes, depth here will be about 9m, this is where I descend. Once on the bottom I take a north bearing on the compass and head for the first reef, this will take about 8 minutes. Before moving off and during your swim, check for any currents.

The sea bed is covered in sea grass and slopes gently down to the ridge of the first drop off where the depth is 15m, at this point you should find a double bowl area, below this area at 24m there is a broken anchor. From the centre of the two bowls take a northerly compass bearing and cross the deeper area towards the double arch, the approximate distance is 40 meters.

The unusual Double Arch at Xwejni Bay.

This excellent little reef to the west of the Double Arch is bustling with marine life, with sheer cliffs that drop away to almost 50m.

Once you have had a good look around the arch and maybe taken some photographs, go up on the reef to the west of the arch. This reef is reasonably small in area and you will have no problem in going round the top of it in less than 5 minutes, remember unless you surface you are at least 25 minutes away from a depth of 9m. When you decide to return take an easterly compass bearing which will take you back to the arch, pass over it and follow the ridge of the reef all the way round until you come back to the double bowl, at 15m, this should take approximately 6/8 minutes. From this point take a southerly bearing on your compass, it will take you about 8/10 minutes to reach a depth of 9m and a little longer to reach the main coastline reef. If your navigation has been good you will find the point of land between Xwejni Bay and the Washing Machine. At this point you will have to decide which exit point you are going to use, turn left for E2 and right for E1 although this may be decided for you, for sometimes when returning there seems to be a slight current at this point coming from the west. If this is the case, exit at Xwejni Bay, E2.

DOUBLE ARCH – MARSALFORN

Anchor Reef

From Xwejni Bay slipway drive along the concrete road for 500 metres towards Reqqa Point., on the right hand side will be a single rock opposite a track leading to a cave dwelling, a further 100 metres on, on the right over the wall is the start if a track which used to lead to the salt pans (see aerial photograph).

A red Scorpion fish (Scorpaena scrofa) the photo shows the true colours of the fish. PHOTO: SHARON FORDER

These dramatic reefs drop away to 50m plus at Anchor Reef with a variety of marine life at shallower depths.

Anchor reef has long been the name of this dive site and I have been informed on good authority that there used to be an anchor here. The tales then become a little hazy; one, some visiting divers from a country not too far away, raised the anchor and took it ashore, only to be arrested by the local constabulary, I can only presume that they have been released by now! Two; maybe the anchor which is in two parts near the Double Arch originally came from here? I have been told by a very good source that it was in the museum in Victoria, but they were unable to trace it, so I am afraid it must still remain a mystery!

This interesting dive is only just a short part of the reef which runs from Reqqa Point in the west, with steep slopes which are littered with boulders and rocks, to the Double Arch in the east where the reef has much more dramatic drop offs. The average depth here is 50m plus. Quite often I have seen large groupers just resting on the rocks in this area. Remember you only have one entry/exit point the next closest are some distance away at Xwejni Bay or Reqqa Point.

THE DIVE Minimum time – 45 mins

Take care when going to entry point E1 and especially down the small steps which have been cut out by fisherman. Once in the water descend to around 9m, below you the reef drops away quite sharply, to your left is the start of a 9m ledge, to your right there are a number of ledges ranging from 9m down to 25m. Looking down and to your right you will see a flatish platform at 24m all these are good indications that your exit point is above you. Now descend to your chosen depth, once this is reached head in an easterly direction, after about 12/15 minutes and at a depth of 33m the reef changes from a steep slope to a sheer cliff, continue in the same direction at your chosen depth and around 25/30 minutes into your dive the reef direction will change from a 60° bearing to 120°. Now I suggest you ascend to the top of the reef at 12m and make this your turning point, follow the reef edge in a westerly direction back towards your exit point. Within 50 metres either side of your exit point are two areas of rugged rocks and small boulders to explore, often this area is frequented by large shoals of salema fish which come here to feed. This is an excellent area to complete your safety stops.

Fireworm (Hermodice carunculata) Nothing goes to waste on the seabed!

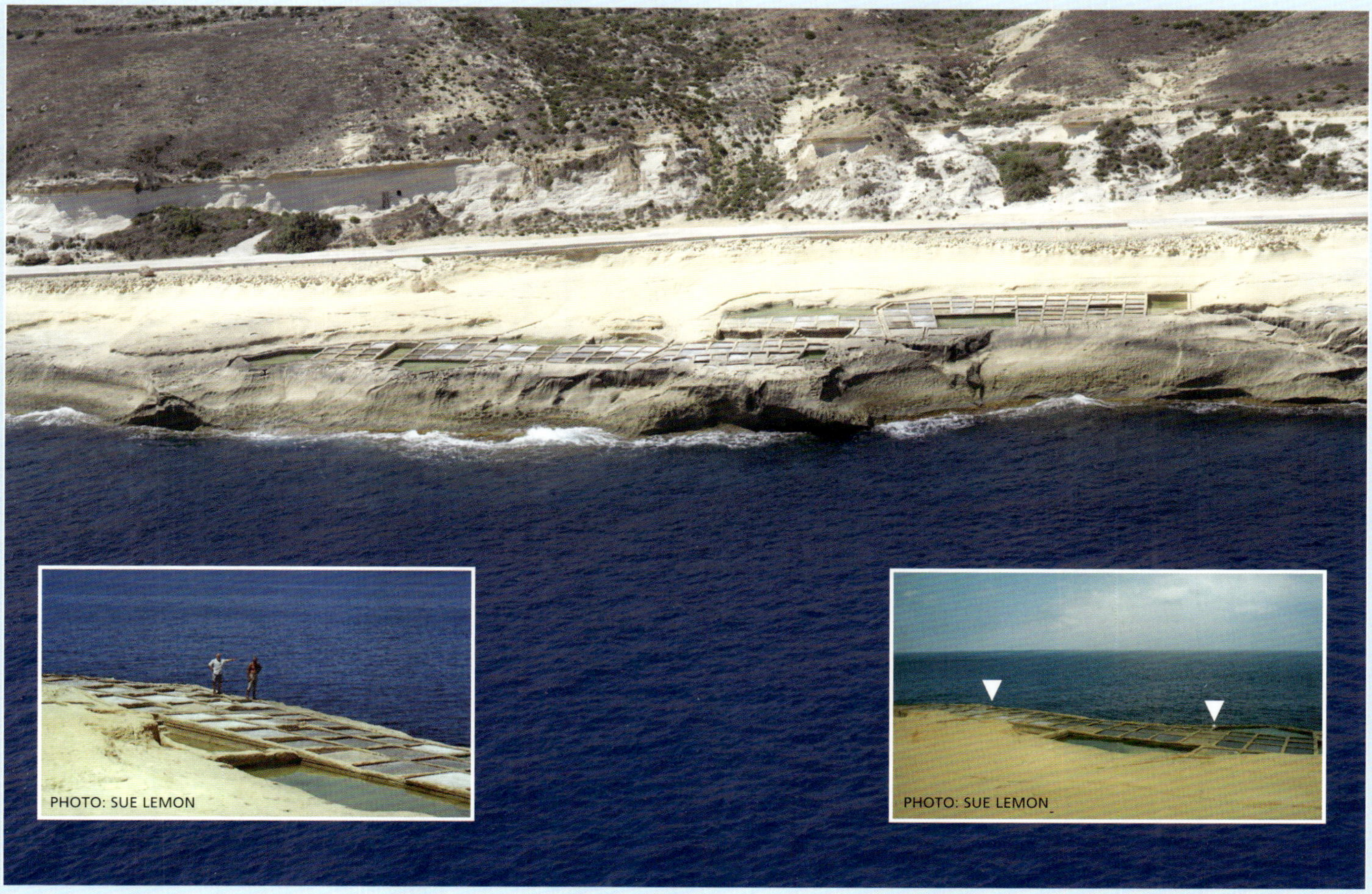

PHOTO: SUE LEMON

PHOTO: SUE LEMON

PGL AERIAL PHOTOS

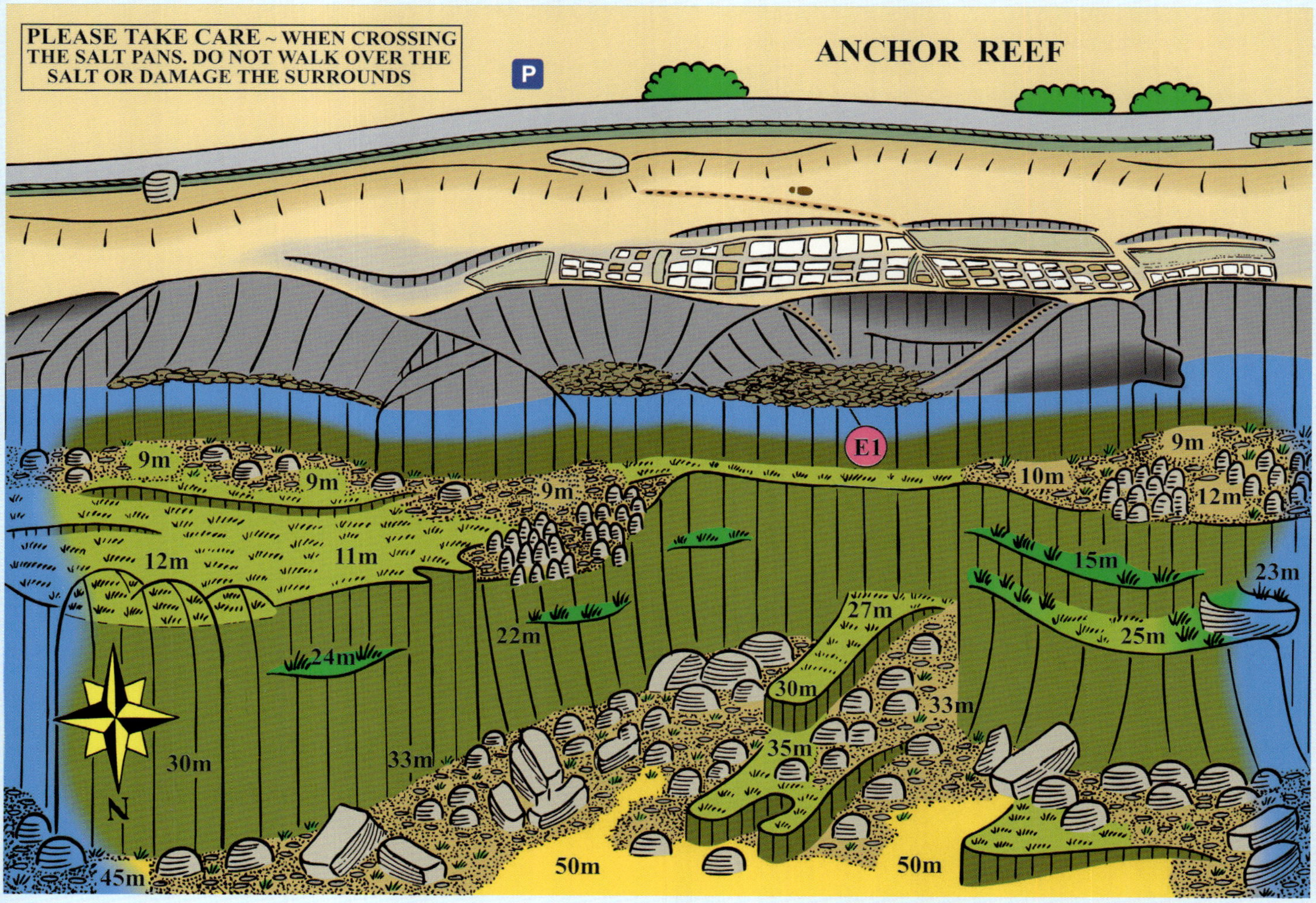
PLEASE TAKE CARE ~ WHEN CROSSING THE SALT PANS. DO NOT WALK OVER THE SALT OR DAMAGE THE SURROUNDS
P
ANCHOR REEF
E1
9m
9m
9m
9m
10m
12m
12m
11m
15m
23m
22m
27m
25m
24m
30m
33m
33m
35m
30m
N
45m
50m
50m

Reqqa Point

From Xwejni Bay slipway drive along the concrete road for approximately 900 metres, here you will find a track which leads down onto the hard sand stone, follow this to your parking space (see aerial photograph). This to me is a very special dive site normally with excellent visibility, a unique plateau at 17m below the surface with its surrounding depths of 50m plus. There is also an abundance of marine life here, which is very good for photography; all this makes it an excellent dive site, possibly the best on the Maltese Islands, maybe my favourite.

The easterly entry/exit for the reef off Reqqa Point.

There are two entry points, E1 and E2, take care when walking to them for the ground is very uneven and the rocks are extremely jagged. E1 at Reqqa Point has a little platform; an exit from here would require a deep-water exit routine. E2 to the west side can be used for entry and exit providing the sea conditions are good. A note of caution, after a storm even though the sea looks calm Reqqa Point can be prone to swell from the North West.

The shallow gently sloping area below the northerly entry/exit point.

The pinnacle at Reqqa Point 17m below the surface.

THE DIVE — Minimum time – 50 mins

The decision of which entry point to use may depend on the weather, but if conditions are good my favourite dive plan would be to enter from the westerly entry point, E2. Once in the water surface swim to your left around the little point, then continue for some 30 metres distance, from here you should have a descent of 35m to the bottom. This gives me a buzz, just slowly drifting down the rock face. Once on the bottom and your plan is to go to 50m, leave the cliff face behind you and head on to the sand. If it is just a bounce dive then turn to your right and use the three large boulders as stepping stones this will lead you up to the flat topped pinnacle at the end of the reef, depth 17m.

The top entrance to the small cave below entry point E1.

REQQA POINT – MARSALFORN

Billinghurst Cave

PGL AERIAL PHOTOS

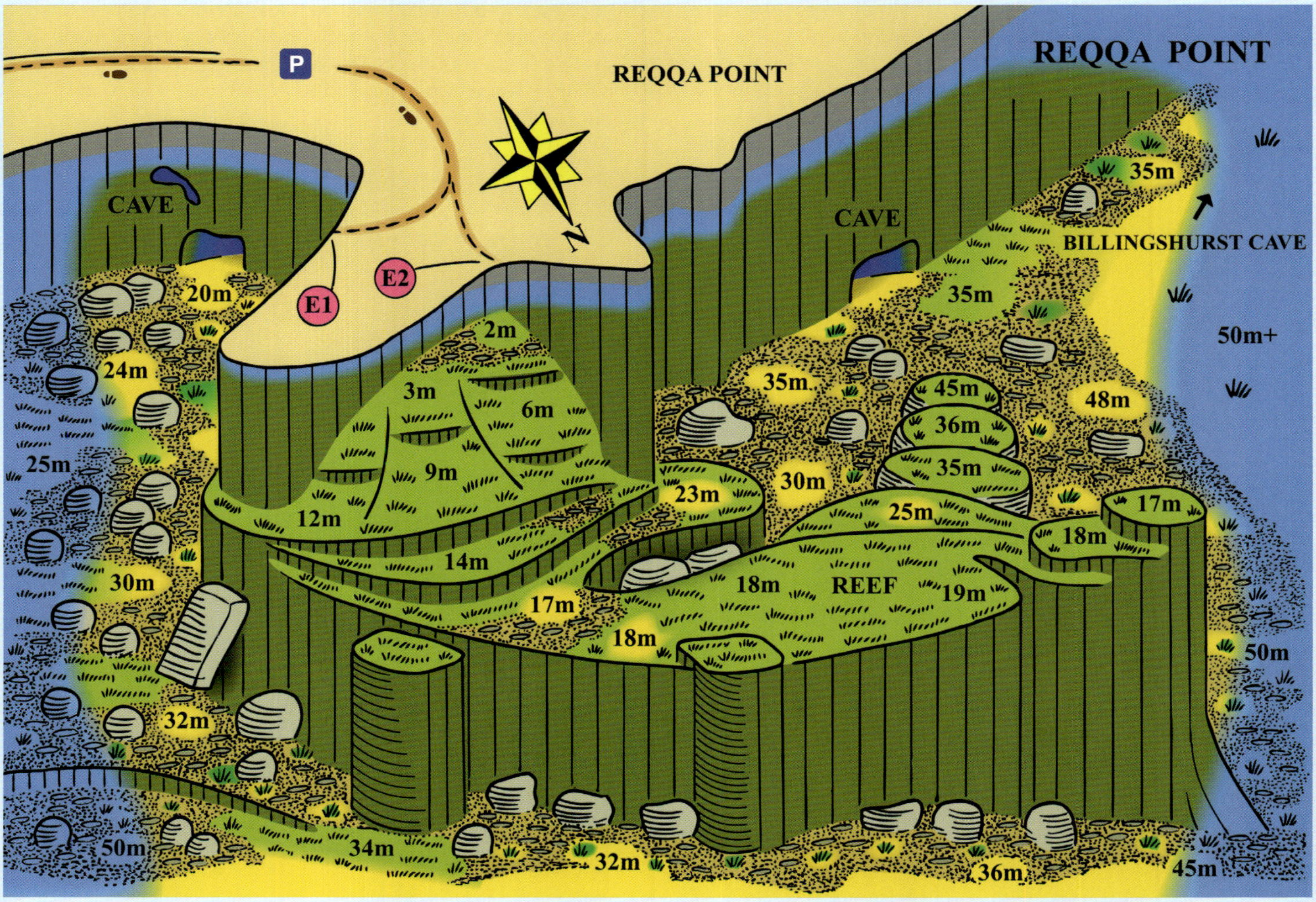

MARSALFORN

This narrow inlet often attracts swimmers and small boats.

To return to the main coastline and your exit point E2 take a southerly compass bearing or just follow the reef. If your dive plan is to use entry point E1, once in the water and you descend to the seabed to 20m, to navigate all the way to the flat topped pinnacle you can use the reef. You will of course, depending on your experience select your maximum depth, bearing in mind that if you stay at 20m or less, this will be a mid-water swim. From the flat topped pinnacle to the main coastline take a southerly compass bearing, or just follow the reef, either will lead you to exit point E2.

When you are below your exit point E2, at the end of both these dives and you have sufficient air remaining, you can continue along the cliff face at your required depth in a southerly direction, remembering that you will have to use exit point E2. Normally at 6m you can see the bottom at 50m, which means you often have visibility of 40m plus; out in the blue a chance of seeing the larger fish which often frequent this area. In my opinion this is an excellent way to end this particular dive.

The parrot fish (Sparisoma cretense) has strong jaws and beak-like teeth, normally swims in family groups.
PHOTO: VICTOR FABRI

It is only a short drive back into the village of Marsalforn where you can find a large selection of very attractive restaurants, cafes and bars, mostly situated around the bay. Fresh fish is almost always on the menus and together with the lovely crispy bread made in Gozo, is a real feast. The nearest telephone is in Obajjar Bay which is next to Xwejni Bay on the road back to Marsalforn.

One of the many overhangs which have been created by huge boulders.

A view from the depths below the pinnacle.

GHASRI VALLEY – MARSALFORN

PGL AERIAL PHOTOS

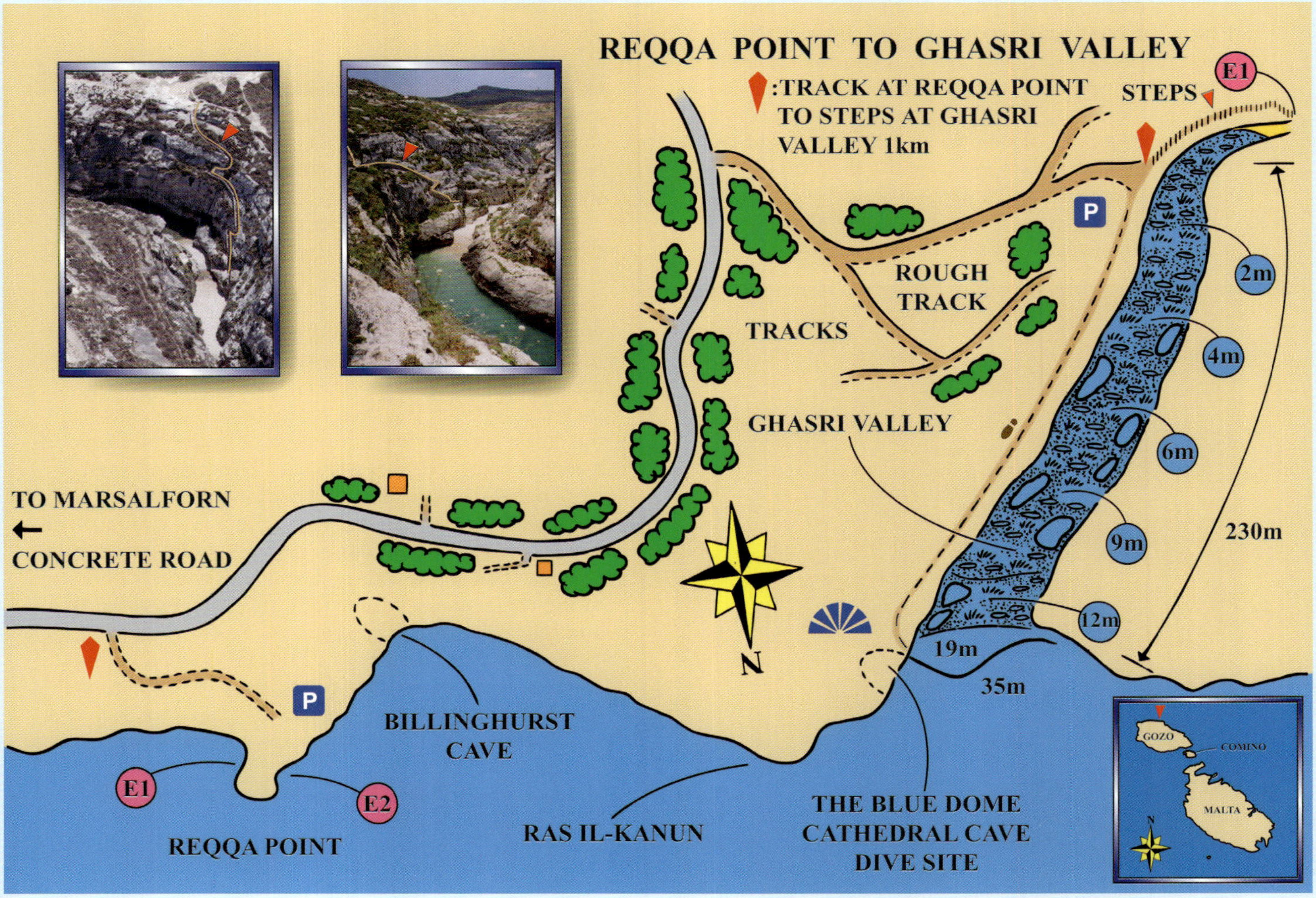

REQQA POINT TO GHASRI VALLEY

↟ :TRACK AT REQQA POINT TO STEPS AT GHASRI VALLEY 1km

STEPS — E1

P

ROUGH TRACK

TRACKS

GHASRI VALLEY

2m
4m
6m
9m
12m
19m
35m
230m

TO MARSALFORN
CONCRETE ROAD

P

E1 E2
REQQA POINT   RAS IL-KANUN   BILLINGHURST CAVE   THE BLUE DOME CATHEDRAL CAVE DIVE SITE

GOZO COMINO MALTA

Ghasri Valley

This dive site is situated on the north coast of Gozo, 3.6km west of the seaside village of Marsalforn. To find this site take the coast road from Marsalforn to Xwejni Bay, from the slipway at Xwenji Bay continue along concrete road towards Reqqa Point, from here travel for a further 600 metres, now turn right down a track and fork left, follow this track almost to the end and turn right into the parking place (see local map).

Blue Dome – Cathedral Cave

This really is a different type of dive well away from the crowds, with its ninety nine steps, 250 metre narrow gorge with shallow waters which lead out into the open sea, together with the magic of the vivid blue colours on the surface in the Dome, has to be seen to be believed. Please do not attempt this dive if there is a swell. Of course I can tell you that most people undertake this dive from a boat, but I am not most people, although on the odd occasion I have used one. It is very important to do a buddy check at this dive site, just to make sure you do not forget something, the last time I dived here I arrived at the entry point minus my fins!

THE DIVE   Minimum time – 50 mins

Once you have negotiated the steps to E1 you will find yourself on a small stony beach, no more than 4 metres wide. Enter the water and enjoy a slow surface swim along this narrow gorge for 8-10 minutes, admiring what nature can achieve. Just before the exit to the gorge descend, **you now have two choices. One;** head towards the open sea, turn slightly to your left and swim in a northerly direction down to 19m, in front of you will see a drop off and to your right the reef will rise to a plateau at 14m, go over the drop off and descend to the sea bed at 33m or your chosen depth. Once you have explored this area follow the reef around keeping it on your right, up and over the large

A diver at the entrance to Cathedral Cave.

boulders and slowly into the cave, your dive time should now be 20-25 minutes.

Two; of course you can follow the coastline reef all the way to the cave which is possible at a depth of 6m. If you wish, here you can complete a safety stop if required if you intend to surface within the Dome. If you do surface it will be safe to remove your regulator for there is a crack in the cave above sea level which allows fresh air inside the Dome. With the light penetration from the cave entrance and the light from the crack, turning the surface water inside the Dome to a vivid blue, this makes a brilliant photograph even from below the surface. Now descend and leave the cave entrance on the north side, there is a plateau with a maximum depth of 20m to explore, when you decide to head back to the exit point take an easterly bearing to the coastline reef, turn right at your chosen depth and follow it into the gorge.

From its entrance to the exit point it will take anything from 10 to 20 minutes, depending on time taken to explore. Of course you can plan your own dive routes from the gorge to the cave and back again.

LEFT: *Diver inside Cathedral Cave admiring the beautiful colour of the sea in the Blue Dome.*

BLUE DOME (CATHEDRAL CAVE) – GHASRI VALLEY

PGL AERIAL PHOTOS

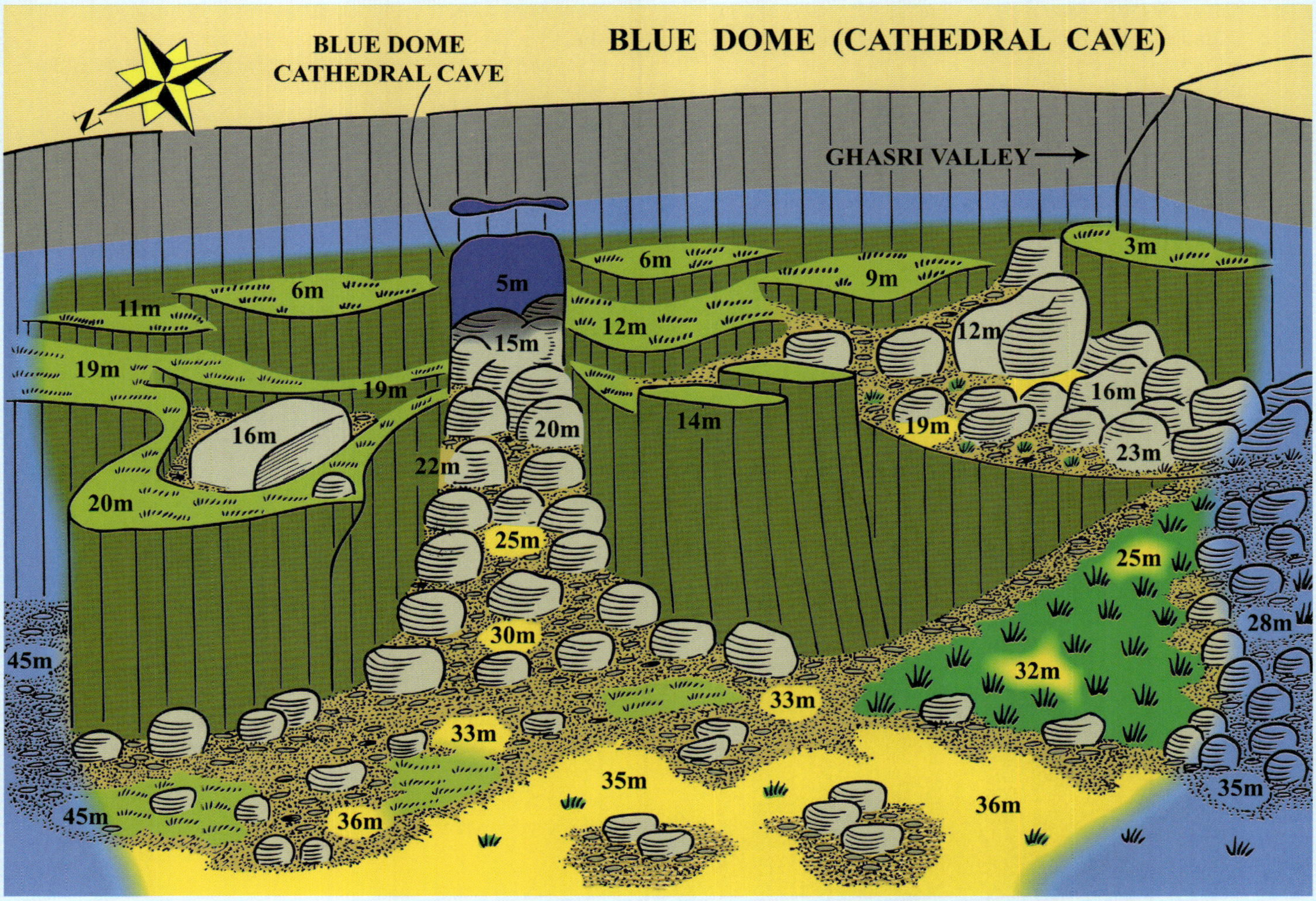

BLUE DOME (CATHEDRAL CAVE)

BLUE DOME CATHEDRAL CAVE

GHASRI VALLEY →

3m, 5m, 6m, 6m, 9m, 11m, 12m, 12m, 14m, 15m, 16m, 16m, 19m, 19m, 19m, 20m, 20m, 22m, 23m, 25m, 25m, 28m, 30m, 32m, 33m, 33m, 35m, 35m, 36m, 36m, 45m, 45m

Malta Boat Diving Sites

Heading out for a days' boat diving.

1. The Bristol Beaufighter

The Bristol Beaufighter was built in Filton, England. The Mk1 was first taken into service in July 1940. It was a twin engine 2/3 seater strike and torpedo aircraft, she had a wing span of 18 metres and almost 13 metres in length, armed with bombs, torpedoes and machine guns in the wings. Using a gyro angling device and a radio altimeter the Beaufighter could make precision attacks at wave-top height with her torpedoes, add to this her long range and able to undertake combat during darkness, made her a formidable fighter aircraft.

On the 17th March 1943, nine Beaufighters of 272 Squadron took off to join up with nine others from 39 Squadron on a shipping strike off Point Stelo, Sicily. Beaufighter 'N' with her pilot Sgt. Donald Frazee and his observer Sgt. Sandery, started to climb to 1500 feet and turned left to search for other aircraft to form up with.

Starboard side undercarriage and engine. PHOTO: SHARON FORDER

Beaufighter on the wartime runway at Ta'Qali which is now the site of the craft village and also home to the Malta Aviation Museum. In the background is Mdina, also known as the Silent City.

PHOTO: BY KIND PERMISSION OF FREDRICK GALEA, MALTA AVIATION MUSEUM

At this time the aircraft began to vibrate violently. The observer reported smoke coming out of his heating pipe, their air speed was around 130 mph and they were losing height at three to four hundred feet a minute. At 600 feet the pilot informed his observer they would have to ditch. There was a slight swell and the aircraft hit the water at about 100 mph, they both managed to get out. By the time they had both floated away from the aircraft, within 15 seconds she had disappeared beneath the waves. Within five minutes they were picked up by a Maltese fishing boat and shortly after that their rescue launch arrived.

The port side engine with the one remaining propeller.

THE DIVE The Beaufighter now lies upside down on a sandy seabed at 38m, which makes her an experienced diver's dive. As you descend you will be able to see what remains of the aircraft, the main fuselage, the wings and undercarriage. This is an excellent dive for the photographer as divers normally stay around the wreckage. Remember that good buoyancy is essential, even touching the sand away from the wreckage will create a cloud and it could drift towards and over the wreckage to the disappointment of the photographer and the other divers.

MALTA BOAT DIVING SITES

Good buoyancy is required on this special dive.

2. HMS *Hellespont*

This Robust-class deep sea paddle steamer tug was built by C & W Earls Shipbuilding & Engineering Co. Hull England and launched on the 10th May 1910. Having spent her first working years based at Haulbowline Dockyard, Queenstown, Ireland, she came to Malta in 1922 and for the next twenty years she worked in the seas around the Maltese Islands. On the night of the 6/7th April 1942 during an air raid she was sunk by German/Italian aircraft, later salvaged, then towed outside Grand Harbour and scuttled three miles off Riscasoli Breakwater lighthouse.

Three Robust-class paddle steamer tugs were built, one of which was the Hellespont.

THE DIVE *Hellespont* now lies on a sandy seabed in an upright position at a depth of 45m; the visibility is normally quite good. The metal fittings for the wooden paddles are still in place but the paddles are long gone. An interesting dive with lots to see and explore, including the engine room where the piston rods and boiler are still in place. There is plenty of natural light for photography. A stunning wreck which has remained remarkably intact.

3. HM Drifter *Eddy*

Built in Aberdeen, Scotland by Alexander Hall Engineering Co Ltd and launched on 6th August 1918. Her first attachment was to a squadron conducting mine clearing duties along the south coast of England at the end of WW1. After the war she was transferred to the Mediterranean fleet and based mostly in Malta.

HM Eddy *mine clearing along the south coast of England.*

At the outbreak of WW2 the *Eddy* was re-commissioned and joined the 403rd Minesweeping Group in Malta. She was armed with a small three pound gun and a Lewis gun. Fitted with an anti-magnetic cable around her side at water level due to the fact she had a metal hull. Her duties included sweeping the approaches to Malta's harbours, unfortunately the *Eddy* was not destined to survive the war.

On the 24th May 1942 she left Grand Harbour under cover of darkness to sweep for mines laid by the Italian E-boats. Whilst on her way back to port the following day at 16.40hrs she struck a mine and sank with a loss of eight crew members, the skipper and ten others survived.

The bow section of HM Drifter Eddy.   PHOTO: GAVIN ANDERSON

The aft section of HM Drifter Eddy *on the seabed, the damage caused by a mine can be seen.*

PHOTO: HUBERT BORG – SEA SHELL DIVE COVE DIVE CENTRE

THE DIVE HM Drifter *Eddy* now lies upright on a sandy seabed approximately 1.3km off St. Elmo Point, at a depth of 56m. There is a large hole on the starboard side which was caused by the mine. The main deck and superstructure has collapsed over the years. Beware there is a lot of sediment inside which will quickly reduce visibility, so do not penetrate this wreck.

4. HMS *St. Angelo*

An auxiliary British tug built by Scott Bowling, originally named HMS *Egmont*, not quite sure when she arrived in Malta. The *St. Angelo*'s duties included serving as harbour transport for the Royal Navy Officers carrying personnel from Fort St Angelo to other destinations. During the war she undertook sea rescue duties and later on as a minesweeper.

The bow section of the St Angelo *at 55m.*

PHOTO: DMITRY VINOGRADOV

THE DIVE She was sunk on the 30th May 1942 and now lies upright on a seabed of boulders and sand at a depth of 55m. First, permission must be obtained from the Harbour Master before diving this wreck, due to the close proximity of the entrance to Grand Harbour and the shipping lanes. HMS Angelo was one of four mine sweepers sunk in this area during May and June 1942.

An unusual photograph on HMS St. Angelo.

PHOTO: DMITRY VINOGRADOV

5. Schnellboot *S-31* (E-boat)

Built by Lurssen at Vegesack Beckedorf Germany launched in October 1939 the *S-31* had three Daimler Benz diesel engines, three propellers, a maximum speed of 38 knots and a range of 800 sea miles. An armament of two torpedo tubes, 2 x 20mm guns and a crew of 24 men. The Luftwaffe received information that HMS *Welshman* was making a solo run from Alexandria to Malta. During the late evening of the 9th May 1942 the German 3rd MTB Flotilla of seven boats left Augusta, Sicily at 22.00hrs to intercept the mine layer HMS *Welshman*.

By 0414hrs the following morning the MTB's were laying mines in Maltese waters; afterwards they

The Schellboot S-31 E-boat, the main part of the hull.

PHOTO: CATHY DE LARA

The stern is open, the rudders and the steering gear can clearly be seen.   PHOTO: CATHY DE LARA

regrouped to search for the British warship. Suddenly the S-31 exploded, probably due to hitting one of her own mines which had cut loose from the mooring ring causing it to rise to the surface and drift into its path. She quickly sank and half the crew lost their lives. HMS *Welshman* supported the island of Malta during the long siege in WW2.

The island population resisted strongly and was collectively awarded the highest decoration for civilian bravery. *Welshman* brought food and essential supplies many times; her role was featured in the UK movie *The Malta Story*.

The torpedo inside its launching tube of the Schnellboot S-31.   PHOTO: DMITRY VINOGRADOV

THE DIVE She now lays approximately one mile from Grand Harbour entrance with a maximum depth of 73m fully intact with torpedoes in the tubes ready for launch. Good Trimix dive.

6. HMS *Southwold*

HMS *Southwold* was a Hunts-class Destroyer, built in Cowes in 1941 by J.S. White, the Royal Navy had 86 in the fleet. With a tonnage of 1050, 86 metres in length and a beam of 9.5 metres and a top speed of 25 knots. She had a crew of 168 and an armament of 3 x 2 barrel 4 inch guns, a number of anti-aircraft guns and submarine depth charges.

After completing her trials she started service as a convoy escort round the Cape to Mombassa. She was

HMS Southwold – a Hunts-class destroyer.
PHOTO: ROYAL NAVAL MUSEUM PORTSMOUTH

The stern gun turret is covered in hard and soft corals, the guns can easily be seen.   PHOTO: CATHY DE LARA

There are portholes still on this wreck.   PHOTO: CATHY DE LARA

MALTA BOAT DIVING SITES

The gun turret makes a good photograph opportunity
PHOTO: GAVIN ANDERSON

The bows of the HMS Southwold. PHOTO: GAVIN ANDERSON

then sent to the Mediterranean to join the 5th Destroyer Flotilla escorting convoys between Alexandria, Tobruk and Malta. In these waters the British were heavily outnumbered by the Italian cruisers and destroyers and on March 22nd 1942 the Italians attacked the convoy MW10. The British laid a smoke screen to prevent the Italians from taking proper range.

They began to dash in and out of the smoke screen firing damaging salvoes at their superior opponents and then doubling up behind the smoke before the Italians could take range. The engagement was broken off that morning, but the Italian fleet approached again in the afternoon. The British ships emerging out of the smoke screen succeeded in hitting the Italian battleship *Littorio*. The Italians responded and the British cruiser *Cleopatra* was hit and was severely damaged, a quick counter attack by the British destroyers including the *Southwold*.

Emerging swiftly out of the smoke blanket they hit *Littorio* again by torpedo and also managed to hit the cruiser *Giovanni delle Bande Nere*. The Italians withdrew, this was recorded for history as the Second Battle of Sirte. The Luftwaffe took over the attacks as they were determined to prevent the convoy from reaching Malta. On the 23rd March 1942 another merchant ship, the *Breconshire*, was hit a few miles off Delimara Point, the weather was deteriorating and she started to drift helplessly towards the shore. The crew on the *Breconshire* managed to anchor the ship 1.5 miles off Zonqor Point.

The next day *Breconshire* was dragging its anchors on the sandy bottom, *Southwold* was ordered to tow her but while trying to pass a line to the disabled ship a floating mine exploded under her engine room. One officer and four ratings lost their lives, she was taken in tow but the damage was so severe she sank.

THE DIVE HMS *Southwold* lies approximately 1.5 miles off Marsascala Bay on a sandy seabed in two sections, the bow is the largest and the stern lies some 300 metres away. The depth varies from 65 to 75m. Good dive planning and safety cover is required for this extended range or tri-mix dive.

Two divers approach the bows of HMS Southwold *lying on her starboard side at a depth of 70m.*
PHOTO: DMITRY VINOGRADOV

Out of order!! PHOTO: CATHY DE LARA

7. Le *Polynesien*

Le *Polynesien* was built for 'The Company of Maritime Freight' in Cirtat, France and launched on the 18th April 1890. She was 152 metres in length with a gross tonnage of 6659, with a maximum speed of 17.5 knots.

This ship was designed to carry 252 passengers and easily recognised by her two black funnels. She began service in 1891 and operated between France and Australia. In 1914 she worked as a troop ship. In the early hours of the 10th August 1918 she was part of a convoy approaching Malta, at 10-30 am she was torpedoed by *UC22*. It took only thirty five minutes for the vessel to sink with a loss of ten lives.

Le Polynesian *of Messageries Maritimes carrying troops in 1914.*

THE DIVE Nick-named the 'plate ship' due to the number of artefacts still aboard, she lies on a sandy seabed almost intact, with depths ranging from 53 to 70m. The wreck is found listed on the port side at an angle of 45° the upper starboard side is the shallowest part of the dive there are two deck guns which can be found, one at the bow and one at the stern. The engine room is quite severely damaged which took the direct hit of the torpedo. Often there are strong currents over this wreck so proper planning and safety cover is required for this extended range or tri-mix dive.

This gun on the forward deck is covered by a rainbow of small fish. PHOTO: CATHY DE LARA

The bows of the Le Polynesian. PHOTO: GAVIN ANDERSON

BELOW: *A diver hovers over the severely damaged engine room.*

A diver descends the shot line to Le Polynesian.
PHOTO: GAVIN ANDERSON

The upper structure of Le Polynesian. PHOTO: CATHY DE LARA

8. Bristol Blenheim

At least nine Blenheim squadrons operated out of Malta during 1941-42. The Bristol Blenheim mark 1V, serial No.Z7858 (code M) started service on the 30th August 1941, allocated to 18 Squadron the following month and in October it was flown to the Middle East. On 13th December 1941 five Blenheims from 18 Squadron took off from Luqa airport. One of them was

Going down the shot line divers get their first sighting of this WW2 bomber. PHOTO: SHARON FORDER

A view from the front of the Blenheim bomber as she is today.

the Z7858 with pilot Frank Jury, D.J. Mortimer air gunner and Tom Black navigator. During their flight to their target they were attacked by a Macchi C200s. Air gunner Sgt Dennis Mortimer was helpless to react as the mid-upper turret with its twin .303 Browning machine guns had jammed.

The bombers port engine was also hit causing the propeller to spin off. The Blenheim was left with smoke pouring from the destroyed engine and only about 30 metres above sea level; she continued towards Grand Harbour, then turned and headed south. When a Maltese fishing boat was spotted just off shore, it was decided to ditch nearby. The Blenheim touched down tail first, despite its battering she remained intact and floated allowing the crew to escape, all three were quickly rescued.

A Royal Air Force Sea Rescue launch went to the crash site. In his book *Call-out* Frederick Galea reveals that a launch arrived to find the aircraft still afloat, they attempted to tow it but before this could be achieved, Z7858 sank. The other four aircraft returned safely to Malta.

A diver enjoys the photographic opportunity this plane allows.

A diver in front of the port side engine.

THE DIVE This Blenheim bomber now lies on a sandy seabed surrounded by small reefs at a depth of 42m, less than a kilometre off Xrobb-il Ghagin on the Delimara peninsular in the south of Malta. It is now a highly rated dive and this WW2 aircraft lives up to its reputation. The wings and engines are upright and mostly intact, although the propeller is missing off the portside engine and some of the rear fuselage lays a few metres in front of the wreckage. Very popular with diving photographers, most position their buddies over the starboard side engine. A number of pieces are missing from the aircraft, almost certainly down to early amateur salvage attempts. Only the depth and difficulty in finding this aircraft has stopped further destruction to the Blenheim, so please take care, do not touch and leave it as it is for others to admire.

9. Filfla Island

Filfla is a small un-inhabited island about 3km south of Ghar Lapsi once used for target practice by the Armed Forces of Malta; it is now a protected nature reserve. This island was made famous as the opening backdrop for the film *The Count of Monte Cristo*. A special permit is required to visit or dive this area and is issued by the Malta Maritime Authorities.

THE DIVE In the immediate area close to the island the depths are up to 10m, further away there are drop offs and areas of large boulders to explore, depths vary between 25 and 40m. To the south of the island is Stork rock which is 6m below the surface, here the seabed then drops away to 60m plus. You have a good chance of seeing large shoals of barracuda large groupers and morays. A word of warning; do not touch the shell rockets or bombs which litter the seabed – they could still be live and dangerous! This off-shore island is seldom dived and if you wish to do so then pre-plan with your dive centre well in advance.

10. Ras ir-Raheb

This headland is almost the most westerly point in Malta and is just a part of the magnificent cliffs some as high as 300 feet which dominate this west coast of Malta.

The sheer cliffs which are on this coast line of Malta.
BELOW: *The yacht* De Water Joffer *on the sand at 32m.*

The Island of Filfla once used for target practice by the Armed Forces is now a nature reserve.   PHOTO : JOE ABDILLA

THE DIVE This is a wall dive with caves at varying depths, at 32m on the sand next to the wall is the wreck of the *De Water Joffer*. Not a lot is known about this wreck, there is a hole on the aft starboard side. She is believed to be Dutch.

The yacht is just part of this dive but good for a photo shoot.

11. Scotscraig

This wreck is located at Ic-Cuumnija, 500 metres north of Anchor Bay on the west coast of Malta. The *Scotscraig* started its life as a passenger/car ferry operating on the river Thames; although relatively small she could carry up to six cars as well as passengers. During the filming of *Popeye* the movie, *Scotscraig* was used as Popeye's boat. After the completion of the film she helped in the construction of the Anchor Bay jetty, she was scuttled in such a way as to be used as a breakwater.

The Scotscraig *barge in Anchor Bay.*
BELOW: *The* Scotscraig *begins to sink before reaching deep water.* PHOTOS: WITH THE KIND PERMISSION OF WILFRED PIROTTA

THE DIVE The *Scotscraig* was being towed out to be scuttled in deep water, but on the way she sunk. Now she sits upright on a sandy seabed at a depth of 21m almost totally intact. During this dive you will most probably see a number of eels, groupers and octopus and the occasional stingray or tun shell on the sand.

The Scotscraig *is an interesting dive with many areas to explore above and below the main deck.*

A diver explores the wreck of the Scotscraig *which lies on a seabed of sea grass, small shingle and sand at 20m.*

MALTA BOAT DIVING SITES

A diver looks for conger and moray below the hull of the Scotscraig.

12. Qammieh Point

Qammieh Point is at the western end of Marfa Ridge, it is the last of the high ground on the north end of Malta. The views towards Gozo and Comino are quite breathtaking.

Many areas to explore created by large boulders on top of each other.

THE DIVE This boat dive is on a reef which runs out in a westerly direction for almost 900 metres from Qammieh Point. On both sides the reef drops away almost vertically to 50m, moving away from the reef the depth quickly increases to 100m plus. Closer in and on the reef, especially on the north side are many large boulders at shallower depths with hiding places underneath their edges where one might encounter octopus or large scorpion fish resting on the seabed.

13. HMS *Stubborn*

HMS *Stubborn* was a 1940 S-Class British submarine launched in November 1942 and commissioned in January 1943. A displacement of 990 tons, length 70 metres with a beam of 7 metres and a crew of 48. Fuel capacity of 92 tons gave her a range of 6,000 miles, with a speed of almost 15 knots on the surface and 9 knots below. She had an armament of 6 forward torpedo tubes and one rear tube, a 3 inch gun and a 20mm Oerlikon gun.

HMS Stubborn *leaving harbour.*

PHOTO: RN SUBMARINE MUSEUM GOSPORT

During the early part of 1943 she operated out of Lerwick on the Shetland Islands, patrolling the Norwegian Sea. During the summer she headed south patrolling around the Scilly Isles. In September of that year she was back in the Norwegian Sea, during her operations she was involved in towing and supporting the X craft which attacked the battleship *Tirpits*.

Above the conning tower.

In the late evening of 11th February 1944 HMS *Stubborn* sighted an enemy convoy of 7 ships, she attacked firing, 6 torpedoes and two hits were claimed; then 34 depth charges were dropped by the enemy before she left the area. HMS *Stubborn* returned the next day and sighted another enemy convoy of 5 ships; she attacked firing 6 torpedoes with two hits claimed. They retaliated by dropping 36 depth charges and HMS *Stubborn* was damaged, she broke the surface, then blowing all her main ballast, she sunk to 500 feet.

She really did have a guardian angel watching over her, for a further 16 depth charges were dropped while she was on the seabed. They decided to wait until darkness before attempting to surface, after many unsuccessful attempts she was able to surface. During the next seven days which it took HMS *Stubborn* to reach Lerwick she was escorted by 4 destroyers, a Norwegian Patrol boat and an air escort of Beaufighters, sometimes being towed and sometimes under her own power she made it.

After a refit in Devonport she returned to Holylock and on the 18th March 1945 she left for Freemantle Australia, via Gibraltar, Malta, Port Said, Suez, Aden, Ceylon and arriving in Freemantle on the 1st June 1945, she then saw action in the Pacific.

HMS *Stubborn* recorded the deepest dive made during the war by a British submarine, reaching 540 feet. She endured one of the worst attacks of the war and suffered the loss of her complete tail fin which held the aft hydroplanes and rudder. This loss was caused by depth charges, but principally from hitting the seabed at 540 feet. During the return voyage from Australia it became evident that the hull aft had suffered more distortion than was originally thought.

Stubborn was one of the few British submarines that had art work painted on her conning tower during the war, it was a mules head. She was sunk on the 30th April 1946, as an Asdic target two miles off Qawra Point on the north coast of Malta.

The bow of HMS Stubborn *showing her three portside torpedo tubes.*   PHOTO: GAVIN ANDERSON
BELOW: *HMS* Stubborn *which lies at a depth of 57m.*   PHOTO: JP BRESSER – DIVE DEEP BLUE

The rear section of HMS Stubborn.

THE DIVE This excellent boat dive to a depth of 57m is for experienced divers only. Descending the shot line through the crystal blue waters and when the Stubborn comes into view you will see that she sits almost upright on a sandy seabed. This wreck is remarkably well preserved with its conning tower, torpedo tubes and propellers, there are two open hatches, but please do not enter. For the photographer, even at this depth, normally the visibility will allow you to take some decent shots.

14. MV *Pippo*

Built in Vella boat yard Marsa in 1975. The hull was planned to be carbon fibre, but ended up being concrete. The boat was completed by A & P Formosa and launched the following year. She was used for surveys and as a cruise boat until sold to Azzopardi Fisheries. During a voyage from Comino to Malta she started taking on water and sank east of Mellieha Bay in October 2004.

MALTA BOAT DIVING SITES

Exploring the bow. PHOTO: HUBERT BORG – SEA SHELL DIVE COVE

THE DIVE MV *Pippo* sits upright on a sandy seabed at 35m. Beware of the ropes floating above the deck, they were used for an unsuccessful attempt to lift the boat, only a compressor and the propeller were salvaged. She is not large enough for penetration but looking around lots of artefacts have been left on board, you can see through the hatch on the deck two of the three engines. Marine life is quite good, with silver bream, damsel fish, crabs, shrimps, nudibranchs and is home for a large grouper who is normally by the rudder.

15. The *Imperial Eagle*

Built in 1938 by J. Crown and Sons Ltd Shipbuilders in Sunderland England, weighing 257 gross tonnes with an length of 45 metres. Named *New Royal Lady*, she was requisitioned by the Royal Navy for transport duties, attached to the U.S. Navy, and then transferred to port defense duties. In 1947 she was sold to John Hall, Kirkcaldy for service on the Firth of Forth and re-named *Royal Lady*.

Later in 1947 she was sold on to General Steam Navigation Co. Ltd. London for Thames dock cruises and

The Imperial Eagle *moored alongside Marfa Quay, Malta.*
PHOTO: BY KIND PERMISSION OF ALEX DUNCAN – ISLE OF WIGHT

re-named *Crested Eagle*. In 1957 she was purchased by Magro Bros. Malta, and after modification to carry 70 passengers and 10 cars, she was re-named *Imperial Eagle* and carried out this service between Mgarr Harbour in Gozo and Marfa Harbour in Malta until the mid-1970's after which time she was used for storage.

The Crested Eagle *moored close to the Tower of London, she was later re-named the* Imperial Eagle.

THE DIVE She was scuttled some 500 metres off Qawra Point on the 19th July 1999 and has come to rest in an upright position at an approximate depth of 38m. An ideal extended range dive with an added extra in the Statue of Christ, a short distance away.

The bows of the Imperial Eagle *which now lies at a depth of 38m.*

MALTA BOAT DIVING SITES

After being re-floated and made environmentally safe the Imperial Eagle was towed out of Grand Harbour during the morning of the 19th July 1999. PHOTO: CHARLIE SCICLUNA

Pope John Paul observes the lowering of the Statue of Christ off St Pauls Island in May 1990. Later moved to a new site off Qawra Pont. PHOTO: WITH KIND PERMISSION OF WILFRED PIROTTA

On the bridge of the Imperial Eagle *still in its original place, the ships wheel.* PHOTO: ALEXANDER ARISTARKHOV

A diver explores what remains of the upper deck of the Imperial Eagle, *which lies within the area of Malta's first marine park.* PHOTO: JONATHAN THOMAS – DIVE DEEP BLUE

The Statue of Christ now near the Imperial Eagle *off Qawra Point.* PHOTO: CATHY DE LARA

Diver above the forward deck of the Imperial Eagle.

ATLAM sub aqua club
MALTA — Established 1955
60TH ANNIVERSARY 1955-2015

Atlam SAC's claim to fame is that it is the oldest diving club in Malta – date of birth: 31st March 1955, but not only...at that time known as the Malta Sub-Aqua Club, it was one of the founder members of the Confederation Mondiale des Activites Subaquatiques – when it was set up in 1959. The CMAS is currently one of the foremost diving authorities in the world.

Tul il-Kosta, Baħar Iċ-Ċagħaq
Naxxar NXR 9038, Malta
email: info@atlam.org
web: www.atlam.org

The change of name from the Malta Sub-Aqua Club to Atlam Sub-Aqua Club – came about following an unexpected bit of local legislation in 1978, where the word Malta was forbidden for use in the name of Associations. The then committee decided to reverse the word Malta to read Atlam – subsequently, even though this legislation was dropped, due to Atlam SAC's popularity, the decision was taken to keep the name, so Atlam it remains to this day!

Being an Atlam member means that every weekend for the greater part of the year one can join a Club boat dive, which opens up access to the remotest and most undived parts of the Maltese Islands. Many of the Atlam divers have learned the ropes within the club, which provides instruction according to the CMAS syllabus. Nitrox and Advanced Nitrox courses are also catered for.

Atlam SAC also organises social events, like barbecues and family boat trips. Photographic competitions are also held regularly. Camaraderie is given a lot of weight in this club. New members and visitors are really made welcome! The members meet Thursday evenings at the new Atlam clubhouse - a seafront premises located at Bahar ic-Caghaq. Atlam designed and had this building purpose made to accomodate and promote diving and related activities. It is complete with conference and lecture facilities equipped with the latest state of the art equipment – there is also, of course, a well stocked bar area!

Atlam issue 'Bubbles' - a bi-monthly e-magazine which may be seen at - https://issuu.com/bubbles_atlam/docs. Available free of charge, anyone interested in being put on the mailing list to keep receiving Bubbles, only has to provide an e-mail address to info@atlam.org or at https://www.facebook.com/groups/132565648913/.

Atlam SAC's 50th Anniversary memorial, placed as a landmark en route to the Um el Faroud wreck at Wied iz-Zurrieq.

The Atlam club premises at Bahar ic-Caghaq seafront.

Sunday morning boat dive.

Gozo Boat Diving Sites

Around the shores of Gozo there are many hundreds of boat dives to list them all would almost be impossible, I have chosen a few of the most popular ones, bearing in mind that some of these dives can be done from the shore. Gozo has so much to offer the scuba diver with dramatic reefs, never ending drop-offs, caves of all sizes, arches, tunnels, blue holes, windows and wrecks all with marine life to match, the diving is just brilliant.

1. Fessej Rock

The pinnacle of Fesse Rock with a dive boat moored off the south coat of Gozo.

This rock is situated some 400 metres outside the entrance to Mgarr ix Xini on the south coast of Gozo. The column of rock rises almost 15 metres out of the sea; below the surface the vertical sides plunge impressively down to almost 50m, where the base is surrounded by large boulders sitting on a sandy seabed. The vertical sides of the column are littered with holes and small fissures, these areas are covered in soft and hard corals and many tube worms.

Fire worms, starfish, coloured nudibranch and of course octopuses are just some of the marine life which have made this reef their home. Looking out into the blue on the southwest side you may see passing shoals of barracuda, dentex and amberjacks.

Is it slight narcosis? No he is absailing!

The dive boat leaves Mgarr Harbour behind heading for one of the many dive sites around the island.

Moving carefully around the algae covered boulders you may spot one of the large groupers that roam this area. On the inside of this rock the shoals of salema fish are easy to recognise, with their blue and gold stripes, passing from one part of the reef to another feeding as they go. Fesse Rock has so much to offer all grades of diver who can control their buoyancy, and for those who do not dive there is always snorkelling.

Fesse Rock has sheer drop offs on all sides to the seabed to 50m plus.

2. Dawra Tas-Sanap and Cave

Tompot blenny (Parablennius gattorugine) distinctive by its horns. PHOTO: IAN FORDER

This dive site is the first sheltered inlet to the southeast of Xlendi Bay and has an underwater landscape to please all divers. A shallow reef, drop offs, massive boulders, an arch, most of the time dentex and groupers roam this area. If all is calm the boat will anchor on the shallow reef which has an average depth of 8m.

There is a deep cave and a natural arch in the surrounding cliffs, which has been created by the sea over thousands of years. There is a massive semi-circular cavern at the base of the archway, below this area there are many large boulders, to both sides and above, the walls are vertical. After you have reached your maximum depth (45m) return to 15m and enjoy the wonderful sight of the big arch in the sunlight and the large shoals of salema fish moving across the reef. Now you can return to the shallow reef for your safety stops and the boat. This is a great dive with much to explore.

A diver explores one of the many hundreds of caves around the coastline of the island of Gozo.

3. Ulysses Cave

Located just over 1km west of Xlendi Bay this is a huge cavern which has been carved by the sea out of the giant vertical cliffs. Just below the surface the walls are covered with a brilliant green algae interspersed with areas of hard and soft brightly coloured corals. Resting on the ledges will be many red scorpionfish and in the fissures, lobsters, small morays and the roaming fire worms always looking for their next meal. The rock formation here is quite spectacular and next to the large opening is a smaller cave with room for two divers.

Large boulders create an underwater landscape with safe havens for marine life. PHOTO: MAX VALLI – ORANGE SHARK H2O

You can surface within this unique cave with its fresh water spring which is mixed with the sea water creating a misty blue halocline. It is an excellent place for a night dive when there is a whole host of marine life to be discovered in the beam of your torch. The maximum depth here is 45m.

A paradise of interesting subjects for you to photograph.

4. Fungus Rock – Dwejra

This large limestone rock dominates Dwejra Bay, originally named 'The Generals Rock' famous for the rare shrub like fungus known as general's root, whose red juice was treasured for its medicinal properties. Used by the Knights of St John against dysentery, bleeding, impotence and other healing properties. The bay behind Fungus Rock is often used by yachts for stop-overs whilst travelling around the islands. The 'Qawra Tower' which overlooks the bay is occasionally open for visiting tourists.

Shrimps (Lysmata seticaudata) can be found in fissures on rock faces. PHOTO: JOE FORMOSA

To view Fungus Rock is only a short walk from Dwejra.

Below the surface this fascinating rock wall drops vertically to a depth of 45m where you will find the area covered in large boulders, these provide excellent habitat for large groupers. From the north-eastern corner of the rock as you begin your slow ascent you will find that the underwater features become more interesting, as ledges and gullies present themselves for closer inspection.

You will find the walls are covered with yellow, golden and red corals and among the marine life that have made this reef their home are tube worms, starfish, fire worms and nudibranch and in the larger overhangs many cardinal fish.

The moray (Muraena Helena) this one has a cleaning shrimp who obviously is not afraid to clean the inside of this predators mouth PHOTO: IAN FORDER

Spiny lobster (Palinurus elephas) in his hideaway. PHOTO: VICTOR FABRI

BELOW: *Posing for a photo is a common occurrence in these crystal clear waters.*

The Lamp of San Dimitri - a legend

The legend of San Dimitri Point is that there was an old widow who lived with her son near to the chapel of San Dimitri. When Turkish invaders came and captured her son, taking him away to become a slave, she ran to the chapel praying to San Dimitri to return her son to her. The painting in the chapel came alive, and San Dimitri on his white horse rode out of the picture to follow the Turkish ships, rescuing the boy and returning him to his mother. Then San Dimitri vanished back into the painting. As a thanksgiving the mother and son promised to light an oil lamp under the painting every day until they died. However one day a big tremor shook the surrounding cliff side; the earth subsided and the chapel sunk to the bottom of the sea. The area has a reputation for abundant fish life, because they are attracted to the lamp of San Dimitri, which still shines to this very day!
Research for this legend kindly carried out by Marthese Matusiak.

ABOVE: *The chapel at San Dimitri Point.*
LEFT: *The picture of San Dimitri above the altar inside the chapel.*

RIGHT: *San Dimitri on his white horse as told in the legend.*

5. San Dimitri Point

San Dimitri Point is the most westerly point of Gozo; here the impressive cliffs rise out of the shimmering blue waters to a height of 80 metres. While admiring the beauty of this area you will realise that the boat is your only exit. Below where the boat will anchor is a shallow plateau with an average depth of 6m, great area for safety stops if required.

Barracuda (Sphyraena sphyraene) which can be seen all year round off this headland.

The first part of the drop off is more of a steep slope leading down to house sized boulders with vertical walls; here you might spot groupers resting on the algae covered ledges. Put these underwater landscapes together with excellent visibility, large shoals of barracuda and truly spectacular fish such as dentex and tuna passing by in the blue makes this a fantastic dive.

The excellent visibility found at this site.

6. Hekka Point

This dive starts from a brilliantly coloured cavern which is completely submerged, the top of which is just below the surface and its stony base at 15m. Out of the cavern follow a steep wall to the right which leads to a massive completely submerged cave full of pristine corals, this is by far the highlight of the dive and worth spending time to explore, you have an excellent possibility of finding seahorses. The view to the outside blue of the ocean is breathtaking and a chance to see the big fish such as dentex tuna, and shoals of barracuda passing by.

Billinghurst Cave/Tunnel entry point now has hand rails. During the summer season there is usually an exit ladder here.

Inside Billinghurst Cave - always take an experienced guide.
PHOTO: J.P. BRESSER – DEEP BLUE DIVE CENTRE

Caves entrances make a great opportunity for a silhouetted photo.

7. Billinghurst Cave

This dive is often done from the shore with the entry point by the side of the cave entrance and if there is no ladder your exit will be Reqqa Point. In my opinion if you are not familiar with this cave you should seek a professional dive guide from your dive centre. This spectacular cave is situated on the north coast of Gozo not far from Reqqa Point. The cave/tunnel entrance is approximately 30 metres wide and 20 metres high and faces due north with very little light penetration, after about 30 metres in you will begin to lose all natural light.

Approximately 60 meters into the cave over a bottom of fine sand and shingle, several loose boulders form an upward slope leading to a massive cavern where you will be able to surface; the ceiling of this cavern is about 5 metres above the water level. The sight of the blue open water with the sun shining through from the outer reef on the way out of this cavern is very impressive.

It was in 1984 a group of divers from St Andrews University SAC were exploring what they called Booming Cave and the Railway Tunnel, when they reached the cavern they found a plastic bag containing a soggy book, which read: 'We are Billinghurst SAC and we have invited others to sign the book and leave a message'. It was around this time it became known as Billinghurst Cave. After a number of dive trips to Gozo, St Andrews discovered the bag and book were missing, so it was duly replaced. If cave diving is your thing, then Gozo is the place, for there are many to suit all tastes, but possibly Billinghurst is the icing on the cake.

8. Double Arch

For the experienced diver this world renowned unique Double Arch is a must. Located not far from Marsalforn on the north coast of Gozo with its two arches leading to a flat table top reef at 17m and surrounded by drop offs to depths ranging from 28 to 45m. This dive is listed as a shore dive but of course some of you would much prefer to do it by boat, either way it is a fantastic dive.

This could be the top arch of the two, at this dive site.
PHOTO: MAX VALLI – ORANGE SHARK H2O

The Double Arch from 38m plus. PHOTO: JOE FORMOSA

9. Calypso Tunnel/Cave

Just a short distance to the west, from the seaside resort of Marsalforn, is the lovely Xwejni Bay. The landmark here is the large lump of sandstone which has been shaped over the years by the wind and sea. The reef wall where the dive site is located is a continuation of the same wall at the Double Arch and lies some 100 metres off the reef below the sandstone landmark. On the face of this vertical wall there are two narrow horizontal cracks at 21m, below at 35m is a spectacular arch.

Divers can easily pass through all these openings into a semi cave area; this is due to two very large holes in the roof, and looking back these resemble a face. This is a very impressive and interesting dive with a maximum depth of 35m. You can of course shore dive this site if sea conditions are very good, but in my opinion the boat is the best option.

The divers are leaving Calypso Cave via the mouth; the eyes are in the top of the photo.

BELOW: *Posing for a photo in the mouth area of Calypso Cave.*

Comino Boat Diving Sites

1. Lantern Point

Lantern Point, sometimes called Lighthouse Point, or in Maltese, Ras L-Irqieqa, is probably the most popular dive on Comino, and with good reason.

Lantern Point, Comino where the dive boat will moor.

The underwater topography here is simply stunning, and includes tunnels, caves and swim-throughs, a sheer wall, massive boulders, and a maximum depth of 50m, ideally take a torch. The boat will usually anchor to the south of the point, quite close to the Lantern which gives the point its name. Below the boat is a large, flatish plateau with an average depth of 8m, just the place to end your dive and safety stops There can be unpredictable currents here, so maybe the dive plan will have to be altered.

Divers ascending from the chimney to the plateau on the south side of Lantern Point.

The chimney is often the start of the dive, close to the Lantern at a depth of 4m the entrance is large enough for divers to enter one at a time and exits at 18m and is relatively straight. Your torch will illuminate the corals, fans and sponges which decorate the walls. On exiting the tunnel you will find yourself in a gully leading down to 25m, with the sheer wall of the headland to your right.

Above the reef and below the boat.

Continue straight ahead towards a huge boulder known as "The Mushroom" at 28m. It is possible to swim under this massive rock using a series of swim-throughs for a complete circuit of the central pillar that gives the boulder its name. Take your time and light up your surroundings for an array of beautiful sponges, corals, fans, and occasionally lobsters or huge urchins.

Almost at the exit of the chimney at 18m.

Leave the Mushroom on the south side heading for the plateau reef wall, which would now be on your left, depth 25m, to your right large boulders, sandy areas sloping away to 50m.

Look out for large groupers resting on the rocks, continue down to 35m where there is a U shaped cave near the headland. On reaching the headland ascend to the top of the reef at 20m, look out in the blue for a chance to see larger fish such as dentex and amberjacks. Follow the reef with the drop off on the left, keeping your depth at 18m, once you reach the gulley at the start of the wall you can either, return through the chimney to the plateau or ascend the reef wall. Once on the plateau take your time to explore this area, you will normally find octopus and other marine life, also you will see bubbles being released from the chimney through the porous limestone rock forming a curtain, which is good for an unusual photograph.

2. Lantern Point West

Also known as Inner Lantern Point, this site is on the opposite side of the thin peninsula of rock from Lantern Point. Depths here range from 30m to less than 5m, and it is suitable for all levels of diver. The underwater landscape is almost as beautiful as Lantern Point: here you have a sheer wall, a shallow cave, and lots and lots of large boulders lying against each other, giving several swim-throughs. In fact the more you dive this site, the more swim-throughs you will discover,

The cliffs at Lantern Point west.

some obvious, some not so. If you can dive this site in the afternoon you will benefit from natural sunlight on the wall. You can start the dive anywhere along the wall that forms the coastline, or even around the headland of Lantern Point.

There are two large inlets which can be seen on the aerial photograph: these are interesting to explore when conditions are calm. The wall itself is covered in colourful growth, including sponges of all colours. Look out for octopus, comber and multi-coloured ornate and cuckoo wrasses. Beyond the boulders the seabed slopes down to a sandy area around 30m. On this side you will find some of the tallest boulders, their tops only 12m below the surface. Towards the end of your dive, swim

A red scorpion fish (Scorpaena scrofa). PHOTO:JOE FORMOSA

with the wall on your right until you reach a little plateau 6m deep. Here an overhang starts to form above the surface, and within the plateau you will find two large well shaped holes carved out of the limestone by wave action over the centuries. You can see the rounded stones responsible lying at the bottom of the holes.

Moving further on you will reach a shallow cave on your right, with an entrance at 5m. Within the cave there is an air space above you, and it is possible to continue along the wall in a U-shape until you exit at only 2m deep. Before you go too far, look behind you at the cave entrance and the overhanging rock framing a dazzling blue window. A great photo opportunity.

The top of the drop off at Lantern Point.

3. Crystal Lagoon

This shallow, popular dive site is suitable for all levels of diver with depths ranging from 5m to 16m, and is just a short distance from the famous Blue Lagoon.

Crystal Lagoon with its jetty and entrance to the tunnel.

It features a long, well-lit tunnel as well as a mixture of sea grass, boulders and dazzling sandy patches; this area is a nursery for young fish and is great for photography. Just past the tunnel in this little cove is a jetty where your boat will moor allowing non-divers to go ashore. The tunnel is large enough for small boats to pass through, so please be careful where and when you ascend. Usually the dive starts at the entrance of the tunnel, depth 5m. The tunnel is reasonably wide, with vertical walls, and a seabed of rocks and gravel, it is a good place to find beautiful nudibranchs. Once you exit the tunnel at 8m, turn right where you can explore a false tunnel.

A diver has obviously spotted something of interest.

Snakelocks Anemone (Anemonia viridis) has around 170 tentacles.   PHOTO: JOE FORMOSA

Continuing to your right you will see a rocky overhang, which gives the appearance of a rhino's head; the ceiling is covered in marine growth and often attracts nudibranchs this is also an excellent location to find large groupers.

Here there is a pinnacle which rises up above the waves, it is known as Mushroom Rock, it is over 10m tall. Explore the base where you may find lobster, octopus, cuttlefish, reef fish, trigger fish and even barracuda. To return to the lagoon you can use the tunnel or go round the headland the seabed is made up of boulders, sea grass and sandy patches, 10m, this is the octopus's garden... check out their empties (shellfish they have eaten). Here usually are several flying gurnards picking their way across the sand. Try not to spook them and you may be rewarded with a wonderful display of their iridescent blue wings. Moving north into the lagoon itself you will find all sorts of juvenile fish and cuttlefish as well as items dropped from boats.

Exploring the boulders local marine life.

4. *P31* Patrol Boat

The Armed Forces of Malta Maritime Squadron decommissioned the *P31* Kondor-class offshore vessel in the latter months of 2004, ending her thirteen year chapter in Malta's history.

The P31 *Patrol Boat leaves Grand Harbour for an exercise.*
PHOTO: JOSEPH TONNA

The P31 *gently sinks slowly to her resting place.*
PHOTO: DAVID P. ATTARD, ARMED FORCES MALTA

Being made environmentally safe for her new surroundings, the *P31* patrol boat was scuttled as a diver attraction on the 24th August 2009 off the island of Comino. She now lies on the seabed, at 21m, with a slight list to the portside, surrounded by sand and areas of sea grass, midway between Lantern Point and the small island of Cominotto. Given time this wreck will be home for many fish and other marine life.

The *P31* began her life in former East Germany, she is a Kondor-class boat designed and built on the Peenewerft, Wolgast, East Germany in the 1960's. Like her sister ship the *P29*, she is 52 meters in length, with a width of 7 metres and weighs approximately 360 tons and was primarily a mine sweeper. In August 1992 the *P31* and the *P30* left Germany undertaking a three week long journey to Malta, seeing some of the worst seas in their lifetime. For two days they battled through force nine winds, climbing enormous waves and ploughing down into their troughs. After entering calmer seas off Dover their next port of call was Brest, home of the French Navy's Atlantic fleet.

Whilst crossing the Bay of Biscay they encountered thick fog, the *P31* developed a fault with her radar and the *P30* guided her along to the port of Vigo in Spain. After a further two days at sea they entered the Straits of Gibraltar and into the Mediterranean, finally the ships arrived in Malta where they were greeted by the crews' family, friends and the Armed Forces of Malta's top brass.

The last patrol by the *P31* was in September 2004, she was then sold to the Malta Tourism Authority to be scuttled as a diver attraction.

ABOVE: *The bow of the* P31 *Patrol Boat.*   PHOTO: SHARON FORDER
BELOW: *Divers over the bridge and chimney of the* P31.

The P31 *on active service patrolling around the coast of the Maltese Islands.*
PHOTO: ARMED FORCES MALTA

COMINO BOAT DIVING SITES

Divers enjoying the good visibility on this wreck.

THE DIVE After you have entered the water and before you descend, check out the wreck as sometimes it can be seen from the surface When I am below the bow I like to move away a little and look up at it, rising up towards to the surface some five metres high. You can also see that she has a slight list to port. With the *P31* being at a shallower depth than the *Rozi* or the *P29* patrol boat, only time will tell how much damage will be done by the sometimes severe winter storms. Maybe her only saving grace is that her bow faces in a westerly direction. She is protected from north and easterly storms by Comino and the north eastern coastline of Malta.

The diver has found a cuttlefish, who seems to be trying to take shelter beneath the upper structure of the P31.

Diver explores the inside of this wreck

PHOTO: MAX VALLI – ORANGE SHARK H2O

As you travel over the sand along the side of the *P31* check out the number, A126, for some people this may be a photo opportunity also keep an eye out for the marine life which has started to move towards this diver attraction, to use as a safe haven.

Moving on to the deck you will find a depth of approximately 16m, at this point you may wish to penetrate the wreck. Although light penetrates into many parts of the interior of the ship, for other areas you will need a torch This can be done through the bow deck hatch; doors in the main structure, and the two rear holds. On the port side, below where the mast was and just in front of the chimney, you can enter the wheel house and central area but you have to exit through the same door.

The port side and bridge of the P31 on the sand at 22m.

The *P31* was meticulously planned to the highest standards for divers, so the hazards are minimal if not non-existent. Safety is paramount feature so please remember your penetration procedures. Depending on your experience or at least for the first time you should take a dive guide or request his or her advice on this dive. Now you will probably begin to explore the main deck, bearing in mind the depth here is 16m.

The ship's chimney with its dolphin logo.

The stern is quite open, but as stated before there are two openings to the holds, a small one to the rear and a much larger one just behind the upper structure and chimney, check out the logo. Moving along the side the upper structure towards the bow, you will pass the chimney and the bridge, unfortunately the mast has been removed due to the fact that originally it was too close to the surface and could have been a hazard to shipping. At first it was laid along the top of the upper structure, during a storm it became unstable, so

The P31 stern - sadly the rudders are now buried in the sand.

A shoal of two-banded sea bream (Diplodus vulgaris).

for safety reasons it was totally removed.

For those who are qualified to dive the *P29*, the sister ship of the *P31*, they will see the ship's mast in place.

Entering the bow deck the first thing you will see something which looks like a round seat, this was the mounting for the 14.5mm AAMG anti-aircraft machine gun, in front of this is the forward hatch. The railings around the bow deck will possibly show the first signs of marine life making this their home. Moving up and on to the bridge, here the depth is approximately 12m; you can explore this area where many of the gauges and other instruments have been left in place. If you are not using a shot line you will need to deploy your delayed surface marker buoy.

Fish to be found here are saddle bream, parrot fish and hopefully dusky groupers if they return will be safer here than on the Rozi or the *P29*.

A diver heads for the surface leaving the P31 *below.*

5. Alex's Cave/Blue Lagoon

Alex's Cave is situated within the largest islet to the south of the Blue Lagoon it is a remarkable underwater cave, including a chamber with fresh air, suitable for all levels of diver.

Almost above the P31, ahead the islet where Alex's Cave is found.

The boat will normally moor near the pinnacle known as Mushroom Rock just at the easternmost point of the large islet; here there is a tunnel which has an average depth of 6m, which leads to the Lagoon where you can normally find nudibranchs and scorpion fish. There is a crack in the roof which gives a bright feel bringing out the colours of the corals and sponges. On leaving the tunnel at 8m you are directly in front of the Mushroom Rock, which has a reef at its base, with lots of hiding places for octopus, turn right and head towards the sandy seabed at 16m; to your right is a headland with a perfectly square notch cut out of it.

Follow the boundary between sand and reef heading west and behind a large boulder is the entrance of Alex's cave, which is very wide. You might hear and see small boats taking tourists a little way into the entrance 14m above you. The first leg of the cave is well lit due to a crack in the rock above, until you reach the left-hand bend where it becomes completely dark. Using your torch explore the side walls and ceiling of this wonderful underwater chamber. It is 20m long and about 4m high and wide and easy to navigate, as you can always see the light of the entrance.

This makes Alex's Cave a great first cave dive, the floor of the cave is fine sand, so good buoyancy control is a must. The walls and ceiling are inhabited by shrimp, both with and without claws, and there is also a resident conger eel called Alex. When you have reached a dead end, about 10m deep, slowly ascend to your right and you will find a chamber above sea-level with room enough for half a dozen divers at least. The air here is fresh, since there is a small crack through which you will see some sunlight. Descend again to the seabed, then I suggest that you turn off your torch and enjoy the intense blue arch which is the exit.

Like most dives around the Maltese Islands, good idea to take a torch if only to illuminate the beautiful colours.

Exploring Alex's Cave looking for a subject to photograph.
PHOTO: MAX VALLI – ORANGE SHARK H2O

BELOW: *Divers surface in Alex's cave for it has a crack in the roof*
PHOTO: MAX VALLI – ORANGE SHARK H2O

6. Anchor Reef, Cominotto

This dive site is located on the west side of the small island of Cominotto; the diving here is just as dramatic as on its big brother. Normally the boat would moor by the southern tip at Cominotto Corner, depth 10m.

This dive usually starts by the large V-shaped cut-out in the cliffs. To the southeast the cliffs drop away underwater giving a wall all the way to Cominotto Corner; depths are between 15m and 25m, with lots of interesting overhangs and ledges. Take a torch to explore two swim throughs and you will find lots of colourful marine growth, along with plenty of invertebrates such as tube worms, hermit crabs and octopus. For the more experienced divers there is a drop off for a deep and exciting wall dive, with depths up to 50m. In this area at 35m is a relic from Malta's maritime history a large WW2 anchor, completely encrusted in corals and sponges. There is boat traffic in the area, more so during the summer, so bring your DSMB just in case.

7. Santa Marija Reef

Located on the north side of Comino on the same headland where the Comino Caves are. Suitable for all grades of diver with a maximum depth of 22m, the boat will anchor in 10m. This dive site covers a large area with two main guide routes: your guide will select which route according to your group's qualifications. There are numerous gullies, caverns, swim-throughs and caves to explore. An excellent dive for the photographer as there are lots of opportunities for wide angle shots.

The large swim through to the north has a large colony of red anemones in its roof, schools of salema fish that feed on the algae, red mullet, saddle bream, painted combers and cuttlefish are just some of the marine life that have made this reef their home.

8. Comino/Santa Marija Caves

Almost the perfect dive? This dive site is situated on the rugged northeast coast of Comino. Its interconnecting caves/caverns and the fantastic feeling of close contact with the saddled bream in a feeding frenzy makes this a very popular dive with most divers.

The swim-through in the shape of a Z as if Zorro had carved it with his sword.   PHOTO: MAX VALLI – ORANGE SHARK H2O

Your dive boat will anchor in the little bay; from here you will be able to see some of the caves from the surface, below the boat the gentle undulating seabed is made up of sand, Posidonia (sea grass) and some small boulders, with a maximum depth of 16m. Once in the water and descending, the saddle bream will be there to greet you expecting to be fed; normally this happens at the end of the dive. When and if you feed them, start with one person and form a circle around them, once the fish have moved in to feed other divers will find it possible to feed them by hand.

Normally the dive will start at the entrance of the

A boat is moored to the left of the cave entrance and the area of sand where the saddle bream are waiting to be fed.

COMINO BOAT DIVING SITES

Inside the Santa Marija cave system.
PHOTO: MAX VALLI – ORANGE SHARK H2O

The exit of the Santa Marija cave.
PHOTO: MAX VALLI – ORANGE SHARK H2O

cave at 5m, which extends all the way through the headland; there are at least two routes through it. Once in the cave bear round to the right and you will see a small tunnel giving way to a wide open area with a brilliant azure blue exit beyond. Explore the right hand wall and on your exit from the cave look to your left; you will see a wonderful swim-through in the shape of a Z, almost as if Zorro carved it with his sword. This is a fantastic photo opportunity, as well as being possible to swim through.

Looking at the headland, which is quite an impressive sight, seems to be resting on three pillars of rock, with a large horizontal crevice filled with corals, sponges, tube worms and nudibranchs. On your return through the cave you may spot: a beautiful hole in the roof creating dancing sunbeams; if you ascend to the surface you may even surprise some tourists who have climbed down into the cave; now for the short tunnel giving you access to the west sandy cave. When you return to the area under the boat you will be able to feed the fish or, if you have a camera, take some exceptional photographs of the fish feeding and being almost unable to see your buddy due to the number of fish surrounding him.

I have been diving this site for almost thirty years and each time it still gives me a buzz. I do not normally feed the fish myself, but this practise has been carried out here for as long as I can remember. The photographic opportunity with the light blue of the sea, the hundreds of silver fish on a sandy seabed is too good to miss. Whether you feed the fish, take photographs or just watch this spectacular show I cannot see how you will not be impressed.

Mark Dove in the red bandanna returning from a dive. A big 'thank you' for your input on the Comino boat diving section within these pages

Mostly saddle bream on a feeding frenzy!

9. Elephant Rock

Sometimes referred to as Santa Marija Tunnel, situated on the north east coast of Comino and sheltered from any south westerly seas. This 30 meter long tunnel which runs through the headland is the highlight of the dive, once again do take a torch or you may be disappointed. Here the seabed is littered with boulders, sand and small areas of Posidonia (sea grass). Inside the tunnel the floor is partly covered in calcified seaweed, which looks like red rose petals, the walls are covered in red and yellow sponges. Look out for the red and black faced blennys.

10. Sultan Rock

The dive is located off the south east coast of Comino in the south Comino channel; this dive site has a maximum depth of 18m. Around this rock the seabed is littered with massive boulders, sand/shingle and areas of Posidonia (sea grass).

In March 1889 the ironclad battleship HMS *Sultan* with a gross weight of over 9,000 tons ran aground, this incident happened during torpedo practice. During the following years she was heavily salvaged and virtually no wreckage remains, although from time to time artefacts are found.

Comino / Blue Lagoon

Comino is the smallest of the three main islands, its total area is about 2.5 square km, not more than ten permanent residents including a priest and policeman.

For most of the year its rocky landscape is covered in wild flowers and thyme. The Blue Lagoon is excellent for swimming and also a wonderful sight. The hotel on the island is only open during the summer period, boat taxis run from both Gozo and Malta.

The small sandy beach across the Blue Lagoon on the little island of Cominotto.

The small jetty on Comino just in front of the refreshment bars.

The Blue Lagoon and Wignacourt Watchtower built around 1816.
PHOTO: BDR. ALFRED AZZOPARDI, AFM

Sunset.

Sunflower.

The Maltese Islands – It's not all about diving!
Sue Lemon

Chadwick Lakes.

Bougainvillea.

Oleander.

Hibiscus.

Three generations of Lemons!

Malta – Places to visit when you are not diving

Malta is 27 km long and, at its widest point is 14.5 km although towards the north of the island there is a place where both coastlines can be observed. The island's coastline is characterised in two different ways; most of the south and southwest is dominated by sheer cliffs rising from the sea. On the south east to the north coast, it is reasonably flat and in most areas the land gently runs down to the sea. It is on this coastline that the capital Valletta with its two harbours is situated, as well as most of the residential areas. There are many places in Malta to visit too numerous to mention, the whole island is steeped in history; the following are just a few to whet your appetite.

Valletta

Valletta, the capital was built by Jean de la Valette, French Grand Master of the Order of the Knights of St John of Jerusalem, after the epic siege of 1655. Within its limited boundaries is reflected some of Malta's rich heritage of archaeology history, architecture, art and

The Port des Bombes was built in 1721 and forms part of the outer bastion on the main road into Floriana and Valletta.

culture. The island's historic Grand Harbour, being one of the finest natural ports in Europe, and the three Cities of Vittoriosa, Cospicua and Senglea, all of which can be viewed from the Upper Barracca Gardens.

Republic Street

Republic Street is the main thoroughfare, which runs the length of the City, half way along this street is Republic Square, the real centre of Valletta. This was formerly called Queens Square and still has a statue of

There are many lovely places in this capital city of Valletta where one can rest their weary legs, after enjoying the sights.

Queen Victoria to recall the period of British rule. There are many interesting buildings in Republic Street also cafes and bars which offers a glimpse of the true southern European style.

St. John's Cathedral and Museum

One of the most compelling sights in the Maltese Islands – a real must for all those sensitive to great art and the appeal of history – is the Conventual Church of the Order of St John in Valletta. It is a veritable treasure house full of the most impressive works of art dating from the 16th century.

The Cathedral of St John built between 1573 & 1577 by Girolamo Cassar and is considered to be his masterpiece. Plain outside but beautiful inside.

BELOW: *An aerial view of Valletta showing the city walls and the main entrance to the city leading to Republic Street. In the foreground is Valletta's main bus station.*

MALTA – PLACES TO VISIT

The front view of the Auberge de Castille where the Prime Minister has his office in Valletta.

In the centre of the photograph is the Grand Master's Palace, to the right is Palace Square and above, Republic Square.

Upper Barracca Gardens

From the terrace of the Upper Barracca Gardens *(below)* there are excellent views of Grand Harbour, the Three Cities and Lascaris Wharf where the cruise ships usually moor.

The Manoel Theatre

This little theatre in Old Theatre Street is a real jewel because of its cultural history as well as its architectural design. It was built in 1731 in the time of the Grandmaster Monoel de Vilhena, whose name it bears, initially it was called 'The Theatre of the People', later becoming 'The Royal Theatre' and finally in 1868 as a tribute to its founder 'Manoel Theatre'.

The Manoel Theatre is one of the oldest in Europe still showing regular performances.

PHOTO COURTESY OF THE MANOEL THEATRE

The Grandmaster's Palace

This grand and beautiful palace was the home of the Republic of Malta's' Parliament The first building on this site was built by Grandmaster Jean de la Cassiere 1572-1581 and was designed by Gerolamo Cassar along with much of the rest of Valletta at the time. You can visit parts of the palace also the Armoury; the palace is a treasure trove of sights for the determined sightseer and Palace Square has been completely refurbished.

The Siege Bell which looks out over the entrance to Grand Harbour, is a memorial which honours the 7,000 service personnel and civilians who died during the 'Siege of Malta' 1940-1943.

MALTA – PLACES TO VISIT

Grand Harbour

One of the finest natural harbours in Europe has had a very colourful and chequered history with many visitors. The walls of the capital city Valletta dominate one side of this harbour, to the south eastern side are the fortified towns of Cospicua, Senglea and Vittoriosa known as the three cities. It was an important British naval base during two worlds wars, today things are much quieter, but busy, the dockyards are still very much in use and the harbour is visited by many cruise ships and naval vessels.

The entrance to Dockyard Creek with the bastions of Senglea, where you can get good views of Grand Harbour and Valletta.

Vittoriosa – Maritime Museum

This museum on Vittoriosa Wharf was opened in 1991 and is housed in what was a former Royal Navy bakery. It highlights the most important moments of Malta's maritime history; exhibits include two ceremonial barges, several models of sailing ships as well as a number of authentic guns and cannons.

Dockyard Creek with the building in the background which now houses the National Maritime Museum.

Mosta – The Mosta Dome

The Maltese architect Giorgio Grognet de Vasse designed Mosta Dome. it is one of the largest unsupported domes in the world. During World War II a 500 lb. bomb fell through the roof, hitting the floor and the bomb did not explode. At this time there was congregation inside and even to this day people talk about the bomb that did not explode. A replica of the bomb can be seen in the church.

The Vedette (look-out tower) at Senglea, the men once posted here are symbolised by carvings of two eyes and two ears.

Built between 1833 and 1860 the church of St Mary in the town of Mosta, is much better known as the Mosta Dome, its sheer size will not fail to impress.

BELOW: *Golden Bay – a very popular beach.*

Mdina – The Silent City

In days gone by this ancient walled city was the capital of Malta, but now it is known as the Silent City. Once through the main gate of this Medieval City you will find yourself going back in time with its palaces, cathedral, museums and narrow streets leading to the ramparts, where on a clear day the views are quite breath taking. Within walking distance of Mdina is Rabat, here also there are many places of interest to visit St. Paul's Grotto, St. Agatha and St. Paul's Catacombs, the Buskett Garden and the Verdala Castle to mention but a few.

Crowning a hilltop at the centre of Malta is the beautiful city of Mdina, also known as the Silent City. The magnificent cathedral dome and the surrounding city walls can be seen from quite a distance.

Marsaxlokk – Fishing Village

The Turkish forces invaded here in 1565, Napoleon landed here in 1798 and more recently in 1989 George Bush and Mikhail Gorbachev had their historic meeting outside the bay. But for visitors this is much better known as Malta's largest fishing village; a fish market is held here every Sunday and a street market is held daily on the seafront promenade. In the harbour you will see many Maltese colourful fishing boats; almost always an eye is painted on the bow of the boats to protect the fishermen from the evil eye of the Devil. This is a tradition which goes back to Phoenician times.

At the Sunday fish market you can purchase the best of what can be found in the Maltese waters. A taste of Malta at its very best!

BELOW: *The walled city of Mdina, known as the Silent City, used to be the capital of Malta.*

Aviation Museum and Craft Village

Ta'Qali which is the site of one of the well-known wartime airfields where British fighter aircraft were based during WW2 you will find the Malta Aviation Museum which is a voluntary, non-profit making organisation, creating a collection of unique exhibits related to Malta's rich aviation history. The old buildings have been turned into a craft village with many outlets selling local crafts. Ta'Qali is also home to the National Football Stadium and park.

This Hawker Hurricane was ditched about a mile offshore from the Blue Grotto in 1941, recovered in 1995 and being restored by the Malta Aviation Museum.

One of the many outlets in Ta'Qali craft village.

The Limestone Heritage Park and Gardens near Siggiewi are really worth a visit, live demonstrations, citrus gardens, 30ft high waterfall, farm animals and coffee shop. Summer season – Folklore Nights.

Marfa jetty where most dive boats leave for northern Malta, Comino and Gozo. Do not park on the jetty!

Wied iz-Zurrieq – Blue Grotto

Situated on the southwest coast of Malta these grottoes are at the base of the sheer cliffs that rise from the blue sea near the pretty little village of Wied iz-Zurrieq.

The slipway at Wied iz-Zurrieq where the small pleasure boats leave to visit the Blue Grotto.

These are the spectacular sea caves of the Blue Grotto.

MALTA – PLACES TO VISIT

Explore Malta and Gozo
The open top bus service operates a 'hop-on hop-off' system, with three different routes around Malta and one on Gozo. Boat cruises are another enjoyable way to see the sights and coastline on an island cruise, normally stopping at the Blue Lagoon on Comino for a swim and lunch. There are shorter cruises around Grand Harbour and the surrounding creeks.

A cruise boat close to the coastline where there is a huge cavern at Fomm ir-Rih Bay.

An open top bus which is a great way of seeing the sights around Malta and Gozo.

BELOW: *The new aquarium at Qawra designed as a starfish. Ample parking and good places to eat too*

Evening entertainment
For those who like the high nightlife with restaurants, bars and disco music, Paceville, St Julians has all these, plus nightclubs, cinemas and ten pin bowling. For those who like an evening at a more leisurely pace then Valletta, Sliema, Bugibba, St Pauls Bay, Mellieha, and to the south, Marsascala are possible venues. But of course there are many places away from the main tourist areas where there are excellent restaurants and friendly bars where you can spend a most enjoyable evening.

One of the many venues to relax, meet friends and enjoy a meal on the Waterfront, Pinto Wharf, Valletta.

Sporting facilities
Apart from scuba diving, the islands offer a wide variety of sporting facilities. The Royal Malta Golf Club is open to non-members with equipment hire and a restaurant. Other sports available include; windsurfing, sailing, paragliding, fishing, ten pin bowling and horse riding to name but a few. For further details of times and places consult your tour guide, hotel representative or Tourist Information Centre.

Why not spend a day at this green oasis in the middle of Malta? Open to non-members, equipment is available for hire.

Gozo – Places to visit when you are not diving

Gozo, the island of the nymph Calypso, is smaller than its sister island Malta; it is approximately 15km long and 7km at its widest point. It has a character quite distinct from Malta and the countryside is greener and more spectacular. Flat-topped hills characterise the landscape whilst almost all the coastline has rugged cliffs, penetrated by steep valleys and beautiful bays. Life here is more leisurely, rustic and quieter than Malta, the charm of the island makes itself apparent as soon as you land. It is an island where time seems to have stood still, so if you are looking for a restful time then Gozo will suit you.

Most of the Gozo coastline is edged with dramatic cliffs, this photo was taken on the northeast coastline.

Ta' Pinu – National Shrine

The origin of Ta' Pinu goes back to June 22, 1883 when a peasant woman, Carmela Grima, heard the voice of the Blessed Virgin in a little old chapel. In the following years many miracles and acts of grace were manifested. It was believed that the prayers said in the little chapel saved Gozo from the plague, which had stricken Malta. It was decided to build a larger and more magnificent church on the site in honour of the Blessed Virgin. A collection from the Gozitans, including those living abroad, together with donations contributed by community members and much physical work, enabled the people to start construction work in 1920. In 1931 Ta' Pinu was consecrated and in 1932 Pope Pius XI gave it the status of Basilica.

Ta'Pinu Sanctuary dominates the countryside between Gharb and Ghammar, a Romanesque centre of pilgrimage that was given basilica status in 1992.

Mgarr – Gozo Ferry Terminal

Mgarr Harbour, this once small fishing village is now dominated by the new ferry terminal. The church of our Lady of Lourdes overlooks this harbour as does Fort Chambray.

All visitors to Gozo now arrive at the busy harbour of Mgarr.

Mgarr Harbour.   PHOTO: JOE ABDILLA & PAUL GAUCI

Victoria – Rabat

The old name Rabat simply means 'the city'. On the occasion of the jubilee of Queen Victoria in 1897 the official name was changed in Her Majesty's honour. Even today, many locals still call it by its original name, Rabat. The town is picturesque, a stroll along the streets to look at the colourful shops and why not visit St George's Church built between 1672 and 1778. The paintings in the dome are the works of Battista Conti of Rome, Paolo Azzopardi carved the richly decorated statue of St George in the year 1841. The area surrounding the Church itself is steeped in history showing objects and indications of former cultures and settlements dating back to Roman times.

Sometimes the streets are filled with a variety local market stalls.

The impressive Cathedral which stands within the Citadel.

The Citadel

The Citadel, also known as 'Gran Castello' owes its origins to the late medieval era, and was re-fortified by the Knights in the 17th century to provide refuge and defence against the numerous attacks by the Turks and Corsairs during that time. It was built at a most strategic point on a hill in the centre of the island above the capital Victoria, it offers stunning views from the ramparts around the Citadel.

The Cathedral

The Cathedral in the Citadel designed by Lorenzo Gaf'a was built between 1697 and 1711. At the time it was constructed, money was short and would not run to a dome. The Italian painter Antonio Manuele, who created a wonderful impression that the flat roof was a dome, brilliantly overcame this problem. There is a Cathedral museum which houses many sacred silver and gold items.

Perched on a hillside the Citadel, from its ramparts Malta can be viewed 6km away.

Citadel Folklore Museum

This most impressive Folklore museum is situated in four houses dating back to the 1500's. The collection includes domestic objects and agricultural implements, craft products, sacred articles and some traditional costumes. As well as the interest with the exhibits, it is interesting to walk through the old houses to gain an impression of the life of the nobility on Gozo in the late medieval period.

Music from the Calypso Island being played at the entrance to the Calypso caves high above Ramla Bay.

Marsalforn – popular resort

This fishing village on the north coast has developed over the years into Gozo's most popular seaside resort. Once again it is very quiet and peaceful, a very pleasant place to sit at one of the bar/restaurants on the quayside. From here it is just a short drive along the coast road to Reqqa point, where you will be able to view the shapes that have been created in the sand stone cliffs by the wind and sea, also the many salt pans which are still in use today.

The concrete road, Marsalforn.

Marsalforn Bay Harbour and small sandy beach.

Xlendi – Picturesque bay and village

Tucked away in the south of the island, this long narrow bay dominated by towering cliffs on its northern side, at the end of the bay there are promenades and many water edge café's, round this natural bay there are footpaths and steps leading to viewpoints.

The picturesque bay of Xlendi with its little beach, swimming area, bars and restaurants.

Dwejra

This proposed World Heritage site on Gozo's western dramatic coastline where the land meets the sea; nature has created a number of wonders for the visitor to see, the Azure Window, the Blue Hole, the Inland Sea and Tunnel. Many well-known movies have been made here using this area as a backdrop, recently *Game of Thrones* and *Sinbad*.

The Inland Sea is an area of water linked to the sea via a tunnel in the cliffs. Boat trips are available here, which will take you through the tunnel where you can view the dramatic coastline and the Azure Window. Waves and rough seas breaking on the rocks over thousands of years created this window, arch 20 metres high.

This is where the boats leave from which take you through the tunnel to the sea outside

The scene is set, the filming of Sinbad *at Dwejra.*

Fungus Rock

Known also as the General's Rock, Fungus Rock stands proudly in the sweeping bay alongside Dwejra. It was here that Fungus Gaulitanus, a fungus much prized by the Knights for its medicinal powers, once grew. This rare plant for centuries was kept under constant guard and anyone caught stealing it was instantly put to death. Due to its height, the Fungus Rock was almost unreachable from the sea; therefore the Knights constructed a hoist resembling a funicular, on the watchtower. This tower known as 'Qawra Tower' can still be seen. Sadly, it has been proved in recent years that the fungus has no known medicinal powers.

The visitors area of Dwejra with its small chapel and watering holes. PHOTO: JOE ABDILLA & PAUL GAUCI

Fungus Rock situated a short distance from Dwejra.

Northeast Coastline

The coastline from Mgarr to Marsalforn is made up of undulating cliffs and huge boulders, with its picturesque inlets and sandy bays. Further on to San Dimitri Point and round to Xlendi the cliffs are sheer and dramatic, the shore is only reached in a small number of places which requires fitness and care.

Ir-Ramla (Red Bay) with its red sandy beach is ideal for swimming, there is a statue of the Madonna in the centre.
PHOTO: JOE ABDILLA & PAUL GAUCI

The quiet secluded bay of San Blas, with its steep path to the beach, but worth the effort. PHOTO: JOE ABDILLA & PAUL GAUCI

Hondoq Bay has a small sandy beach.

Ggantija – Prehistoric Temples

The megalithic temples of Ggantija near the village of Xaghra are an outstanding example of the pre-historic monuments to be found on the Maltese Islands. These are considered to be the oldest free standing structures yet discovered in the world. Ggantija means 'giant woman' and the huge stones of these two temples, according to the latest analysis, were built around 3600 BC, earlier than the first pyramids in Egypt which was 2800 BC, and Stonehenge in England around 2400 BC.

The entrance to the megalithic temples of Ggantija.

A Taste of Gozo

One of the greatest pleasures when visiting any country is its local cuisine. The fields are abundant with Mediterranean produce like green peppers, aubergines and courgettes, and each day a wide variety of fish is brought into the tiny harbours only an hour or so after the catch. To go with these is Gozo's delicious crispy bread as well as Gozo wines, which are served young and chilled. There are some very attractive restaurants nestling in the small bays where you can dine next to the waters edge with a view of the fishing boats. Others to be found are perched high up within the ancient bastions of the capital city of Victoria, with spectacular views of the terraced countryside.
Look also for the intimate weathered courtyards with worn flagstones and old walls covered in flowers, where small tables and candlelight provide the most romantic of settings. Sometimes compromise on the setting and search out the family run bars, which specialise in local dishes and by balancing your budget you will also get an enjoyable first hand taste of Gozitan cuisine.

Sue, Sharon and Ian are taking a rest – I am still working!

Dive safely in Malta

Look for a PDSA approved dive centre and know that you are diving with **the best** the islands have to offer.

Setting the standard

PDSA MEMBER — SAFETY · QUALITY · PROFESSIONAL

The **Professional Diving Schools Association** of Malta, Gozo and Comino is a collective of diving professionals, all committed to a diving experience that lives up to the highest standards.

Visit **pdsa.org.mt** for more information

Dive safely and enjoyably. Dive with a PDSA member, and ensure that you get the very best out of Malta, Gozo and Comino

PDSA
MALTA, GOZO
& COMINO

Dive centre locations

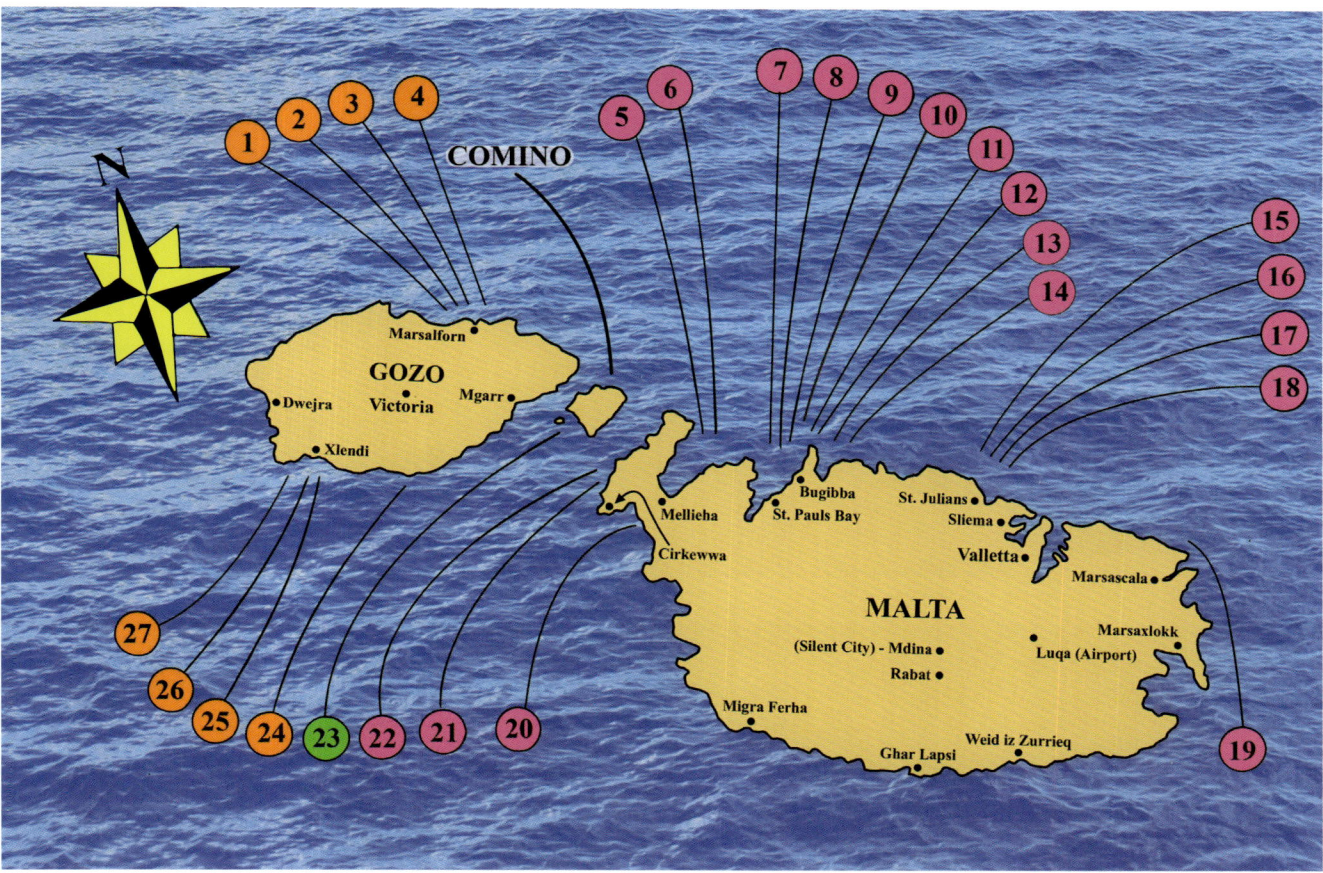

1. **Atlantis Diving Centre**, Qolla St, Marsalforn, Gozo
   www.atlantisgozo.com
2. **Gozo Aquasports**, Rabat Rd, Marsalforn, Gozo
   www.gozoaquasports.com
3. **Calypso**, The Seafront, Marsalforn, Gozo
   www.calypsodivers.com
4. **Blue Waters Dive Cove**, Kuncizzjoni St, Qala, Gozo
   www.divebluewaters.com
5. **Aquaventure**, Mellieha Bay Hotel, Mellieha, Malta
   www.aquaventuremalta.com
6. **Sea Shell Dive Cove**, Tunny Net Lido, Mellieha Bay, Malta
   www.seashell-divecove.com
7. **Octopus Garden**, Gillieru Harbour Hotel, St Pauls Bay, Malta
   www.octopus-garden.com
8. **Aquatica**, St Pauls Bay, Malta
   www.scubadivingmalta.com
9. **Maltaqua**, Mosta Rd, St Pauls Bay, Malta
   www.maltaqua.com
10. **Scubatech**, Alka St. St Pauls Bay, Malta
    www.scubatech.info
11. **Buddies**, Pioneer Rd, Bugibba, Malta
    www.buddiesmalta.com
12. **Dive Deep Blue**, Annanija St, Bugibba, Malta
    www.divedeepblue.com
13. **Dawn Diving**, Maskli Street, Qwara, Malta
    www.dawndiving.com
14. **Mad Shark**, Triq il Qawra, St Pauls Bay, Malta
    www.madsharkmalta.com
15. **Starfish**, Corinthia Hotel, St Georges Bay, Malta
    www.starfishdiving.com
16. **Divewise**, Dragonora Point, St Julians, Malta
    www.divewise.com.mt
17. **Dive Systems**, Tower Point, Exiles, Tower Road, Sliema, Malta
    www.divesystemsmalta.com
18. **Diveshack**, Qui-Si-Sana Seafront, Sliema, Malta
    www.divemalta.com
19. **Dive Med**, Zonqor Point, Marsascala, Malta
    www.divemed.com
20. **Orange Shark H2O Divers**, Golden Sands Resort & Spa, Malta
    www.orangeshark.eu
21. **Paradise Diving**, Paradise Bay Hotel, Cirkewwa, Malta
    www.paradisediving.com
22. **Orange Shark H2O Divers**, Ramla Bay Resort, Marfa Bay, Malta
    www.orangeshark.eu
23. **Diveshack**, Comino Hotel, Comino
    www.divemalta.com
24. **Gozo Diving**, Mgarr Rd, Xewkija, Gozo
    www.gozodiving.com
25. **Moby Dives**, Triq Il-Gostra, Xlendi Bay, Gozo
    www.mobydivesgozo.com
26. **St Andrews Dive Cove**, Xlendi Bay, Gozo
    www.gozodive.com
27. **Utina Diving College**, Xlendi Bay, Gozo
    www.utina-diving.com

Malta dive centres

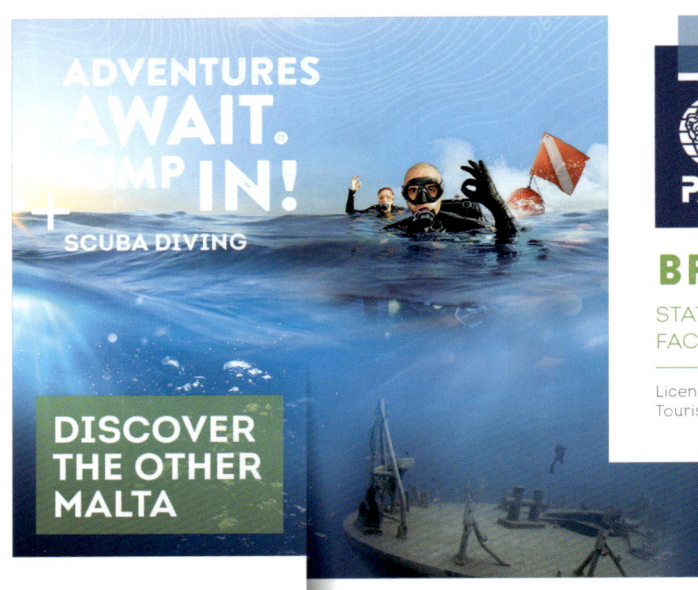

TAILOR-MADE TRIPS

Full range of PADI courses

Daily dive excursions to several dive sites around the Maltese Islands

BRAND-NEW
STATE-OF-THE-ART FACILITIES AND CAFÉ

Licensed by the Malta Tourism Authority.

GET IN TOUCH!

Aquatica,
Mosta Road, St Paul's Bay,
SPB 3418, Malta
(+356) 2157 9753 /
(+356) 7906 3462
info@scubadivingmalta.com

aquaticamalta

www.scubadivingmalta.com

scuba diving at it's best

**PADI Courses
Escorted Diving
Equipment Rental & Sales
Accommodation**

AquaVenture Ltd
Mellieha Bay Hotel, Mellieha, Malta
(+356) 21 522 141
info@aquaventuremalta.com
www.aquaventuremalta.com

- Family run with friendly & experienced staff
- Committed to diver safety & satisfaction
- Padi 5 star IDC centre
- Centrally located in Bugibba
- Scuba courses from complete beginner to instructor levels
- 'Small Group' escorted dives for personal attention
- Daily shore and boat dives around the 3 islands
- Assistance in booking accommodation and airport transfers in Malta
- Free transport from/to accommodation in Malta

buddies divecove malta

Your Diving Partners in Malta

Dive Centre: Buddies Divecove Malta
24/2, Pioneer Road, Bugibba, Malta

Tel: +356 2157 6266
Fax: +365 2157 1042
Mobile: +356 9947 8975
Email: dive@buddiesmalta.com

www.buddiesmalta.com

MTA Lic No: Dive/0059

Malta dive centres

Dawn Diving

- Learn to Dive
- Diving Courses Run Daily
- Guided Diving

Mob: +356 99431703
www.dawndiving.com
info@dawndiving.com

Find us on: facebook

PADI 5STAR DIVE CENTER

PADI® The Way the World Learns to Dive®

P.A.D.I.
5 Star Gold Palm Centre
DSAT Technical Centre

Hotel or Apartment Diving Packages.
Malta/Gozo/Comino Trips
Introduction Dives.
Guided Dive Packs.
Courses /Specialties.

The Adventure Starts Now !

BS-AC
Premier Centre & Technical Centre

Facilities include:
Dive Shop.
Equipment Rental.
Car parking.
Pool & Sundeck

A Warm Welcome !

DIVE DEEP BLUE LTD.
Deep Blue Lido, 100 Annanija Str., Bugibba/Qawra. Malta.
Tel:(+356)21 583946 Fax:(+356)21 583945
Internet:http://www.divedeepblue.com   email:dive@divedeepblue.com

---

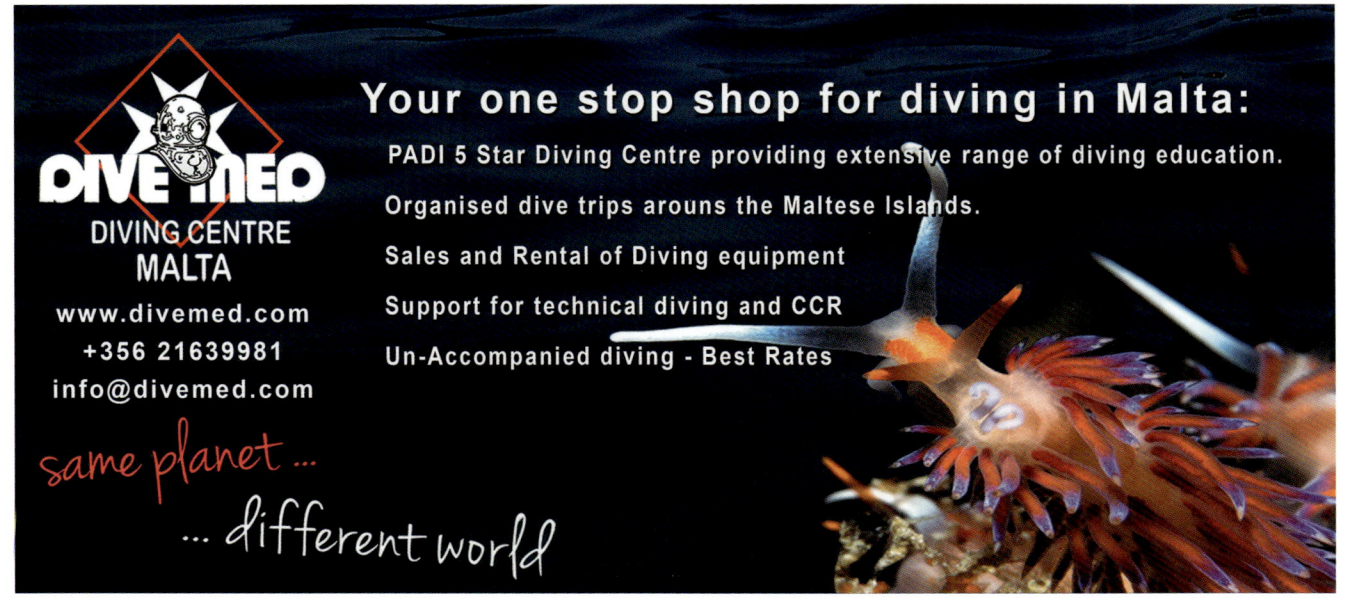

DIVE MED
DIVING CENTRE MALTA

www.divemed.com
+356 21639981
info@divemed.com

Your one stop shop for diving in Malta:

- PADI 5 Star Diving Centre providing extensive range of diving education.
- Organised dive trips arouns the Maltese Islands.
- Sales and Rental of Diving equipment
- Support for technical diving and CCR
- Un-Accompanied diving - Best Rates

same planet ...
... different world

Malta dive centres

Malta dive centres

MALTAQUA
Celebrating 45 years — providing the highest standards in diver training

Dive Shop
- Snorkeling & Diving Gear Sales & Rental
- Servicing of Dive Equipment
- Scuba Wear
- PADI Materials
- Air, Nitrox & Trimix Fills

Dive School
- Try Dives
- Kids Courses
- Beginner Courses
- Continued Training
- Technical Courses: Open & Closed Circuit

Adventure Dives
- Escorted Dives Daily
- Cave, Wreck, Night and Boat Dives around the Islands of Malta, Gozo & Comino

Holiday Services
- Accommodation
- Airport Transfers
- Car Hire
- Boat Charter
- Classroom Hire

Mosta Road, St Paul's Bay, SPB 3114 Malta
t: (+356) 2157 1111, 21572558
e: dive@maltaqua.com w: www.maltaqua.com

At Mad Shark we are a fully qualified CMAS and PADI training facility, we can offer a large variety of courses from beginner to instructor level in german and english language, dives accompanied by instructor by boat or from shore.

Mad Shark Diving Malta-Gozo

Triq il Qawra; St. Pauls Bay SPB 1904
phone: 21 584 274; mobile: 99 241 872
dive@madsharkmalta.com
www.madsharkmalta.com

SCUBA DIVE TODAY...

Orange Shark Malta — H2O Diving Centers

Radisson Blu Golden Sands, Mellieha:
+356 23561950
Ramla Bay Resort, Marfa Bay, Mellieha:
+356 21521329 [Diveline]
E: info@orangeshark.eu
orangeshark.eu

- SCUBA DIVING & TRAINING • SCUBA DIVE EXCURSIONS
- BOAT DIVING • SNORKELING & SNORKELING EQUIPMENT
- SALES & EQUIPMENT RENTAL

Malta dive centres

Paradise Diving Malta, PADI 5* Resort

Forget the dive shop on the high street and chill out on our beach. Boat diving every day May - October off Malta, Gozo and Comino. Dive times at 9.00, 12.00 and 15.00. Winter diving from shore. PADI courses all year round. Beach facilities include sunloungers, showers, beachbar, restaurant, watersports and optional 4* hotel onsite. Perfect for those travelling with non divers.

Winners of the Malta Tourism Award for best instructor, 2006, 2007, 2009, 2010 and again in 2011 with Mark Dove.

Paradise Bay Hotel, Cirkewwa, Malta
+356 21574116, 21524363, 99491877

info@paradisediving.com
www.paradisediving.com

Malta dive centres

Gozo dive centres

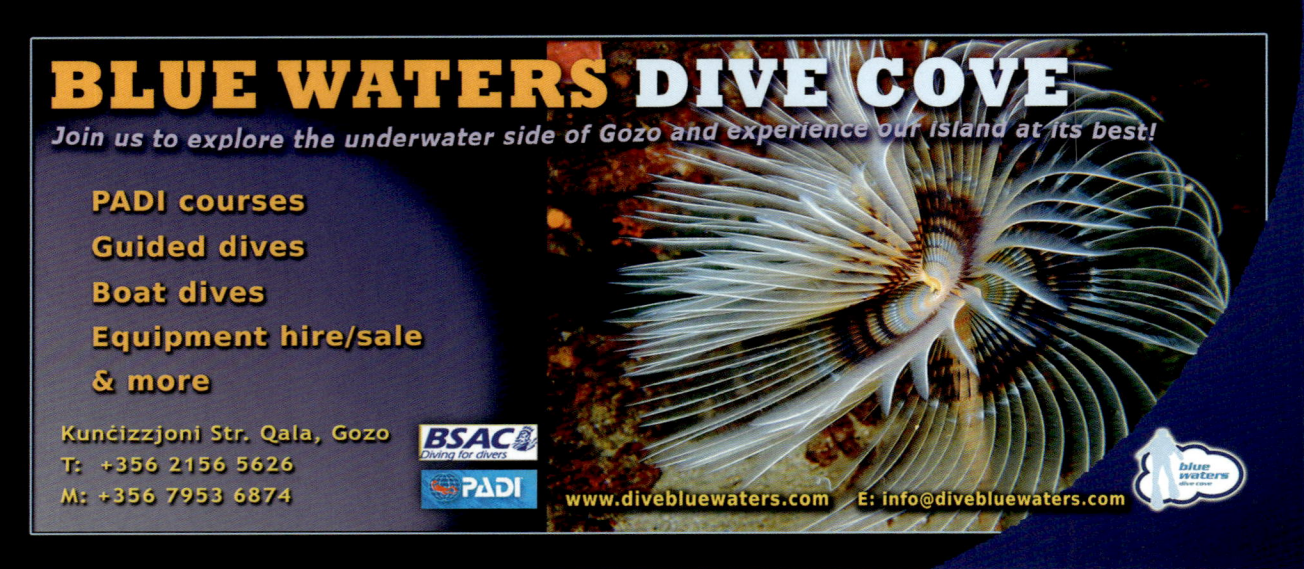

Gozo dive centres

Celebrating over 30 years of quality service!

Over 50% of our business is repeat business

- PADI courses from beginner to Instructor
- Shore, hard boat and RIB diving available
- Well stocked dive shop
- Technical courses, Nitrox and Trimix Available
- Rebreather Friendly

The friendliest dive centre in the Med!

TRANSFERS • ACCOMMODATION • CAR HIRE • AIR UP TO 300BAR

Tel: +356 21563037 | dive@gozoaquasports.com | www.gozoaquasports.com

GOZO aquasports

GOZODIVING
Explore Deep - Caves - Wrecks

It may be Dark ... It may be Deep ...
... but It does not have to be on Air

RECREATIONAL & TECHNICAL DIVING
www.gozodiving.com
www.gozotechnicaldiving.com
Guided & Unguided Dives, Diver & Instructor Training
Equipment Sale & Rental - (+356) 7900 9565 / 9575

MOBY DIVES

Discover the Magic of Gozo

In the heart of beautiful Xlendi Bay, Moby Dives has an excellent reputation for Scuba Training, organisation and professionalism whilst maintaining a friendly atmosphere. We are sure that you will have a truly memorable holiday in Gozo.

We also offer a comprehensive range of accommodation options at affordable prices, on site at our Ulysses Aparthotel. Combine this and our bar/restaurant and you have everything you need all under one roof.

So join us and dive in with Moby Dives

t: +356 2155 1616
e: info@mobydivesgozo.com

WWW.MOBYDIVESGOZO.COM

Gozo/Comino dive centres

St. Andrew's Divers Cove

Xlendi Bay, Isle of Gozo, Malta
e-mail: standrew@gozodive.com
web site: www.gozodive.com
tel. +356 21551301 fax +356 21561548

For all your diving and holiday needs including:

Airport Transfers, Accommodation (hotels, apartments and farmhouses), Car Hire.

Accompanied or Unaccompanied Diving and Courses (PADI, BSAC, CMAS).

Plus Dive Shop, considered the best stocked in the islands, exceptional prices. Agents for: Apeks, SeaWay, Waterproof

For further information contact Diana, Joe or Mark

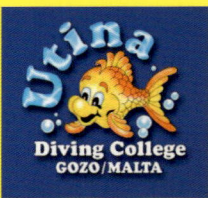

**PADI 5* GOLD PALM RESORT
AND
INSTRUCTOR DEVELOPMENT
CENTRE**

Come and Dive with the Utina Team

We are a small Friendly School in Xlendi Bay
and can Tailor Dive Trips to Suit YOU!!

www.utina-diving.com

Tel.00356 2155 0514

utina@gozomail.com

Mob. 00356 7955 0514

Our PADI 5-Star Instructor Development Centres are in Sliema (Malta) and on the island of Comino.

COMINO, one of the smaller Maltese islands famous for its Blue Lagoon, is only 1 square mile in size. A perfect getaway. No roads, no cars, no hassles. Simply SUN, SEA & DIVING!

We Offer:
- Try a Dive - all equipment provided
- Full range of PADI Courses
- Guided Boat & Shore dives at the best dive sites around Comino, Gozo & Malta
- Cavern & Wreck Specialty Courses
- TEC Diving

TEL (+356) 21345671 / 21529821
MOB (+356) 7799 3483 / 9942 3215
info@divecomino.com
www.divecomino.com

WE ARE OPEN FROM MAY TO OCTOBER

Acknowledgements

I would like to thank the people below who have assisted me in one way or another in producing this book, without their help it would not have been possible.

Dr.Michael Refalo – KOM.,BA(Hons)., LLD., FRSA 1936 – 2015
  Minister for Tourism – High Commissioner for Malta in London

Malta Tourism Authority

George Lanham – for his patience and the professional way in which he has designed the book, also his assistance with the covers

Joe Abdilla (Pilot) and Paul Gauci – Aerial Photography

Sharon and Ian Forder – computer assistance, web design, colouring illustrations, dive buddies, fellow underwater photographers, friends

Chris Gray – a friend and dive buddy, who had the original idea that I should produce a book

Bent Matusiak – a friend and dive buddy, also his wife Marthese, sons Andreas and Michael, for their help, friendship and genuine hospitality

Joseph Borg and Michael Vella De Fremeaux, Miller Distributors Ltd. Malta

Joe and Tess Abdilla – Hospitality and friendship

Mark Dove – for the detailed information given on boat diving Comino

Martin Stanhope and his staff – Buddies Dive Centre

Max and Paola Valli – Orange Shark H2O Divers

Brian and Stephania Azzopardi, John (Jack) Dabill – Atlantis Dive Centre

Agnes and Mike Upton, Simone Brinch-Iversen, Anna Catania
  Maltaqua Dive Centre

Simone Schiberras and his staff – Dive Systems

Stephen Clough – Design of front covers and posters

Lina Fabri – for her never ending help, patience and lovely sense of humour

Ivan Consiglio – a friend that keeps us in touch with the Maltese Islands

Ian Gaunt – for his tireless work on colouring the original illustrations

Paul and Mariella Mizzi – The Foto Grafer – original Aerial Photographs

Diving Instructors and dive buddies – Dave Whitlam, Gerrard De Waal

Paul and Debbie Adams

David Mallard – for his painstaking task of research on the *X127* Lighter

George Zammit Briffa – Manager, Captain Morgan Cruises Malta

Joseph Roger Sammut, Joseph Bianco, Charlie Scicluna (retired) – Malta Maritime

Joe & Paul. Thank you!

PHOTOGRAPHY

Joe Abdilla and Paul Gauci – Aerial Photos

Sharon Forder – Spyder Design

Ian Forder – Spyder Design

Joe Formosa – Atlam BS-AC

Victor Fabri – Atlam BS-AC

Max Valli – Orange Shark H2O Divers

Cathy and John De Lara

Gavin Anderson

Dmitry Vinogradov

Jonathan Thomas – Dive Deep Blue

Sergey Markov – Dive Systems

Wilfred Pirotta – Atlam BS-AC

Alexander Aristarkhov

Kevin Debattista

Derek Chircop – Scubatech Dive Centre

Jesper Kjoller – DYK Magazine

Hubert Borg – Sea Shell Dive Cove

Colin Stead

Anthony Chetcuti – Pilot Officer

George Zammit Briffa

Joseph Tonna

David P. Attard

Charlie Scicluna

Joseph Caruana – Maritime Museum

Mark Baluci

Bettina Rohbrecht

I would like to thank all the above persons for donating their photographs.

All photographs in this publication which are credited, the copyright remains with the photographer.

Photograph index

Alex's Cave	194
Amberjack	50, 153
Anchor	72, 134
Anchor Reef	160, 161
Anchor Bay	71
Anchor Bay Cave	72
Anemone	100, 190
Aquarium	204
Arrowhead Rock	44
Auberge de Castille	200
Aviation Museum	203
Azure Window	150
Barracuda	94, 185
Beaches – Gozo	209
Beaufighter	168, 169
Bell Cave	52
Ben's Arch	16, 84, 88
Billinghurst Cave	163, 186
Blenheim bomber	174, 175
Blenny	16, 183
Blue Dome	166
Blue Grotto	203
Blue Hole	4, 143, 148
Blue Lagoon	197
Bream	38, 78, 79, 136, 144, 193, 196
Bumblebee shrimp	16
Calypso Cave entrance	187, 207
Cardinal fish	52, 144
Chadwick Lakes	14, 198
Chimney	188
Cirkewwa	10, 15, 75, 78, 82, 84
Cirkewwa Anchor	78
Cirkewwa Arch	76
Cirkewwa Tunnel	76
Citadel	206
Comber	16, 38, 114
Comino Caves	195, 196
Cominotto	197
Conger	30
Coral	92
Crabs	38, 95, 112
Crocodile Rock	145
Crystal Lagoon	190
Cuttlefish	19, 26, 122, 192
Damsel fish	140
Delimara	41, 42
De Water Joffer	175, 176
Dive boats	6, 20, 168, 181, 182
Dive centre	15
Diver groups	110, 117, 181, 184, 188, 196, 198
Divers marine life	17, 42, 58, 91, 92, 99, 122, 146, 192
Dockyard Creek	12, 201
Double Arch	158, 187
Dwejra	2, 18, 143, 146, 154
Eating out	204
Elephant's Trunk	62
Exiles	108
Fan Worm	95, 144
Farm House	13
Fesse Rock	182
Festa	13
Finger Reef/Crib	60, 61, 62
Fireworm	60, 160
Fish feeding	196
Flowers of the Maltese Islands	198
Fortizza Reef	112, 114
Fort St Elmo	26
Fra Ben Cave	99
Fungus Rock	184, 208
Ghar Lapsi	57, 60, 61, 64
Ghar Lapsi Cave	60, 61
Ghasri Valley	164
Goby	95
Golden Sands	201
Gozo	205
Gozo Ferry	11
Grouper	15, 44, 78, 150, 158
Gurnard	62, 64
Hannah's Reef	84
Heka Point	186
HMS *Eddy*	169, 170
HMS *Hellspont*	169
HMS *Maori*	22, 23, 24
HMS *Southwold*	171, 172
HMS *St Angelo*	170
HMS *Stubborn*	17, 178
HMS *Talbot* base	117
Inland Sea	18, 143, 152, 208
Jellyfish	100, 144
John Dory	54
Kartozzin	11
Kalkara Creek	12, 32
L'Ahrax	92, 94
L'Ahrax Tunnel	91
Lantern Point	188, 189
Limestone Heritage	203
Lizards Head	64
Lobster	41, 95, 184
Luzzu	6, 20, 157
Madonna	82
Manoel Island	116, 118
Manoel Theatre	200
Marfa Harbour	203
Marsa Sports Club	204
Marsalforn	157
Marsascala	35
Marsaxlokk	202
Mdina	202
Meagre	152
Mercanti Reef	104
Mgarr Harbour	205
Migra Ferha	67, 68
Mini Blue Hole	38
Moray	52, 80, 95, 152, 184
Mosta Dome	201
MV *Cominoland*	124, 126
MV *Imperial Eagle*	179, 180
MV *Karwela*	124, 125
MV *Pippo*	179
MV *Rozi*	1, 16, 78, 79, 80
MV *Xlendi*	121, 122
Neolithic Temples	209
Nudibranch	31, 44, 94, 95, 100
Octopus	99, 114, 128, 140
P29 Patrol Boat	85, 86, 210
P31 Patrol Boat	18, 191, 192, 193
Paradise Bay	88,
Parrotfish	164
Photography under water	18, 19, 58, 60, 61, 95, 140, 183
Pilot fish	42
Plaque	52, 86, 107, 181
Pleasure Cruiser	204
Pope John Paul	180
Popeye Village	71
Port des Bombes	199
Qammieh Point	177
Qawra Point	96, 100, 102
Ras il-Hobz	131, 132, 134
Ras ir-Raheb	175
Ray	62
Red mullet	140
Reefs	60
Reqqa Point	162, 164
Salema fish	58, 132, 157
Salt seller	157
San Dimitri Point	185
San Dimitri Chapel	185
Schnellboot *S-31*	170, 171
Scorpion fish	154, 160, 189
Scotscraig	176, 177
Sea hare	94
Sea horse	95, 104, 136
Senglea	201
Shark sucker	36
Shellfish	96
Shrimp	16, 184
Siege Bell	200
Soft coral	58
Sponge	102, 153, 154
Squid	95, 144
SS *Le Polynesien*	173, 174
SS *Margit*	29, 30, 31, 32
St Elmo Bay	23, 24
St Johns Cathedral	199
St Pauls Island	12
Statue of Christ	180
Sugar Loaf	82
Sunset	198
Swimthrough	18
Ta'Pinu	205
The Author	3, 60
Torpedo DPV	15, 17, 42, 48, 49, 85, 86, 183, 196
Transport	11, 204
Triggerfish	140
Tugboat *2*	106, 107, 108
Tugboat *10*	35, 36
Tug boat *St Michael*	36
Tun shell	96
Turbot	128
Turtle	19
Ulysses Cave	183
Um el Faroud	16, 47, 48, 49, 50
Upper Barracca Gardens.	200
Valletta	12, 199, 200
Wied iz Zurrieq	47, 54, 203
X127 Lighter	117, 118
Xatt L'Ahmar	124, 128
Xlendi	14, 139
Xlendi Cave	139
Xwejni Bay	159
Young Divers	10, 15, 88

Aerial photograph index

Please note that this index is in numerical page order

Malta

	PAGE
Wied iz-Zurrieq (Blue Grotto)	3
Cirkewwa (Marfa Point)	4, 74, 75
St Pauls Islands	12
Valletta – St Elmo Bay	21
St Elmo Bay – Valletta	25
Fort St Elmo – Grand Harbour	27
Kalkara Creek – Vittoriosa	28, 33
Marsascala – Zonqor Point	34
Zonqor Point – Marsascala	37
Mini Blue Hole – Marsascala	39
Delimara Point – Marsaxlokk	40
Delimara Point – East Reef	43
Delimara Point – South Reef	45
Wied iz-Zurrieq	46, 53
Um el Faroud – Scuttling	48
Wied iz-Zurrieq – West Reef	51
Wied iz-Zurrieq – East Reef	55
Ghar Lapsi	56, 63, 65
Black John – Ghar Lapsi	57, 59
Migra Ferha	66, 69
Anchor Bay – Mellieha	70, 73
Cirkewwa (Marfa Point) E2	77
Cirkewwa (Marfa Point) E1-E2	81, 83
Cirkewwa – *P29* scuttling	84
Cirkewwa (Marfa Point) E1-E3	87
Cirkewwa – Paradise Bay E3-E4	89
L'Ahrax Point	90
L'Ahrax Point – Tunnel & Reef	91, 93
Slugs Bay – The Jetty	96
Slugs Bay – 4 x 4 routes	97
Qawra Point	98, 101
St Julians – Sliema	103
Dragonara Point – Paceville	105
Tugboat 2 Scuttling – Exiles	106
Exiles – St Julians Point	109
Sliema – Fortizza Reef	111
Sliema – Coral Gardens	113, 115
Manoel Island – Sliema	116
Manoel Island – Entry Point	119
Filfla Island – South of Malta	175
P31 Arrival Grand Harbour	191
Valletta – City Gate	199
Upper Barracca Gardens	200
Grandmasters Palace	200
Seige Bell	200
Golden Sands Bay	201
Mdina – The Silent City	202
Marfa Jetty Marfa	203
Aquarium Qawra	204

Gozo

	PAGE
Xatt L'Ahmar – Ghanjsielem	120
MV Xlendi Scuttling	121
Xatt L'Ahmar – Entry Points Wrecks	123
MV Karwela & Cominoland scuttling	127
Xatt L'Ahmar – Red Bay	129
Ras Il-Hobz – Ghanjsielem	130
Ras Il-Hobz – Entry Point	131
Ras Il-Hobz – Middle Finger	133
Mgarr ix Xini	135, 137, 223
Xlendi – Xlendi Bay	138, 208
Xlendi – Tunnel & Reef	141
Dwejra – Inland Sea	142, 143, 208
Dwejra – Little Bear – Crocodile Rock	145
Dwejra – Big Bear – Little Bear	147
Dwejra – Blue Hole – Coral Gardens	149
Dwejra – Blue Hole – Azure Window	151
Dwejra – Tunnel – Azure Window	153
Dwejra – Inland Sea Tunnel	155
Marsalforn – Harbour and Bay	156, 207
Xwejni Bay – Marsalforn	159
Anchor Reef – Marsalforn	161
Reqqa Point – Billinghurst Cave	163
Ghasri Valley – Marsalforn	165
Ghasri Valley – Steps – Entry Point	167
Fessej Rock – South Gozo	182
Fungus Rock – West Gozo	184, 208
Mgarr Harbour	205
The Citadel – Victoria	206
Coastline Xwejni Bay – Reqqa Point	207
Ir-Ramla (Red Bay)	209
San Blas Beach	209
Hondoq Bay	209

Comino

Ras L-Irqieqa (Lantern Point) Comino	6, 188
Crystal Lagoon – Cominotto – Comino	188
P31 Scuttling – Comino	191
Comino Caves – North Comino Channel	195
Blue Lagoon – Comino	197

Mgarr ix-Xini

INDEX

	PAGE
Tugboat Rozi	1
Copyright	2
Contents	3
Shore Diving Locations – map	4
Shore Diving Index	5
Boat Diving Locations – map	6
Boat Diving Index	7
Foreword	8
A note from the Author	9
Introduction	10
Travelling information	11
To the Maltese Islands	11
Passport & Visa regulations	11
Ferry Service – Malta Gozo	11
Public Transport – buses	11
Car Hire & traffic laws	11
The Maltese Islands	12
The People	12
Language	13
The Weather	13
Weather Chart	13
Religion	13
Medical Care	14
Shopping	14
Currency	14
Phone cards	14
Electricity	14
Water	14
Dive Centre License Authority	15
Sharon & Ian Forder photo page	16
Islands for Divers	17
Dive Centres & Schools	17
Diving for the disabled	18
Government protection	18
The sea around the Islands	18
Marine life	19
Underwater photography	19
Night diving	20
Key to Symbols	20
Special Diving Notes	20
Shore Diving Malta	from 21
Joe Formosa thank you page	95
Calypso Sub Aqua Club	110
Shore Diving Gozo	from 120
Malta Boat Diving Sites	168
Atlam Sub Aqua Club	181
Gozo Boat Diving Sites	182
Comino Boat Diving Sites	188
Comino	197

	PAGE
Sue Lemon's page	198
Malta – Places to Visit	199
Valletta	199
Republic Street	199
St Johns Cathedral & Museum	199
Upper Barracca Gardens	200
The Manoel Theatre	200
Grandmaster's Palace	200
Grand Harbour	201
National Maritime Museum	201
Mosta Dome	201
Golden Sands Beach	201
Mdina – The Silent City	202
Marsaxlokk	202
Aviation Museum	203
Ta'Qali Craft Village	203
Limestone Heritage Park	203
Marfa Jetty	203
Wied iz-Zurrieq	203
Blue Grotto	203
Explore Malta & Gozo	204
Aquarium Qawra	204
Evening Entertainmant	204
Royal Malta Golf Club	204
Sporting Facilities	204
Gozo – Places to Visit	205
North Coast	205
Ta'Pinu	205
Mgarr Ferry Terminal	205
Victoria – Rabat	206
The Cathedral – Victoria	206
The Citadel – Victoria	206
The Cathedral	206
History & Folklore Museum	207
Marsalforn	207
Xlendi	208
Dwejra	208
Inland Sea	208
Fungus Rock	208
Ir-Ramia (Red Bay)	209
San Blas Bay	209
Hondoq Bay	209
Prehistoric Temples	209
Chilling Out	209
Professional Diving Schools Ass.	210
Dive Centre Locations – map	211
Malta Dive Centres	212
Gozo Dive Centres	218
Comino Dive Centre	220
Acknowledgements	221
Photograph index	222
Aerial Photograph index	223